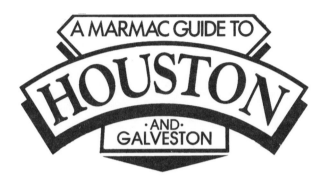

A MARMAC GUIDE TO

HOUSTON

·AND·
GALVESTON

A MARMAC GUIDE TO

HOUSTON

·AND·
GALVESTON

Edited by
George L. Rosenblatt

PELICAN PUBLISHING COMPANY
GRETNA 1996

The Marmac Guidebook series was created by Marge McDonald of Atlanta, Georgia. As owner of a convention and sightseeing service in Atlanta for fourteen years, she learned from visitors and those relocating to Atlanta what information was important to them. She also served as president and CEO of the Georgia Hospitality and Travel Association for four years and in 1978 was named Woman of the Year in Travel by the Travel Industry Association of America.

We would like to thank the Greater Houston Convention & Visitors Bureau, the City of Houston, the Galveston Island Convention and Visitors Bureau, the Greater Houston Partnership, the City of Houston Aviation Department, the Port of Houston, the Houston International Protocol Alliance, Dancie Perugini Ware Public Relations, the Houston Museum of Natural Science, the Houston Museum of Fine Arts, and the many restaurateurs, hoteliers, and public relations professionals who made this book possible.

Information in this guidebook is based on authoritative data available at the time of printing. Prices and hours of operation of businesses listed are subject to change without notice. Readers are asked to take this into account when consulting this guide.

Manufactured in the United States of America
Published by Pelican Publishing Company, Inc.
1101 Monroe Street, Gretna, Louisiana 70053

CONTENTS

MAPS

KEY TO LETTER CODE

E	Expensive
M	Moderately Expensive
I	Inexpensive
CH	Entrance Charge
NCH	No Charge

FOREWORD

The Marmac guidebooks are designed for the resident and traveler who seek comprehensive information in an easy-to-use format and who have a zest for the best in each city and area mentioned in this national series.

We have chosen to include only what we can recommend to you on the basis of our own research, experience, and judgment. Our inclusions are our reputation.

We first escort you into the city, introducing you or reacquainting you as we relate the history and folklore that is indigenous to it. Next we assist you in *learning the ropes*—the essentials of the community, necessary matters of fact, transportation systems, lodging and restaurants, nightlife and theater. Then we point you toward available activities—sightseeing, museums and galleries, shopping, sports, and excursions into the heart of the city and to its environs. And finally we salute the special needs of special people—the international traveler, senior citizens, the handicapped visitor, children, and students. New residents will discover a whole chapter of essential information just for them. A special feature is a detailed chapter on nearby Galveston.

The key area map is placed at the opening of the book, always at your fingertips for quick reference, the margin index, keyed 1-6 and A-F, provides the location code to each listing in the book. Subsidiary maps include a downtown street map keyed 7-12 and G-L, intown and out-of-town touring maps, and a Galveston map.

The Marmac guide serves as your scout in a new territory among new people or as a new friend among local residents. We are committed to a clear, bold, graphic format from our cover design to our contents, and through every chapter of the book. We will inform, advise, and be your companion in the exciting adventure of travel in the United States.

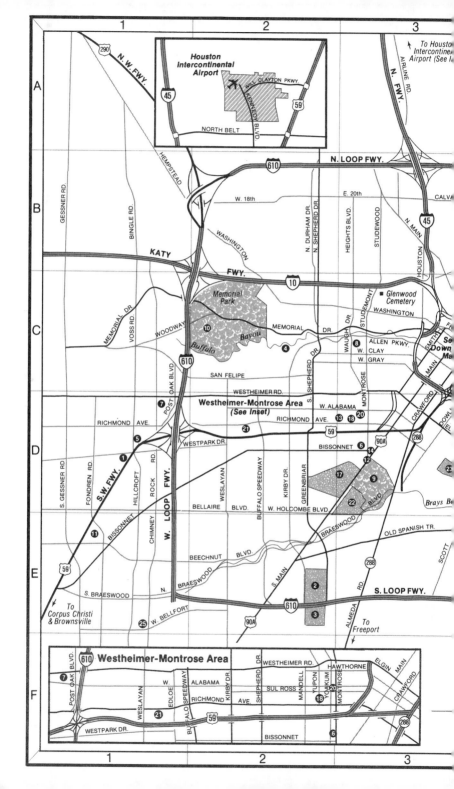

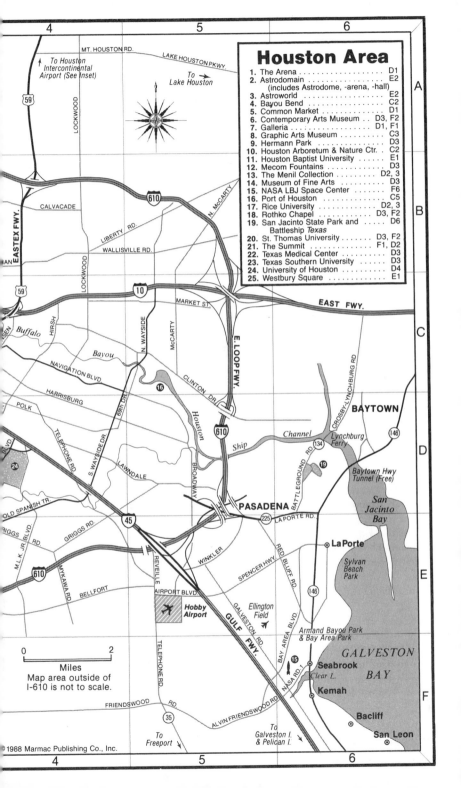

Houston Area

1. The Arena D1
2. Astrodomain E2
   (includes Astrodome, -arena, -hall)
3. Astroworld E2
4. Bayou Bend C2
5. Common Market D1
6. Contemporary Arts Museum . . D3, F2
7. Galleria D1, F1
8. Graphic Arts Museum C3
9. Hermann Park D3
10. Houston Arboretum & Nature Ctr. . C2
11. Houston Baptist University E1
12. Mecom Fountains D3
13. The Menil Collection D2, 3
14. Museum of Fine Arts D3
15. NASA LBJ Space Center F6
16. Port of Houston C5
17. Rice University D2, 3
18. Rothko Chapel D3, F2
19. San Jacinto State Park and D6
    Battleship *Texas*
20. St. Thomas University D3, F2
21. The Summit F1, D2
22. Texas Medical Center D3
23. Texas Southern University D3
24. University of Houston D4
25. Westbury Square E1

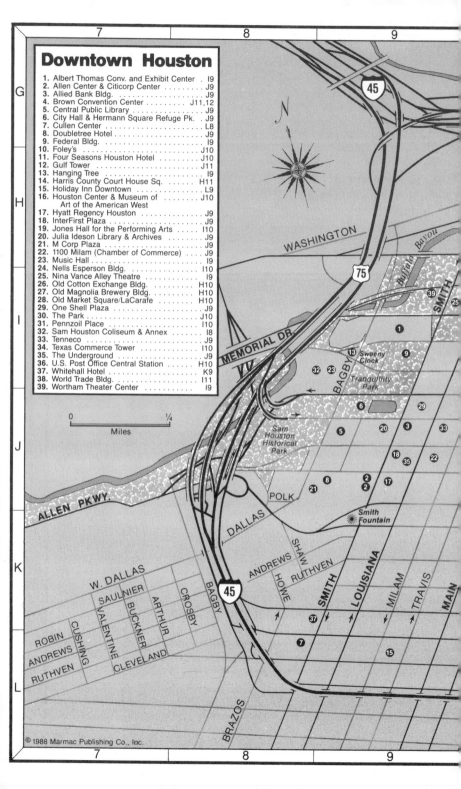

Downtown Houston

0   ¼
   Miles

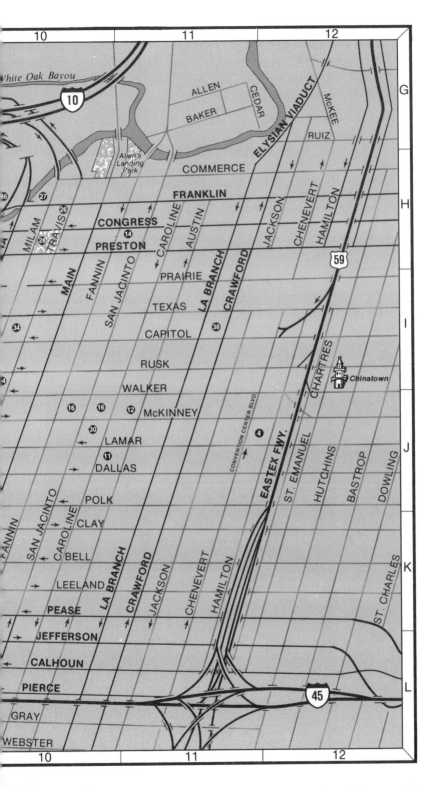

Sam Houston Statue   *Greater Houston Convention & Visitors Bureau*

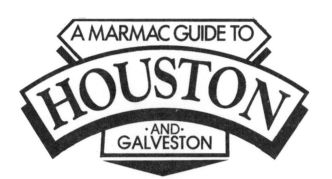

A MARMAC GUIDE TO

HOUSTON

·AND·
GALVESTON

HOUSTON PAST

The City's Namesake

The man for whom this city was named led a colorful life, at times defying reason, and often restless in his wanderings, but a born leader. A native of Virginia, Samuel Houston was a descendent of Sir Hugh of Padivan, the founder of Hughstown Castle of Scotland. Later the spelling changed and became Houston. During his lifetime Houston was governor of Tennessee and Texas, a U.S. Senator, signer of Texas' Declaration of Independence, twice president of the Republic of Texas, general in command of the troops that led Texas to victory in its war with Mexico, and an adopted Cherokee chief.

Houston's family had taken him to Tennessee at an early age where, living close to a neighboring Indian tribe, he became intrigued with their life and lore. He was later to marry Tiana, the daughter of the Cherokee chief, and great-aunt of Will Rogers. He practiced law and became governor of Tennessee. His future looked bright indeed, until suddenly his first wife, Eliza, left him; with that he resigned his post and elected to live with the Indians. Adopted as a son of the Supreme Chief, Oo-loo-te-ka, he served his tribe as an advisor. Later he was to move on to Oklahoma where he continued to direct the affairs of the Cherokees. He had long nurtured a plan to immigrate to Texas, where the affairs of the American colonists in the Mexican state had captured his interest.

Working his way down through Arkansas, he arrived in Texas as settlers chafed under the bridle of edicts emanating from the government in Mexico City. The tall, vigorous politician from Tennessee captured the imagination of the colonists, and before long he was put in command of the cause for Texas independence.

Had he heeded the warnings of U.S. president Andrew Jackson, a good friend from his days in Congress, he would never have persisted in his resolve to free Texas from Mexico. Had he listened to his critics, Texas today might still be part of Mexico, and, most likely, so might much of the western United States. Had he listened, the United States might yet be confined to its eastern lands, deprived of the opportunity to exploit the vast resources and wide-open spaces of the West.

But Houston was restive and determined that the small band of Texas heroes who had been wiped out while defending the Alamo at San Antonio had not died in vain. The battle cry, "Remember the Alamo!" was echoed as he positioned his small army at the San Jacinto peninsula. There he awaited the right moment to attack Gen. Antonio Lopez de Santa Anna's superior forces that had massed to put down the rebellious Texans. Houston had deployed between 700 and 800 men, clearly outnumbered by Santa Anna's 1,600.

On April 21, 1836, while the Mexican Army was taking its "siesta," General Houston sounded the attack and in less than 20 minutes it was all over. Santa Anna was captured, the treaty of surrender was signed, and Texas was a free nation; the Republic of Texas was born.

This battle has been called the most decisive of our times, because just nine years later, Texans voted to join the Union, and the annexation by the United States precipitated the Mexican-American war. The United States won that war, along with much of what was to become the western half of our nation.

The City's Founders

With its independence, Texas saw the arrival of many pioneers and prospectors from the East seeking the good life in the new republic. Among them were two New York land speculators shopping Texas for an ideal interior location to establish a port city for trade with the outside world.

The brothers John and Augustus Allen had heard of a canal-like stream called Buffalo Bayou that merged with the San Jacinto River to the east and meandered toward fertile farms and cotton fields at its western extreme. Failing to acquire land at Harrisburg near the junction of that river and bayou, they followed the stream farther inland until they came upon its confluence with White Oak Bayou, a likely enough spot for vessels to turn around and head back out to sea. That spot, where they stepped ashore to found their townsite, is now Allen's Landing Park at the foot of Main Street in downtown Houston.

In August 1836, the brothers struck a deal purchasing close to 7,000 acres from the widow of John Austin for a little more than $9,000 and, with a wise political gesture, named their town Houston, in honor of their friend and hero, General Sam.

Capital Gained

The Allens made another astute move when they talked the Texas congress into moving its headquarters from nearby Columbia to Houston. Thus, with their townsite as the capital of the new Republic of Texas, it follows that Gen. Sam Houston was soon named its president.

They advertised their city in newspapers both in Texas and in the United States, boasting that it would become a great commercial center and a leading world port.

The city fathers who followed the Allens imitated their lead with a spirit of boosterism, and down the line their prognostications on Houston proved right on target.

Seat of Government Lost

One of the few major goals that never came to fruition in Houston was the plan to make it the permanent seat of government. Actually the Texas congressmen arrived from Columbia even before the Capitol building was begun, and they folded tent and headed for the hills of Austin before it was ever completed. Houston held on to its role as the capital only from 1837 to 1840 and again for a short span in 1842. For a while, then, it seemed that founding the city had been a colossal mistake.

After Houston lost its coveted role in government, the value of Texas money took a nose dive, there was little trading going on, and the ravages of cholera and yellow fever nearly decimated the town. Things began to look bleak and there was even talk of abandoning Houston.

But the majority of settlers doggedly held onto the dream that one day the bayou could be developed into a major shipping lane. Progress was slow at first, since the land routes into the city were impassable during frequent monsoon-type rains that created such mud bogs even oxen sank helplessly up to their knees.

Rails Spur Shipping

The coming of the railroads, however, was the spur needed to boost progress along the bayou. Houston visionaries and power brokers wasted no time in hubbing the rails at Houston with Galveston and all points into the interior. And it wasn't long before Houston was called "The City Where 17 Railroads Meet the Sea."

Port Dream Comes True

All this time the Port of Galveston held a strong lead in competition with Houston, but the idea of developing the bayou persisted. Off and on over the years Houstonians continued pressing for measures of improvement, widening and dredging Buffalo Bayou a little more each time.

Then, in 1900, Mother Nature dealt the island city of Galveston a devastating blow, which became known as one of the world's worst natural disasters. Islanders awakened early one September morning to a surprise hurricane and tidal wave of incredible force sweeping over the entire island, leaving up to 8,000 known dead in their wake. During the ensuing years, as Galveston worked to recover and rebuild, Houston was making headway toward the final phase of development of its port, and by 1914 it came of age. In that year President Woodrow Wilson pressed a button in the White House and, by remote control, fired a cannon that officially opened the Port of Houston to the world. As a feat of engineering, the port and the 50-mile ship channel that made it possible were such a marvel at the time that Will Rogers was prompted to say, "Houston is the only city that dared to dig a ditch to the sea."

Oil in Her Veins

A little more than a decade before this event occurred, Houston had discovered oil in her veins. According to the *Guinness Book of World Records*, the world's greatest gusher was the Lucas well at Spindletop, east of the city. When it blew in, the gusher could be heard more than a mile away, and that mighty roar sent prospectors scurrying across Texas in hot pursuit of the "black gold." Many a fortune was made practically overnight, and thus the legend of the land of the "giants" and the big rich was born. Following Spindletop another huge discovery was made north of Houston at Humble. Those finds alone ultimately spewed forth two of the petroleum industry's top giants: Texaco and the Humble Oil & Refining Co. (now called Exxon Company U.S.A.).

By the time oil was pouring in at record levels, Houston entrepreneurs were getting ready for the next move. Sinclair Oil was the first to build a major refinery here, and others followed, setting up along the banks of the bayou. In typical Houston fashion, business leaders saw to it that the crude found its way from the fields through pipelines right into Bayou City refineries, where ships and rail cars lined up to take the by-products out to waiting world markets.

Thus, drenched in oil, many Houstonians focused on other enterprises. Oil field tools and equipment were vital to the highly competitive drilling industry, and native sons like Howard Hughes, Sr. invented such things as the oval cone drill now in universal use. The multiplicity of these endeavors fixed Houston as the oil field equipment manufacturing capital of the world.

Diversification

During the two world wars, particularly the second, many new industries were introduced that became vitally important to Houston's economy. There were mass conversions of existing factories to wartime production, and still others opened. Steel manufacturing and ship building became major industries as did plastics, synthetic rubber, and, using salt, gas, sea water, oil, and sulphur, explosives. The age of petro-chemicals had come into its own and, again, Houston took the lead as the world center for this new industry.

By the close of World War II, Houston had developed another rich resource—natural gas. It wasn't long before Easterners and Midwesterners became familiar with terms such as "Big Inch" and "Little Inch," which were pipelines that Houston-based Texas Eastern Transmission Corporation laid for transporting gas for heating wintry states in the north.

The People of Houston

From the beginning Houston attracted foreign immigrants, predominantly Germans and Bohemians (Czechs). The Mexicans were already here, and joining the waves of early immigrants were thousands of East Texas and Louisiana Acadians, who arrived to seek a better life in the oil fields and continue the age-old tradition of working area rice fields. While slavery was forbidden in Mexico, many Texan colonists were involved in the illicit trade, and thus many blacks were brought in to work the rich cotton and farmlands along the Brazos River.

The majority of Houston's settlers though were Southern whites seeking a new life during the post-Civil War Reconstruction era. They brought their Old South ways with them, but since Houston straddles the gateway to the Southwest, Southern gentility often gave way to a harsher frontier spirit. Thus the newcomer will observe today that many native Houstonians seem a mixed breed of Southerners with outgoing, robust Southwestern ways, influenced with an unusual blend of Mexican and Cajun "joie de vivre."

But in many other ways the Houstonian is a paradox, like Houston itself, resisting all attempts to be pinned with any label or description.

Houston is Houston. In ways, it remains a self-centered youth with an unshakable faith in its own destiny, an undying belief in itself and in the idea that nearly anything is possible.

HOUSTON TODAY

A Lot Has Happened Since 1836

Even the visionary Allen brothers who founded Houston would be astounded if they could return today to see what is happening to the bayou town they inaugurated in 1836.

These two New York land speculators promoted their new settlement with some fanciful claims, but even they couldn't possibly have foreseen that in just 150 years it would be the fourth most populous center in the country with over three million inhabitants.

Some say that the gangly bayou town is coming of age . . . that the rawboned blue-collar kid is developing into a well rounded, cosmopolitan center of commerce. Certainly with its miles of refineries and hundreds of other heavy industrial sites, Houston still wears her blue-collar label prominently. But with new input from space sciences, medical research, and diverse white-collar fields of endeavor, she is taking on a dressier image.

Houston's promising investment opportunities, minimum taxation, low cost of living, temperate climate, and overall potential have captured the imagination of the world, and new immigrants continue to arrive daily despite fickle unemployment in various industries.

Within the city limits sprawl 600 square miles of urb and suburb linked by 340-plus miles of completed freeways and tollroads. Encompassed in that area are industrial sites, billion-dollar office parks, warehouse districts, shopping centers, condos, hotels, and subdivision housing.

All Around Town

Unlike many of the nation's other cities, Houston has several major business districts. The oldest and largest is the downtown central business district, proclaimed by a magnificent futuristic skyline rooted primarily in finance and energy companies.

This core has been called the playground of today's most notable architects. The aesthetic designs prompt many visitors to take advantage of the American

20

Institute of Architects' Tour conducted on the third Sunday of each month (except December and August) at 2 pm. Information 622-2081. CH (nominal).

Uptown Houston boasts the tallest building in the nation outside of a central business district. The art-deco Transco Tower, at 65 floors, is the striking feature among hundreds of new buildings constituting the Galleria/Post Oak area. The area concentrates elite shops, restaurants, hotels, and clubs together with office buildings and apartments.

The South Main corridor is the third key district, the site of the world-famous Astrodomain and the renowned Texas Medical Center. Many medical support firms are in the area, along with lodging and some of the city's finest dining.

Outside these areas are many other major developments such as Greenway Plaza and the city's newest emerging skyline on the northwest corner called North Belt.

The Oil-Port Duo

While the city continues to diversify into a much broader business base than one might expect, the big bulge in the bicep continues to be energy in all its related forms. And any discussion of energy from oil should be in juxtaposition with shipping, since the exploration and refining industry practically grew up with the Port of Houston. Together they constitute the backbone of the city's economic base.

Before the great oil discoveries in the fields north and east of Houston, there was a concerted community effort to make good the founders' dream of developing a major world port. Eventually this was accomplished with the widening and dredging of Buffalo Bayou to accommodate every class of ocean-going vessel.

Who would have thought that the first steamboat, Laura, that made it up the twisting path of the sluggish bayou, would blaze the trail for the more than 5,000 ships a year that call on the Port today? And that the high banks' groves of cedar, pecan, magnolia, and oak would be replaced with several major refineries and more than 150 other types of industrial plants stretching along the inner half of the 50-mile channel to the Gulf?

Many of those companies manufacture such basic products as fertilizers, chemicals, plastics, and synthetic rubber. But the Port handles a vast variety of other goods as well, including heavy machinery and oil tools, sand and gravel, steel, agricultural products, sulphur, paper, and automobiles. Houston definitely has achieved its initial goal, for today the Port ranks first in the nation in international tonnage moved and second only to New York in total tonnage.

The Changing Profile

While much of the central spotlight remains on energy, there is growing diversity in other ventures entering the mainstream, making marked changes in the city's complexion.

A major shift in this direction occurred at the close of World War II, when city fathers foresaw the importance of establishing excellent medical care in a city even then experiencing a population explosion. In 1945 the Texas Medical Center was organized for the development and coordination of what has become one of the largest, if not the most mixed-use, medical facilities in the world. The center is still expanding, and already there are 38 different hospitals, schools, and other institutions. It has gained greater renown in the prevention and treatment of children's diseases, cancer research, and open-heart surgery. As a center of study, the complex maintains a faculty of 10,000 and draws students from all parts of the globe, introducing a new kind of brain pool to Houston.

The Space Age

Another major image change took place in 1962, when the National Aeronautics and Space Administration opened its 1,620-acre training and flight-control center here. At the peak of the Mercury/Gemini/Apollo programs NASA employed more than 5,000, mostly white-collar personnel involved in space sciences and related industries.

It is noteworthy that more than 125 companies followed NASA to Houston. But even before that, the city had a standard bearer in space-age pursuits at Rice University, the first to establish a curriculum in space sciences. That was followed by the implementation of similar programs at the University of Houston, which later opened a branch campus at Clear Lake, providing strong academic support for the space effort.

NASA virtually transformed what was once a cow pasture on the city's southeastern fringe. Today the growth continues all the way down to Galveston Bay, where housing, hotels, shopping centers, low-rise office parks, and giant resort developments have all been evolving.

The International Look

The best indicator of Houston's growth as an international city is its Intercontinental Airport, which several years ago added a third terminal, twice the size of the two originals. International arrivals generated a fourth terminal that opened in 1990 and is dedicated solely to foreign service. In 1993 more than 2.6 million international passengers went through Intercontinental, disembarking from flights that at least 11 airlines operate in direct and nonstop service to and from 33 foreign destinations, thus making Houston the nation's ninth busiest airport for international passengers.

The majority of foreign arrivals stem from international trade. It is known that about 550 foreign companies have offices in Houston and, conversely, more than 2,000 Houston-based firms operate abroad in more than 100 nations. Foreign interest is at such a peak there are now 55 nations with consular offices here.

The Convention and Visitor Trail ─────────

When Houston hosts a convention, and that ranges between 300 and 500 times a year, there is a trail of delegates from around the world.

Houston has long boasted more than 1.7 million square feet in exhibit halls situated mainly in four complexes, namely Astrodomain, the George R. Brown Convention Center, the downtown Civic Center, and The Summit. The largest at the moment is Astrodomain, anchored by the world-famous Astrodome and augmented by Astrohall and Astroarena. Second is the new Brown Center. Third in size is the Civic Center complex, which includes Albert Thomas Convention and Exhibit Center, Sam Houston Coliseum, the Music Hall, Wortham Center, and Jones Hall for the Performing Arts. The fourth is The Summit at Greenway Plaza. The George R. Brown Houston Convention Center contains 470,500 square feet of exhibit space plus 43 break-out meeting rooms, a major theater, a ballroom, and parking for 3,000 cars. The center will ultimately cover a wider area on the east side of downtown next to Chinatown.

A wide range of events are booked into these buildings; the Greater Houston Convention and Visitors Bureau reports convention business with 351 conventions in session during the course of 1992. Houston's major league sports teams also use these facilities, with the Rockets (basketball) playing in The Summit (where they won the 1994 National Basketball Association championship against the New York Knicks), and the Astros (baseball) and the Oilers (football) in the Astrodome.

And while conventioneers are pouring in from around the world, the Houston area is host to 4 million-plus tourists a year, making it the top visitor destination in Texas.

Cognizant of this growing role in corporate, convention, and visitor business, the hotel industry is hitching its wagon to the Gulf Coast star. At this writing there are about 33,000 rooms in major Houston hotels and motels.

The Third Coast ──────────────────────

In addition to promoting convention and visitor activity, the convention and visitors bureau is aggressively involved as liaison for Houston with the motion picture industry. Texas has become known in the movie circles as the "Third Coast" in filming, and Houston is getting a major share of this new and lucrative business. In fact, it was the forerunner among Texas cities in establishing a sales staff to solicit films and the first to form a private motion picture council to better serve the industry. Twenty-six productions were completed here in 1986, generating $10.8 million in revenue.

The Entertainment World ───────────────

As in its industrial circles, Houston has a broad mix in entertainment, ranging from country/western nightlife to esoteric dance programs, and from jazz to Gilbert and Sullivan. It is one of few cities in the country with its own grand opera, symphony, ballet, and professional theater, plus a Broadway musical production company.

The Academic Scene

Some of Houston's more than 35 colleges, universities, and institutes are visitor attractions in themselves. Rice University, established in 1912, and arguably the flagship of Houston's excellence in science and engineering, is on South Main, the only Ivy League-looking campus for miles.

The state's second largest institution is the University of Houston with a total enrollment of 48,000. It is worth a stroll around the main campus just to see the numerous works of outdoor art and magnificent new architecture. (See VISUAL ARTS.)

Texas Southern University opened in 1934 and is the state's largest predominantly black campus. The University of St. Thomas is Houston's largest Catholic school and was designed by the famous architect, Philip Johnson. Other institutions of higher learning include Houston Baptist University, the South Texas College of Law, University of Texas Health Science Center, Baylor College of Medicine, Prairie View A&M School of Nursing, and Texas Woman's University-Houston Center.

The Houston Independent School District is the nation's fifth largest with nearly 200,000 students.

Climate and Dress

At this point we would dispel all myths about Texas brags. We're not going to say come on down, the weather is great . . . we're simply going to say, y'all come but dress comfortable.

Here are the unvarnished facts: the average temperature year-round is 68.6 degrees Fahrenheit, while the average precipitation is close to 49.14 inches. As former mayor Louie Welch once quipped, "If you don't like Houston's weather, just wait five minutes." He's the same source for the observation that "Houston has two seasons: summer and February." We can offer a dry run with afternoon temperatures in the high 90s in summer or a "blue norther" dipping overnight into the low teens during the brief winter months.

Yes, it's humid and it rains much of the year, but we can almost guarantee you'll never shovel snow, and about the only ice you'll see is at a skating rink. You can shed your winter wear from early March to early December and during that time should stick to cottons and other lightweights. However, at times from early December through late February, you definitely should have a top coat, sweater, and rain gear handy. But not to worry about summer or winter . . . Houston is climate controlled with air conditioning everywhere, above ground, underground, and even outdoors in some spots.

This can be a dressy town, especially evenings at fine restaurants and chic parties. Otherwise it tends to be fairly casual, even at cultural events.

The most practical fabrics are cottons, linens, rayons, and silk for the summer and light woolen blends and ultra-suede for winter. Houston men continue to stick with traditional conservative attire, especially those who are older and more professionally oriented. The young of both sexes lean toward jeans.

MATTERS OF FACT

There are many telephone numbers that you may need at your fingertips, whether you are a visitor here, a new resident, or even if you've lived in Houston a long time. Some of the contacts that might be of interest to you for more specific needs are already listed in chapters such as INTERNATIONAL TRAVELER, NEW RESIDENTS, TRANSPORTATION, and others.

The following list recapitulates a few of those numbers, but most fall under the heading of miscellaneous.

AAA—524-1851.

Ambulance—Houston Fire Department dispatcher; 222-3434.

American Red Cross—526-8300.

Area Code—713.

Automobile Registration License and Title—224-1919 (Harris County Tax Assessor/Collector's Office).

Better Business Bureau—868-9500.

Chambers of Commerce—
Clear Lake Area Chamber of Commerce; 488-7676.
Galveston Chamber of Commerce; 1-409-763-5326.
Greater Houston Partnership (Houston Chamber of Commerce); 651-1313.
Houston Citizens Chamber of Commerce; 522-9745.
Northwest Chamber of Commerce; 440-4160.

City Hall—247-1000.
City Parks & Recreation (schedule of events in public parks); 845-1000 or 845-1111.
Civic Center; 853-8000.
Office of the Mayor; 247-2200.

Climate—Annual averages (calculated over the past 50 years, according to the National Weather Service)
Rainfall: 49.14 inches (149.78 cm).
Snow or ice: almost zero.
Clear days: 97.
Days above 90° F. (32° C.): 89.
Days below 32° F. (0° C.): less than fi day.
Dryest month: March.
Coldest month: January.
Warmest month: July.
Wind: South/Southeast prevailing.

Consumer Product Safety Commission—653-3448 (U.S. Govt.).

Consumer Services—Houston Associated Credit Bureau; 652-3434.

Convention Sales & Services—
Clear Lake/NASA Area Convention & Visitors Bureau; 488-7676.
Galveston Island Convention & Visitors Bureau; 1-409-763-4311.
Greater Houston Convention & Visitors Bureau; 227-3100 or 1-800-446-8786.

Dentist—Dentist Referral Service; 961-4337.

Doctor—Harris County Medical Society
(open 9 am-5 pm, Mon-Fri);
790-1838. Otherwise call the Houston
Emergency Ambulance service; 911,
or go directly to the hospital emergency room nearest to you, or contact
the hotel manager.

Driver's License—
General Information; 681-6187.
Information on testing locations;
681-6187 (Texas Dept. of Public
Safety).

Emergency Counseling—
Center for Counseling; 529-3555.
Crisis Hotline of Houston; 350-0700.
Family Connection Crisis House;
523-6825.
Runaway Hotline; 1-800-392-3352.
The Shoulder; 649-7200.

Emergency Rooms—
Ben Taub General Hospital (D3),
1504 Taub Loop; 793-2000.
Lyndon B. Johnson General Hospital,
5656 Kelley; 636-5000.
Veterans Administration Hospital
(E3), 2002 Holcombe Blvd.;
791-1414.

**Equal Employment Opportunity Com-
mission**—653-3320 (U.S. Govt.).

FBI—868-2266.

Federal Information Center—(800)
366-2998 or TDD (800) 326-2996.

Fire—911 or 227-2323.

Harris County—755-5000.
Precinct 1; 755-6111.
Precinct 2; 455-8104.
Precinct 3; 463-6300.
Precinct 4; 755-6444.
County Judge: Harris County Judge
Jon Lindsay; 755-6666.

Harris County Heritage Society—
655-1912.

Hospitals—Harris County Hospital District; 746-5800.

Houston Independent School District—
Information; 892-6390.

Human Resources—Texas Dept. of
Human Resources; 526-3531.

Institute of International Education—
621-6300.

IRS—541-0440.

Lawyer—
Houston Bar Association; 759-1133.
Houston Lawyer Referral Service;
237-9429.

Legal Aid—Gulf Coast Legal Foundation;
660-0077.

Library—Central Public Library; 236-1313.

Local Laws—
Pertaining to alcohol sales and consumption—Everyone must be 21 or
older to drink in public places in
Texas; liquor stores open 10 am-9 pm;
closed Sun and certain holidays; most
bars stay open until 2 am; no alcoholic
beverages sold on Sundays until after
12 noon. Even first offenders are sen-
tenced to jail for DWI. (See NEW
RESIDENTS chapter for more
details.)

Metropolitan Transit Authority—Route
information and schedules; 635-4000.

Motorists Assistance Program—
225-5627.

Newspapers—
Major dailies:
The Galveston *Daily News*; 488-1009
(Houston).
The Houston *Chronicle*; 220-7171.

Passport Offices—653-3153.

Pets—City of Houston information,
225-3301; Humane Society, 433-6421.

Pharmacy (24-hour)—Eckerd Drugs;
447-0358.

Poison Control Center—654-1701.

Police—Emergency; 911 or 222-3131.

Population—About 1.5 million city; 3.7
million statistical region.

Port of Houston—670-2400.

Post Office—Central Station (H10), 401
Franklin; 227-1474.

Radio Stations—
AM—
KCOH (1430) Music, talk.
KGBC (1450) Middle-of-the road,
Spanish, R&B.

KIKK (650) Country/Western.
KILT (610) Country/Western.
KJOJ (880) Middle-of-road.
KKBQ (790) Country.
KNUZ (1230) Middle-of-road.
KPRC (950) News/talk show.
KRBE (1070) Contemporary hits.
KTEK (1110) Christian news, talk.
KTRH (740) News/talk/sports.
KYOK (1590) Urban contemporary.
KYST (920) Bilingual.
FM—
KACC (91.3) Noncommercial top 40.
KHCB (105.7) Christian.
KHMX (96.5) Adult contemporary.
KHYS (98.5) Urban contemporary.
KIKK (95.7) Country/Western.
KILT (100.3) Country/Western.
KKBQ (92.9) Country.
KLITE (93.7) (See KLTR.)
KLOL (101.1) Album rock.
KLTR (93.7) Light rock.
KMJQ (102) Urban contemporary.
KODA (99.1) Adult contemporary.
KPFT (90.1) Alternative public access.
KQQK (106.5) Bilingual Top 40/Tex-Mex.
KQUE (102.9) Nostalgia/oldies.
KRBE (104.1) Top 40.
KRTS (92.1 & 104.9) Classical.
KTSU (90.9) Jazz (affiliated with Texas Southern University).
KUHF (88.7) Noncommercial classical; National Public Radio.
KZFX (107.5) Classical/Rock and Roll/60s, 70s and 80s.
Sheriff's Office—Citizens complaints; 221-6000.
Social Security—(800) 772-1213.
Social Services—United Way Helpline; 957-4357.
SPCA—869-8227.
Television Stations—
KHOU-TV, Channel 11 (CBS); 526-1111.
KHSH-TV, Channel 67 (Home Shopping Network); 331-8867.
KHTV-TV, Channel 39 (Independent); 781-3939.

KNWS-TV, Channel 51 (All News Station); 974-5151.
KPRC-TV, Channel 2 (NBC); 771-4631.
KRIV-TV, Channel 26 (Fox); 626-2610.
KTMD-TV, Channel 48 (Telemundo); 974-4848.
KTRK-TV, Channel 13 (ABC); 666-0713.
KTXH-TV, Channel 20 (Paramount); 661-2020.
KUHT-TV, Channel 8 (PBS); 748-8888.
KXLN-TV, Channel 45 (Univision); 662-4545.
Texas Alcoholic Beverage Commission—880-3003.
Texas Employment Commission—2040 North Loop West; 956-4170.
Texas Medical Center—
Administration; 797-0100.
Visitor Information; 790-1136.
Texas Rangers—957-6161.
Tickets—
Front Row; 977-5555 or 847-5555.
Houston Ticket Co.; 877-1555. Ticketmaster; 629-3700.
Northside Tickets; 447-8833.
Ticket Connection; 524-3687.
Time Zone—Central (on daylight savings time April-October).
Traffic Laws—Seat belts, infant seats required by law. May turn right on red; may turn left on red when moving from one-way street onto another one-way. Consuming alcohol while driving is illegal. Maximum speed limit on freeways 55 MPH. (See TRANSPORTATION.)
Traveler's Aid—668-0911.
U.S. Customs—Forms and publications; 671-1000.
Veteran's Administration—Benefit information and assistance; 664-4664.
Weather—Forecast and local weather; 529-4444.
Boating and recreation forecast; 228-8703.

TRANSPORTATION

With the existing variety of transportation systems including land, rail, air, and sea, traveling to and from Houston is no problem.

But in a city approaching 600 square miles that still has no method of mass rapid transit other than a public bus system, it is vital that visitors and newcomers be familiar with the alternatives for moving about in this highly mobile city with its nearly 2.2 million registered vehicles.

TO HOUSTON

Air

Houston has two commercial airports, Intercontinental and William P. Hobby. Together, operating at nearly full capacity, they served more than 28.8 million passengers in 1993. Combining the services at both airports, Houston has nonstop flights to 114 U.S. cities, plus 34 direct and nonstop destinations abroad, thus conveniently connecting Houston to more than 148 points around the globe.

Intercontinental Airport is the city's largest, covering 9,000 acres, and there are 19 airlines spread out among four terminals. The design of all four terminals is similar as follows: the lower level is devoted to a subway route and pedestrian tunnel; the street level is for baggage claim, car/taxi/limo pickup, and auto rentals; and level three is primarily for enplaning, deplaning and people amenities. Ticket counters are on level 3 in all terminals except the IAB, where they are at street level.

All the auto rental pick-up and drop-off points are located near the airport on Kennedy Boulevard and Will Clayton Parkway, with counters at the terminals.

The Mickey Leland International Airlines Building (IAB) handles all international arrivals and departures at Houston Intercontinental Airport (IAH). Federal inspection service facilities can process arriving international passengers in 45 minutes or less.

IAH terminals have signage and audio assistance in English and Spanish, while at Customs the directories are also in German, French, and Arabic. At IAB, passengers can exchange more than 70 currencies between 6:30 a.m. and midnight, when all scheduled international flights arrive and depart. Intercontinental Airport's three runways (9,400 ft., 10,000 ft., and 12,000 ft.) can serve any present or foreseeable aircraft in commercial use.

Hobby (HOU) was once the city's only airport but it is busier today than it ever was and is still growing. A recent multimillion-dollar expansion and renovation program has provided an additional concourse, an expanded baggage-claim area, renovated concourses, new dining and cocktail facilities, plus a new garage with covered parking for 3,500 cars.

Five major airlines, several commuters, and hundreds of private aircraft and cargo planes use Hobby daily. Hobby has most of the conveniences and services found at Intercontinental.

Airlines Serving Houston

Intercontinental Airport terminals and Hobby Airport-based airlines are shown in parentheses. Telephone numbers are for reservations and information. Numbers preceded by 1-800 are toll-free. Airline service and numbers may change without notice, and some (800) numbers may be regional and not dialable from all parts of the country.

Domestic

America West
(Terminal B) 1-800-247-5692
Continental & Continental Express
(Terminal C) 821-2100
Delta and ASA
(Terminal B & Hobby) 448-3000

Northwest
(Hobby) 1-800-225-2525
Southwest
(Terminal A & Hobby) 237-1221
United
(Terminal A & Hobby)
1-800-241-6522

International

Aeromexico
(IAB) 939-0777
Air Canada
1-800-776-3000
Air France
(IAB)1-800-237-2747
American
(Terminal B & Hobby)
1-800-433-7300
Aviateca
(IAB) 1-800-327-9832
British Airways
(IAB) 1-800-247-9297
Cayman Airways
(IAB) 1-800-422-9626

Continental
(Terminal C & IAB) 821-2100
KLM
(IAB) 1-800-777-5553
Lufthansa
(IAB) 1-800-645-3880
TACA
(IAB) 1-800-535-8780
TWA
(Hobby) 222-7273
USAir
(Terminal A) 1-800-428-4322
Viasa
(IAB) 1-800-327-5454

Ground Services To and From Houston Airports

Buses and Vans. Airport Express provides motor-coach service between Intercontinental and various locales around the city. The service has varied considerably over the years in terms of locations served—hotels, terminals or both—as well as in pricing and scheduling. All these elements have tended to be confusing and, just when you think you've figured them out, at least one seems to change. Most consistent has been use of buses to/from Intercontinental and vans to/from Hobby, plus the need to allow at least 60 and 40 minutes, respectively, for actual travel time.

Probably the best counsel for anyone planning to use this means of transfer is simply to call Airport Express at 523-8888 for the most current information, fares, and instructions. Passengers with more time than money can save 50% or more over what a cab would likely cost, but will require substantially more time and patience.

Some hotels and motels offer courtesy car service to/from Airport Express stops if not the airport itself. Ask your hotel/motel management whether they offer such a service and at what, if any, price.

The **Metro public bus** system operates a varying schedule of buses linking downtown with both airports.

The 50 Harrisburg-Airport route functions from early morning to late evening every day, taking passengers to/from Hobby in about 40 minutes for 85 cents (exact change).

The 102 Intercontinental Express links downtown with Intercontinental airport early morning through early evening on Mondays through Fridays only. The trip takes about an hour and costs $1.20 (exact change).

These are city buses with no special provision for luggage. Fares, routes, and stops can change with virtually no notice. For the best information on where, when, and how to catch these buses, call Metro Information at 635-4000.

Taxis. At Intercontinental there are taxi dispatch offices just outside the South entrance of each terminal. By zone, the fares range from a low of $29 for Downtown, up to $52 for the far East Side near NASA.

There are about 50 different taxi companies in Houston. Because of its large fleet of over 1,500, **Yellow Cab,** 236-1111, is the most highly visible at the airports and around town.

One of Houston's best-kept transportation secrets is affiliated with Yellow Cab: **Towne Car.**

Towne Car service costs no more than regular cabs to or from airports, and is available by reservation or direct call, although mainly for longer or more involved hauls.

What makes Towne Car distinctive is also the source of its name: dark blue Lincoln Towne Cars subtly marked with Towne Car livery. The cars invariably offer sparkling clean, air-conditioned interiors, an ocean of clean trunk space, and the most conscientious and dependable of drivers. One professional traveler has been using the same Towne Car and driver for nearly a decade and swears it's the only way to go to and from the airport.

Helicopters. These birds can be more squirrelly than whirly, as regular helicopter service to/from Houston airports has proven anything but regular. At this writing, there is none. Check with the City of Houston Aviation Department to determine whether choppers have returned and at what price.

Aircraft Rental and Charter

Two major fixed-base operators are located at Intercontinental Airport. They are **Garrett General Aviation Service Division,** 443-7300, and **Qualitron Aero Services,** 443-3434. The Garrett passenger terminal is at 17250 Chanute, and Qualitron is at 17725 Kennedy Blvd.

There are numerous fixed-base operators at Hobby, 13 of which are considered major operations. Check with Hobby Airport Operations, 643-4597, for a listing by ramps.

Automobile ———————————————————————

Houston is at the junction of I-10, crossing the country from east to west; I-45, originating at Galveston and terminating at Dallas; and I-610, the "Loop" encircling the city.

It is advisable to stop at a Texas Highway Department Information Center coming into Texas or at a major gasoline station to pick up a map, and ask for assistance on getting into Houston. Once you are in town the **Greater Houston Convention & Visitors Bureau,** 801 Congress, 227-3100, can assist. Ask your bell captain or car rental agent for directions on leaving the city.

Consider using the Sam Houston Tollway/Beltway 8 system, which flows freely even at rush hours and can save lots of time and aggravation — even if you must go a bit out of your way to use it. Tolls are payable at various segments, with the maximum payout totalling about $4.

Bus ————————————————————————————

Greyhound/Trailways has a terminal downtown at 2121 Main (L9), 1-800-231-2222.

Rail ————————————————————————————

AMTRAK, 1-800-872-7245. Amtrak has a passenger station downtown (H9) at 902 Washington Ave. Three trains a week link Houston with Los Angeles, three with Miami, and three with Chicago.

The Texas Limited, 864-9991, offers train excursions between Houston and Galveston Thursday-Sunday.

Package Tour

There is a trend in the United States for vacationers to take the simple route in holiday planning by paying a bottom-line price for a "package tour" that can include anything from the basic hotel room and ground transfer, to more extravagantly deluxe offerings such as chauffeured limo, helicopter transfer, and champagne treatment all the way. These are priced accordingly from budget to luxury and are sold through travel clubs, hotels, travel agents, tour operators, and card holder clubs. Another type of package may be a "weekend special" which most lodgings put together themselves and, again, the offerings run the gamut. Check with your local travel agent or directly with the hotel of your choice.

AROUND HOUSTON

Bus Charters

There are several major companies offering this service. They are **Gray Line,** 223-8800; **Kerrville,** 236-1887; and **Texas Bus Lines,** 523-5694.

Public Transportation

Metropolitan Transit Authority (Metro) operates the public bus system. The fare on all local rides is 85¢; an express ride is $1.20, and Park N Ride fares vary. In the Downtown area there is a Texas Special circulatory route from 10 am to 3 pm, Mon-Fri with a 30¢ fare. Exact change is required on all boardings, except passengers who have monthly passes or ticket books. Transfers available.

Downtown stops are easily identified with the bus code colors of red, white, and blue. In outlying areas they are metal poles labeled "Bus Stop." Park N Ride lots are also marked.

The average waiting time during peak periods is 10-15 minutes; during the normal time of the day, 20-30 minutes; during late night, early morning or weekends, 45-60 minutes.

Tickets, maps, and route and schedule information are available at MTA offices (I10), 705 Main; 635-4000. For information on Metrolift vans for disabled or senior passengers, call 225-0119.

Taxi

Apart from the taxi operations at the airports there are stands at most major hotels and motor hotels. Taxis are permitted to cruise, and you may hail a cab, but it is best to call in advance with a specific address for pickup.

The city has structured taxi fares as follows: the flag drop charge is $1.50 for

Port of Houston   *Greater Houston Convention & Visitors Bureau*

the first 1/9 mile, then it is 30¢ for each additional 2/9 mile; a mile ride costs about $2.70. Waiting charge is $15 an hour. Bear in mind that, depending on the size of the cab, four may ride for the price of one.

While there are about 50 taxi companies in the Houston area, the largest is **Yellow Cab,** 236-1111. Several other alternate choices may include **Liberty Cab,** 999-0088; **Square Deal Cab,** 659-7236; **United,** 699-0000; and **Fiesta Cab,** 225-2666 (bilingual drivers).

Auto Rentals and Leasing

There are more than 170 firms involved in renting and leasing. Most of them rent by the day, week, or month. You should shop for the best deal, but the following are a few suggestions: **Ashbaugh,** 659-8555; **Avis,** 659-6537; **Budget,** 944-1888; **Dollar-Rent-A-Car,** 227-7368; **Enterprise,** 774-7000; **Hertz,** 659-8190; **National,** 654-1695; and **Thrifty,** 442-5000.

Limousine Charters

There are more than 30 limousine companies operating in Houston. Two recommendations: **Action Limousines,** 781-5466 or 1-800-SENDLIMO; and **Limousine Service International,** 524-8468.

Private Car

When driving your own car be sure to plot your course with clear routing instructions.

Special Information on Major Thoroughfares

It should be helpful to the visitor and the newcomer to know that Houstonians refer to certain freeways and expressways in colloquial terms. It can be confusing, for example, when asking for directions to I-10 East and you are told to head out the Beaumont highway. The following key is an attempt at definition.

Interstate 45 North—North Freeway or Dallas Highway.

Interstate 45 South—Gulf Freeway or the road to Galveston (not to be confused with Old Galveston Road, which is not a freeway).

Interstate 610—The Loop (in all directions North, South, East, and West).

U.S. 59 North—Eastex Freeway or Cleveland Highway.

U.S. 59 South—Southwest Freeway.

Interstate 10 East—East Freeway or Beaumont Highway.

Interstate 10 West—Katy Freeway or San Antonio Highway.

Highway 290—Northwest Freeway, the Austin Highway, or Hempstead Highway.

Highway 225 East—LaPorte Freeway.

Highway 3—Old Galveston Road.

Hempstead Highway—Old Katy Road.

Alternate 90—Old Spanish Trail and S. Wayside Drive.

Alternate 90 South—South Main.

Highway 90 North—McCarty St. or Old Beaumont Highway.

Highway 35—Telephone Road.

Highway 288—Almeda Road or the new South Freeway.

The principal through streets and avenues downtown are: Main St. which runs generally north and south; Fannin runs parallel to Main and is a major artery going south; Texas Ave., a crosstown street becomes Harrisburg Blvd. toward the east; Capitol, a crosstown street becomes Memorial Drive going west; Lamar, crosstown street becoming Allen Parkway going west; Travis from downtown puts you on I-45 North; Milam from downtown to U.S. 59 South; Louisiana to I-10 West; Smith to U.S. 59 South; Chartres or Rusk from downtown to U.S. 59 North; Jefferson to I-45 South; Main to Alternate 90 South.

Most Houston streets are wide, the average being 80 feet. Others such as Main Street and Texas Avenue are more expansive. By city ordinance, newly developed streets must be at least 100 feet wide.

Speed limits vary, depending on the area and type of street. Freeways are posted with 55 m.p.h. maximum and 45 minimum. The speed limit on major streets is 35, which becomes 40-45 in outlying areas. Residential streets are usually 30 m.p.h., and in school zones it's a heavily enforced 20 m.p.h. at posted times on school days.

IMPORTANT: Do NOT pass a stopped school bus when its stoplights are flashing, regardless of the direction of your approach and regardless of the impatience of drivers behind you. Police can *arrest* you.

In Texas it is permissible to turn right at a red light, unless otherwise posted, but you must first come to a complete stop and look in both directions before moving on. You may also turn left on red if turning from a one-way street into another one-way. Again, stop and look before proceeding.

During rush hours all major freeways have a contra-flow HOV (high-occupancy vehicle) lane. Anyone driving in the closely monitored HOV without at least one passenger will be stopped and ticketed. Some other streets may have reversible lanes during peak traffic periods.

The following are some helpful driving hints. Remember that Houston, like other major cities, is moving fast. Entry ramps onto the freeways tend to be short, so be careful to ease over to allow people in. Use the maps at the beginning of this book, which are clear and easy to read. Or have a map beside you in the car, your route boldly and clearly highlighted in advance.

Never leave anything of value loaded in a vehicle or trailer, even when locked, overnight.

In warmer months, never leave children or pets in a closed car. Even when the car is vacant, leave a window slightly open to prevent windows from shattering under intense heat. Interior temperature can rise to well over 100° in a matter of minutes.

Visitors will encounter little difficulty in finding desirable parking, except in the core of downtown, where lots and meters can be frustratingly crowded. We recommend open lots and particularly those more distant from the central downtown core. At numerous unstaffed lots you'll need several $1 bills or perhaps a roll of quarters to pay posted maximum fees. There is plentiful parking in underground garages at the Civic Center, ideal for evening cultural performances since they are fairly secure, reasonably priced, and connected to the public buildings in the area via guarded pedestrian tunnels.

In case of emergencies or in need of other auto assistance: **AAA** (D2), 3000 Southwest Freeway (US 59 South); 524-1851. **City of Houston Police,** 222-3131 or 911 for emergencies only; 221-0777 auto theft; TTY/TTD for deaf community only 224-0675. **Houston Fire Dept. or Paramedics Ambulance,** 911 for emergencies only; or 224-2663 (deaf community only).

Tours

More than a score of companies offer a variety of tour programs, some scheduled and others by special arrangement, and ranging from aerial to ground to sea, both in Houston and Galveston. There are also foreign language and industrial tours by special arrangement.

For a regular printed schedule of eleven different daily sightseeing tours contact **Gray Line Tours of Houston** (C4), 602 Sampson; 223-8800.

For a complete list of sightseeing companies consult the **Greater Houston Convention & Visitors Bureau,** 801 Congress. For custom tours by special advance arrangement, try: **Custom Convention Services of Houston** (C4), 812 Delano; 228-9449.

Walking

Downtown sidewalks are generally wide and clean and certain streets lend themselves to window shopping, having points of architectural interest and historical and cultural attractions. Try the Civic Center area with its small parks and plazas.

The downtown pedestrian tunnel system is especially interesting and comfortably air-conditioned. For a quick look at the system, go underground at the Hyatt Regency Houston Hotel and walk northeast one block to the mall under the 1100 Milam Building. (A DOWNTOWN WALKING TOUR is included under SELF-GUIDED CITY TOURS.)

Just west of the downtown area is Buffalo Bayou Park with hike-and-bike trails on both sides along Memorial and Allen Parkway. (See SIGHTS and SPORTS.)

LODGING

With 33,000 rooms, there is hardly a quadrant in the city that doesn't have its share of fine lodging, with the greatest concentration in The Galleria/Post Oak and the North Belt areas near Intercontinental Airport.

There is a hotel, inn, or resort to suit nearly every traveler's needs, budget or taste.

The following selection of hotels, motor hotels, campgrounds, and resorts is keyed to maps at the beginning of the book. If a restaurant, pool or lounge is outstanding, it will be singled out, and unless otherwise stated nearly all hotels have these features.

The following key is used at the end of each listing.

BF—Barrier-free from the front door throughout, including guest rooms and public space. Increasingly, telephones and water fountains are at correct levels for the handicapped, as are elevator buttons, frequently also in braille.
FC—Some foreign currencies accepted at checkout.
FL—Some foreign language personnel at key positions.
PA—Pets allowed. If there are side restrictions we will advise.

Be aware that while hotels have rack rates that may be categorized as expensive, moderate, or inexpensive, they frequently offer discounts or weekend specials that could fall into a cheaper category. Also, rates fluctuate periodically and what may be inexpensive during one quarter may become moderate the next. Be sure to check with the lodging of your choice to determine whether you qualify for a special discount or whether a package rate is available at the time you plan to check in.

E—Expensive, $80 and up for a double room;
M—Moderate, $50-$80 for a double room;
I—Inexpensive, less than $50 for a double room.

Finally, be aware that amenities, decor, facilities, accessibility, courtesy transportation, and specialized services—just like ownership, management, name, and rates—are subject to change without notice.

HOTEL SAFETY RULES

As a public-safety service we include in this chapter the following guidance in case of a hotel fire. All information is taken from a publication of the National Safety Council.

Preliminary precautions start after you check into your hotel. Check the exits and fire alarms on your floor, count the doorways between your room and the exit, keep your key close to your bed and take it with you if you leave your room in case you need to return. In case smoke blocks your exit, check the window latches and any adjoining buildings or decks for low-level escape.

In case of fire, take your key and *crawl* to the door. Don't stand; smoke and deadly gases rise.

If the doorknob is hot—*do not open*—stay in your room. Then open the window, phone for help, hang a sheet from the window to signal for help. Turn on the bathroom fan. Fill the tub with water to wet towels and sheets to put around doors if smoke seeps in. Make a tent over your head with a blanket at a partially opened window to get fresh air.

If the doorknob is *not* hot, leave, close the door to your room, proceed to the exit, counting doorways in the dark, and walk down to ground level. If blocked at lower levels, turn around, walk up to the roof and keep the roof door open to vent stairwell. Wait for help on the roof. **Do not use elevator. Remember to lay low to avoid smoke and gases.**

HOTELS AND MOTELS

ADAM'S MARK HOTEL(D1) 2900 Briarpark Dr.; 978-7400. *E*. This 600-plus-room property is a big-city, upbeat hotel with enough amenities on premises and nearby to keep the whole family entertained. Swim outdoor to indoor, then enjoy a work-out, sauna, or whirlpool. Nearby tennis. Full concierge. *FL, PA (deposit)*. Also large exhibit center and meeting space.

AIRPORT HILTON INN (see Hilton listing).

ALLEN PARK INN (C3), 2121 Allen Parkway; 521-9321. *I to* M. This comfortable motel is convenient to downtown in a quiet location overlooking Buffalo Bayou Park. It is a corporate inn with ballroom, meeting rooms, and suites, 24-hour room and telephone answering service. Features include health club, free parking, some kitchenettes, and special rates for extended periods of stay.

ASTRODOMAIN HOTELS (E2), 8686 Kirby; 748-3221. This complex is made up of four hotels with a total of more than 1,000 rooms and suites. They are **Holiday Inn Astrodome**, M., **Sheraton Astrodome Hotel,** M., the **Radisson**

Suite Hotel Astrodome, M-E. and **Days Inn Astrodome,** I. The hotel is a high-rise with the famous "Celestial Suite" at the top. Ideally situated across from the Astrodomain and Six Flags Astroworld, features include shops in connected facilities. Courtesy car for the nearby points. Lanai rooms. FL. (Texas: 1-800-627-6461; US: 1-800-231-2360).

BEST WESTERN. There are several properties of this chain of motor hotels in Houston.
    Best Western Dome Royale (E2), 3223 South Loop West at S. Main; 664-6425. I. Across from the Astrodomain complex, this 109-room motor hotel is a popular visitor stop. It has a pool, courtesy car to Texas Medical Center. Group rates.
    Best Western Greenspoint (A1), 11211 North Freeway; 447-6311. I. Golf close by, shopping and tennis several miles. Free in-room movies. Courtesy car to nearby Intercontinental Airport.
    Best Western Gulf (D4), 2391 S. Wayside Dr. at Gulf Freeway; 928-5321. I. PA (small).
    Best Western Intercontinental (A2), 6900 Will Clayton Parkway; 446-3041. I. Golf close by, shopping and tennis several miles. Courtesy car for Intercontinental Airport.

CHARLIE FITNESS CLUB & HOTEL, 9009 Boone Rd. between Beechnut and Bissonnet; 530-0000. M. A small but unique hotel with free use of health club. Meeting rooms.

COMFORT INN GALLERIA WESTCHASE (C1), 9041 Westheimer; 783-1400. I. Convenient to shopping, dining, and night life, this motel has a pool, color TV, AM-FM radio, direct-line telephones, laundromat, and meeting rooms. Also smoke alarms and other safety devices.

DAYS INN OF AMERICA. These motels, designed for the budget-minded family traveler, maintain a high standard of management. Two double beds per room, free parking. BF, PA (CH).
    Days Inn (B3), 100 W. Cavalcade; 869-7121. I.
    Days Inn (C5), 10155 East Freeway; 675-2711. I.
    Days Inn (D4), 2200 S. Wayside; 928-2800. I.
    Days Inn (F6), 2020 NASA Rd. 1; 332-3551. I. Close to the LBJ Space Center, Clear Lake Park, and Galveston Bay fishing outlets. Shopping mall one block. Resort atmosphere. Pool. Good family location.
    Days Inn Astrodome (E2), 8500 Kirby; 796-8383. I to M. (See Astrodomain listing for more information.)
    Days Inn West (B1), 9799 Katy Freeway; 468-7801. I.

DOUBLETREE HOTEL (A2), 15747 Drummet Blvd.; 442-8000. I to M. A short distance from Intercontinental Airport, this inn features an 18-hole golf course nearby. *Oakley's Restaurant* specializes in seafood dinners and *Bo Peep's* is a theme lounge with juke box and game room. Special relocation rates, minimum seven-day stay. Courtesy van for the airport. Special services and amenities include free newspapers and shower caps. Pool with side service. BF *(elevator buttons in braille)*.

DOUBLETREE HOTEL AT ALLEN CENTER (J8-9), 400 Dallas; 759-0202. E. An elegant downtown hotel with 341 deluxe rooms. Convenient to both the Civic Center and the George R. Brown convention center. World-class dining in a beautiful restaurant, pastry shop, and lobby bar overlooking the lovely fountain gardens of the Allen Center. Original art in all rooms and 24-hour room service. Also a concierge, meeting facilities, and a full-service business center. Health facilities available. BF, FC, *FL*.

DOUBLETREE HOTEL AT POST OAK (C2), 2001 Post Oak Blvd.; 961-9300. E. An elegant international hotel situated in the heart of the fashionable Galleria/Post Oak shopping, entertainment, and corporate office complex, designed by the world-famous architect, I. M. Pei. Boasts 455 over-size rooms in both traditional and contemporary motifs, 48 spacious suites, a ballroom, and meeting rooms. Beautiful restaurants such as the *Vendome* and *Promenade Room*; also lounge areas and retail outlets. Food and beverage at poolside. Concierge.

ECONOLODGE (B1), 9535 Katy Freeway; 467-4411. *I*. This is a good economy motor inn; ideal for families. No frills. Pool.

THE FLAGSHIP HOTEL (see GALVESTON).

FOUR SEASONS. This fine, award-winning chain is one of the most deluxe in the Americas.
Four Seasons Hotel Houston (J10-11), 1300 Lamar; 650-1300. E. One of Houston's finest downtown deluxe hotels offers elegance in an art nouveau ambiance. A full-service corporate and convention facility. Spacious and beautifully landscaped multi-level lobby features bar and terrace with light meals and entertainment. The *Maison de Ville* formal dining room is accessible via private lobby elevator, and offers Saturday and Sunday brunch and Continental cuisine. Also boutiques and galleries. Heated pool with terraced gardens and side service. Special room services include robe, shoeshine, newspapers, and turn-down service. Other amenities are whirlpool and connection to nearby athletic club. Courtesy shuttle limo anywhere downtown. BF, PA *(on leash)*.

GUEST QUARTERS SUITE HOTEL (D1), 5353 Westheimer Rd.; 961-9000. E. All suite accommodations provide a home-away-from-home atmosphere, complete with fully equipped kitchen, dining area, living room, one or two bedrooms, and grocery deliveries. High-rise contemporary quarters on the West Side with food and beverage service, secretarial services, valet parking, clock radios, and all queen beds. Courtesy cars to restaurants and shops within a two-mile radius. Corporate and convention meeting facilities available.

HARVEY SUITES HOUSTON MEDICAL CENTER (D2), 6800 S. Main St.; 528-7744. Telex: 775774. M *to* E. This hotel across from the Medical Center is ideally situated for patients and their families, and for visitors here for conventions, sports, or leisure at the nearby Astrodomain and Six Flags Astroworld. Courtesy car transfers to the Medical Center, The Galleria, and business complexes. Concierge desk offers wide range of services including tours (Spanish and English), translations, shopping assistance, car and limo rentals, and airline reservations. Suites for business travelers. *FL*. Many full kitchens.

HILTON HOTELS. There are several Hilton Inns, Inc. hotels and inns in Houston, situated in strategic sectors throughout the city. This premier international company offers luxury accommodations in each location.
　Airport Hilton Houston (F2), 500 North Belt East; 931-0101. M *to* E. This hotel has 378 rooms plus a fully comprehensive Conference Center. Situated close to Intercontinental Airport with courtesy car for guest transfers. Amenities include three swimming pools, sauna, two bars, and nightclub. Also townhouses with whirlpool and wet bar.
　Brookhollow Hilton Inn (B2), 2504 North Loop West; 688-7711. E. This Hilton has 204 rooms and an excellent seafood restaurant called *The Anchorage*. Convenient to The Galleria and corporate offices in the area.
　Hilton Hobby Airport (E5), 8181 Airport Blvd.; 645-3000. M. Across the street from Hobby Airport, this new high-rise hotel has 310 rooms and features penthouse suites with private pools. Also jogging track, swimming pool with side service, two restaurants, nightclub with entertainment, and courtesy car for the airport. Ballroom, meeting space. *BF, FL*.
　Hilton Inn Houston West, 12401 Katy Freeway; 496-9090. *I to* M. Situated on the city's booming West Side, this 162-room hotel is oriented to corporate business. Free parking. Meeting rooms. *BF*.
　Hilton Southwest (D1), 6780 Southwest Freeway; 977-7911. M. A high-rise, Western-motif, full-service hotel on the West Side convenient to shopping centers and corporate offices. Continental brunch in an atrium lobby cafe. Ballroom and meeting rooms. Heated pool with sauna. Car rental and airline desks. Free parking. Relocation rates with 10-day minimum stay. *BF, FL, PA (deposit)*. (668-9211).
　Houston Plaza Hilton (D2), 6633 Travis at Southgate and a block from the Texas Medical Center; 524-6633. E. An 18-story luxury hotel featuring rooms and suites complete with wet bar and refrigerator. Also health club which includes a pool, running track, spas, saunas, weight room, and lockers. A restaurant and lounge.

Westchase Hilton and Towers (D1), 9999 Westheimer; 974-1000. M. A deluxe hotel located on the fashionable West Side next to the Carillon Shopping Center. Special features include heliport for transfers to and from Intercontinental Airport and, on request, to The Galleria. Ballroom and fully equipped meeting rooms. Valet parking *(NCH)*, full concierge. Room features include 24-hour news, sports, and movies, and room service 24 hours. Airline and auto rental stations, heated pool, two-hole putter, and guest membership to nearby health and recreational club. Van and limo to and from The Galleria, Hobby, and Intercontinental. *FC, FL.*

HOLIDAY INNS. The world-renowned Holiday Inn green logo can be seen in almost every section of the city, offering its traditional service to America's travelers, whether on business or pleasure. Most offer the same range of services and amenities such as courtesy cars. *FC, FL, PA,* free parking, and ample meeting room facilities.

Holiday Inn Airport—Intercontinental (A2), 3702 North Sam Houston Parkway East; 449-2311. *I to E.*

Holiday Inn Astrodome (E2), 8111 Kirby; 790-1900. *I to E.* Within walking distance to the Astrodome, this 242-room property caters both to the business traveler and vacationing families. Offers pool with side service plus banquet and meeting facilities. *BF (2).* No-smoking floor.

Holiday Inn Crowne Plaza (C1), 2222 West Loop South; 961-7272. *E.*

Holiday Inn Galleria/West Loop (F1), 3131 W. Loop South; 621-1900. M.

Holiday Inn Greenway Plaza (F2), 2712 Southwest Freeway; 523-8448. *M to E.*

Holiday Inn Hobby Airport (D4), 9100 Gulf Freeway; 943-7979. *E.* This 300-room high rise features a beautiful atrium lobby, two restaurants, two lounges, designer-decorated rooms, deluxe and presidential suites, indoor pool with sun deck, exercise room, sauna, and whirlpool. Located three miles from Hobby and nine miles from downtown. Also fourteen conference rooms.

Holiday Inn Houston East (C6), 15157 I-10 East; 452-7304. *I to M.*

Holiday Inn Houston North, 16510 I-45 North; 821-2570. *I to M.*

Holiday Inn Houston/Park-10 West, 14703 Park Row, 558-5580. *M to E.*

Holiday Inn I-10 at Loop 610 (B1), 7611 Katy Freeway; 688-2221. *I.*

Holiday Inn Medical Center (D2), 6701 S. Main; 797-1110. *I to M.*

Holiday Inn NASA (F6), 1300 NASA Rd. 1; 333-2500. *I to M.*

Holiday Inn Northwest, 14996 Northwest Freeway; 939-9955. *I.*

Holiday Inn Southwest (E1), 11160 Southwest Freeway; 530-1400. *I.*

HOTEL SOFITEL (A1), North Belt at Imperial Valley Drive; 445-9000. Toll-free in Houston: 1-800-231-4612; New York: 1-800-221-4542. M *to E.* This $30-million hotel/restaurant complex close to Intercontinental Airport is one of the first of this French chain of hotels to be constructed in the U.S. Three types of French cuisine, traditional, provincial, and bistro. Each room features European period reproduction furnishings with seating area and secretarial, perfumed soaps and shampoos, turn-down service, special hangers, and theatrical lighting in baths. Features 24-hour concierge. Meeting and convention facilities. Heliport nearby. Indoor heated pool with garden terrace. Outdoor tropical pool and gazebo bar. Saunas. Courtesy van to and from Intercontinental Airport and to Greenspoint Mall. Free parking. *BF, FC, FL, PA.*

HOUSTON MEDALLION (B2), 3000 North Loop West; 688-0100. *E.* This 402-room hotel has an atrium lobby and a DJ in the lounge nightly. Sauna and hydrotherapy pool.

HOWARD JOHNSON'S MOTOR LODGES. For traveling Americans, this pioneer of the motor lodge concept offers a dependable standard of accommodation and dining.

Howard Johnson Lodge (A3), 3939 North Freeway; 691-3951. *I.*

Howard Johnson Lodge (E5), 7777 Airport Blvd.; 644-1261. *I to* M. Located in front of Hobby Airport. A large comfortable lodge with relaxed atmosphere. Meeting rooms and small ballroom. Courtesy car to and from the airport.

Nassau Bay Plaza and Marina Howard Johnson (F6), 3000 NASA Rd. 1; 333-9300. *M to E.* On the shores of Clear Lake across from the LBJ Space Center, this 14-story hotel has 240-plus rooms. A full-service hotel featuring live entertainment, fresh seafood specialties, pool with side service, car rentals, and free parking. Access to water sports includes skiing and sailing. Courtesy car for Hobby Airport. *BF, FL.*

HYATT REGENCY HOUSTON HOTEL (J9), 1200 Louisiana; 654-1234. *E.* On the heels of the Atlanta Hyatt Regency success came the Houston Hyatt with the "Portmanesque" design 30-story atrium lobby with inside and outside glass elevators, colorful balconies, and majestic garden lobby. Overlooking the lobby is *Hugo's,* an elegant Continental restaurant. High atop the hotel is *The Spindletop* revolving restaurant and lounge, open for lunch, dinner, and evening cocktails. The Hyatt boasts 959 rooms and 52 suites plus a magnificent ballroom and many meeting rooms. Amenities include full-service concierge, swimming pool with side service, gift shop with out-of-town newspapers, valet parking *(CH),* in-house movies and escalator connection to the Downtown Tunnel system. *BF, PA (on leash).*

LA COLOMBE D'OR (F2), 3410 Montrose Blvd.; 524-7999. *E.* This Old-World type hostelry with only five suites, a penthouse, and a French restaurant, was cited by *Esquire* magazine in a feature titled, "One of the Six Best Small Big City Hotels." It is in one of the few remaining mansions along the once fashionable Montrose Boulevard. The home was built in 1923 by Walter Fondren, one of the principals in the founding of Exxon. All of the original parquet floors, wood paneling, and decorative friezes have been restored. The suites and penthouse (fabulous view of Houston skyline) are appointed in fine antiques and decorative arts. The original library is a quiet corner for reading or conversation before an elegant meal in one of Houston's best restaurants, La Colombe d'Or's own dining room. Suite guests get the real VIP treatment, and can have dinner in their own private dining room. Private functions for up to 500 can be accommodated.

THE LANCASTER (I10), 701 Texas Ave. at Louisiana; 228-9500. *E*. A downtown Houston landmark historic hotel, formerly the Auditorium. This 93-room hotel has been totally renovated and restored to unprecedented grandeur. There are only nine rooms on each floor with custom-made furniture and Italian-marble baths, and each room has VCR and CD players. This is a traditional Old-World hotel with all brass hardware, a doorman, a concierge desk, and valet parking. Also offering several meeting and banquet rooms. Complimentary limousine service available.

LA QUINTA MOTOR INNS, a Texas-based chain from San Antonio, operate several Houston motels plus one on Galveston Island. Dependable service and accommodations. *PA (small)*.
    La Quinta (B1), 11113 Katy Freeway; 932-0808. *I*. Convenient to Town & Country Village and Memorial Center. Meeting rooms. Parking for tour buses.
    La Quinta (B1), 8017 Katy Freeway; 688-8941. *I*. Meeting room.
    La Quinta (E1), 8201 Southwest Freeway; 772-3626. *I*. Convenient to Memorial Hospital, Sharpstown Center, and The Arena theater. Meeting rooms available.
    La Quinta, 17111 North Freeway; 444-7500. *I*. Meeting rooms.
    La Quinta-Astrodome (E2), 9911 Buffalo Speedway; 668-8082. *M*. Complimentary services include local calls, cribs. No-smoking section. Swimming pool with hot-tub. Meeting room.
    La Quinta Hobby Airport (E5), 9902 Gulf Freeway; 941-0900. *I*.
    La Quinta Houston Brookhollow (B1), 11002 Northwest Freeway; 688-2581. *I*.
    La Quinta Houston Greenway Plaza (F1), 4015 Southwest Freeway; 623-4750. *I*. Close to The Summit.
    La Quinta Houston Intercontinental (A1), 6 N. Belt East; 447-6888. *I*. Courtesy car for Intercontinental Airport.
    La Quinta Inn East (C5), 11999 East Freeway; 453-5425. *I*. Shopping mall across the street.

MARRIOTT HOTELS makes a major statement in its Houston-area hotels, all adhering to the quality that has given the Marriott chain an excellent reputation around the world, promoting a dedicated following of business and family travelers.
    Houston Marriott Westside, 13210 Katy Freeway; 558-8338. *M to E*. A 400-room leisure and corporate hotel on the city's West side. A specialty restaurant

plus three lounges and live entertainment. Overlooks a three-acre lake with tributary extending into an atrium lobby. Amenities include health club on premises and close access to Bear Creek Golf World. *FC, FL*.

J.W. Marriott Hotel (F1), 5150 Westheimer; 961-1500. *E*. This hotel across the street from The Galleria, has 518 rooms, plus a 20,000 square-foot exhibit center. Other features include a 24-hour room service and secretarial service, indoor-outdoor pool and fully equipped health club, lighted tennis court, and racquetball. *BF, FC, FL*.

Marriott Houston Airport (A2); 443-2310. *E*. A full-service hotel catering to the business traveler with 576 rooms, 14 suites, two bi-level suites, and four hospitality suites. A new tower has seven additional hospitality suites. Abundant meeting space plus a large ballroom. Features two fine restaurants, one a revolving rooftop dinner spot plus *CK's Flight Room* lounge with live entertainment and dancing. Hotel between IAH Terminals B & C connects to the free subway train linking all four terminals at the airport.

Marriott Medical Center Houston (D2), 6580 Fannin at Dryden; 796-0080. *E*. This 400-room high-rise hotel caters to Texas Medical Center visitors as well as corporate, convention, and tourist business. *FL*. For information call hotel number or the U.S. toll-free number 1-800-228-9290.

Marriott North at Greenspoint (A1), 255 N. Sam Houston Parkway E.; 875-4000. *E*. Near the Intercontinental Airport and adjacent to Greenspoint Mall. Free parking. Features 400 rooms plus indoor/outdoor pool and hydrotherapy pool, saunas, and work-out room. Ballroom and meeting rooms. Complimentary transportation to and from Intercontinental Airport. *FL, PA (small)*.

MOTEL 6, 16884 Northwest Freeway in Jersey Village; 937-7056. This motel features large rooms, swimming pool, pet facilities, non-smoking rooms, color TV, AM-FM radio, and dining facilities. Also two meeting rooms. No charge for cribs.

OMNI HOUSTON HOTEL (C1), Four Riverway; 871-8181. *E*. This delightful hotel is in the center of the West Side commercial center, close to The Galleria, but so hidden away in the woods along Buffalo Bayou that it almost lends itself to being an exclusive resort. This is pure elegance in beautiful surroundings with rustic bike trails and a sparkling manmade lake off the main lobby. There are four bars and restaurants, a mini-health center, twelve conference/meeting rooms, and a British-type pub. Sunday brunch in the *Cafe on the Green*. Valet parking *(CH)*; also free self-parking in garage. *BF, FC, FL, PA*.

PREMIER INNS (F2), 2929 Southwest Freeway; 528-6161. *M*. Convenient to The Summit. Heated pool, meeting and banquet rooms, room service, auto rentals next door, and free parking.

QUALITY INNS. There are several in Houston, all attracting business and family travelers who expect comfortable, clean, and friendly accommodations.

Quality Inn (A2), 6115 Will Clayton Parkway; 446-9131. M. A unique hunting lodge atmosphere on beautiful, spacious wooded grounds, with biking, tennis, nearby golf, and olympic pool. Also a supper club with live entertainment and dancing. Hospitality suites, orthopedic beds, and a conference center are among the amenities. Courtesy car to and from Intercontinental Airport. Big-screen TV and in-room movies. PA (CH). Gift shop and travel agency on premises. Car rentals.

RADISSON SUITE HOTEL—ASTRODOME (E2), 1400 Old Spanish Trail; 796-1000. Telex: 753309. M to E. This property has the ambiance of a European inn with 191 suites with separate bedrooms. Almost within walking distance of the Astrodome and near to the Texas Medical Center. A suite encompasses over 400 square feet and includes kitchenette, telephones, two TV sets, microwave. Exercise room, sauna, game room, pool.

RADISSON SUITES HOUSTON WEST, 10655 Katy Freeway; 467-6411. I to E. High-rise hotel in Town & Country Village. Function rooms. Club with live entertainment.

RAMADA INNS. Situated in outlying areas of the city.

Ramada Hotel (B1), 7787 Katy Freeway; 681-5000. I to M. A high-rise, minutes from downtown. Special amenities are deluxe suites with whirlpool, wide-screen sports TV in lounge, and taped entertainment in club. The *Bridge* is a cheerful restaurant with seafood the specialty. Free parking. Relocation rate offered if stay is 30 days or longer. Plenty of meeting and party facilities. FL, PA. 1-800-228-2828.

Ramada Hotel Astrodome/Medical Center (E2), 2100 S. Braeswood; 797-9000. M to E. Features include heated pool with side service, free parking, barber shop, boutique with designer clothes. All rooms above standard size. Close to Astrodome and Six Flags Astroworld. FC, FL.

Ramada Hotel Northwest (A1), 12801 Northwest Freeway; 462-9977. M. This high-rise hotel has 300 rooms including cabana units, deluxe suites, and penthouse suites with whirlpool. The hotel is convention-oriented with a grand ballroom and eleven meeting rooms with teleconferencing. Lounge and super restaurant. Cable TV and saunas are among the features.

Ramada Inn Central (A3), 4225 North Freeway; 695-6011. M. Convenient to Intercontinental Airport, features include complete meeting, banquet, and convention facilities and executive suite with whirlpool and wet bar. Cable TV in rooms. PA.

Ramada Kings Inn NASA (F6), 1301 NASA Rd. 1; 488-0220. M to E. Close to LBJ Space Center and Clear Lake. Offers 200 rooms and five suites. Meeting rooms. PA. Seasonal rates.

Ramada Limited (D1), 6885 Southwest Freeway; 981-6885. M. This property is a high-rise, convenient to Sharpstown Center and surrounding corporate offices. Features include a show bar with entertainment, free in-room movies, pool with side service, rental car desk, and physical fitness center outside. Special rate for extended stay. Meeting, banquet, and convention facilities. Free parking. Courtesy car to Sharpstown and The Galleria. Bus shuttle to area office parks. BF, FL, PA. 1-800-228-2828.

RESIDENCE INN BY MARRIOTT—ASTRODOME (E2), 7710 S. Main; 660-7993. E. These properties are all-suite hotels. This inn is one mile from the Texas Medical Center and just a short distance from the Astrodomain complex. It offers fully furnished one- and two-bedroom suites which include living room with fireplace and satellite TV. Also fully equipped kitchens. Heated pool, spas, and sport courts. Complimentary services include parking, van service to Medical Center, local phone calls.

RESIDENCE INN BY MARRIOTT—SOUTHWEST (D1), 6910 Southwest Freeway; 785-3415. E. All-suite hotel next to Sharpstown Mall. Furnished studio and penthouse suites. Heated pool. Van transportation, local calls, parking, Continental breakfast, and evening reception. Also spas and sport court on premises. Only four miles from The Galleria.

THE RITZ-CARLTON (C2), 1919 Briar Oaks Lane off San Felipe; 840-7600. E. Marble fireplaces, custom wood molding, objets d'art, and fine furnishings make this hotel one of Houston's most luxurious. The 238-room Ritz-Carlton is geared to corporate executives and distinguished social activities. Featured is a fully equipped business travelers' center. Health club and outdoor swimming pool. Breakfast and lunch only in *The Dining Room* and dinner nightly plus weekend dancing in *The Grill*.

RODEWAY INN—HOBBY (E5), 1505 College; 946-5900. I.

SHERATON HOTELS. These hotels have an international reputation for service and special amenities. Expect to find good restaurants and swimming pools, along with personal attention.
   Sheraton Crown Hotel and Conference Center (A2), 15700 JFK Blvd.; 442-5100. M to E. A major hotel with over 418 rooms, convenient to Intercontinental Airport. Oriented to business travel with 255-seat, fixed-stage amphitheater, large ballroom and 12 meeting rooms, health club, saunas, access to World Houston Golf Club, and H & H Guest Ranch. Courtesy car for Intercontinental Airport. Free parking. BF, PA (small deposit). 1-800-325-3535.
   Sheraton Grand Hotel (F1), 2525 W. Loop South; 961-3000. M. This 300-room modern hotel features Continental breakfast weekdays in the lobby bar. The bar and grill have entertainment six nights, closed Sundays. Full service

concierge desk open until 1 am. Ballroom and meeting rooms available. Courtesy car for The Galleria, churches, and some office buildings. Valet parking. *PA (small CH)*.

STOUFFER PRESIDENTE HOTEL (F1), 6 Greenway Plaza East; 629-1200. *E.* This is an award-winning hotel in the heart of the Greenway Plaza convention, corporate, and entertainment complex. Offering 389 deluxe rooms, 17 suites, ballroom, and 19 meeting rooms. *City Lights* on the 20th floor has great views of Houston. Poolside service for beverage, an exercise room, locker rooms for men and women, saunas, and access to a private athletic club. Valet parking *(CH)*. Full service concierge. Courtesy car for The Galleria and Medical Center. Sunday brunch specials. *BF, FL, PA.* 1-800-468-3571.

SUPER 8 (D2), 4020 Southwest Freeway; 623-4720. *I.* Convenient to The Summit and Galleria, this 211-room hotel has individually controlled air conditioning and heating. Pool, meeting and banquet space. Courtesy car to area office complexes, malls, and medical centers.

TIDES II MOTOR INN (D2), 6700 S. Main; 522-2811. *I.* A block from Texas Medical Center. Features hospitality desk with Spanish language tours and other assistance. Courtesy car for Medical Center. Free parking. *BF, FL.*

TRAVELODGE HOUSTON (F2), 2828 Southwest Freeway; 526-4571. *M.* This is a hotel convenient to The Summit and surrounding corporate offices. Self-service free parking. Concierge desk. *BF, PA.*

WESTIN GALLERIA (F1), 5060 W. Alabama; 960-8100. Telex: 79-1480. *E.* This deluxe establishment anchors the southwest end of The Galleria mall. Sunday brunches, Continental dining. Also breakfast, lunch, and dinner in the *Cafe Plaza.* Heliport nearby, full concierge (bilingual), valet parking *(CH)*. *FC, FL.*

WESTIN OAKS (F1), 5011 Westheimer; 960-81300. Telex: 499-0983. *E.* This luxury Westin at the east end of The Galleria offers 406 spacious rooms and suites plus ballroom and meeting facilities. Restaurants and entertainment areas offer elegant and casual dining. A sidewalk-style cafe and deli overlooks the Galleria ice rink. *The Roof,* a 21st-floor club, offers Sunday brunch and is open from 5 pm-2 am, nightly. This hotel has consistently won AAA's Four Diamond Award for years. It is of traditional design and European service, including full concierge and valet parking. Also jogging track and health facilities available. Car rentals. *FC, FL, FP.*

WYNDHAM HOTELS. This international chain of hotels is widely known for its distinctive architecture and attentive service.

Wyndham Greenspoint Hotel (A2), 12400 Greenspoint Drive; 875-2222. *E.* Emphasizing convenience and full service for the business traveler, this hotel features tastefully appointed guest rooms and a mix of 31,000 square feet of meeting space including a 15,200 square-foot ballroom. Also a recreational center, outdoor pool, sauna, and athletic club nearby. Free shuttle service to and from Intercontinental Airport.

Wyndham Warwick Hotel, 5701 Main; 526-1991. *E.* A luxury hotel since late oil magnate John Mecom lavishly restored it years ago, the rich and famous have long reposed within this AAA four-diamond winner. It gleams in the leafy heart of the museum district and at the edge of the medical center.

ALTERNATIVE LODGING

Bed and Breakfast

THE BED & BREAKFAST SOCIETY OF TEXAS 523-1114. *I to E.* Affiliated with an international network of such associations, the society aims to provide unique accommodations at a reasonable price. It appeals to business and pleasure travelers who prefer the kind of friendliness and individualized care extended in private homes. Accommodations are checked for cleanliness, comfort, and security and are located throughout Houston and surrounding areas. They vary from quaint small cottages in charming old neighborhoods to high-rise condominiums, to suburban homes with pools and tennis courts. Many homes are convenient to the Texas Medical Center, the Astrodome, NASA, and Rice University, as well as shopping and business centers.

Campgrounds

The Houston area has a number of campgrounds and trailer parks with facilities ranging from basic hook-ups to complete community services parks with stores, pools, and golf. Check with individual parks and locales before going, as rules, schedules, and procedures can change drastically.

Alexander Deussen Park (A6), 12303 Sonnier; Out Highway 90 to C.E. King Parkway, directly on to the West side of Lake Houston; 454-7057. *I.* Includes 309 acres of wooded parkland, water skiing, swimming in designated area, fishing, restrooms, lighting, picnic grounds, ball fields, boat ramps, private concession stand, park security. No hunting. Water and electric hook-ups and sewer station. Pets on leash. Alcoholic beverages permitted. Two weeks maximum camping. No motor vehicles off roadway.

Dwight Eisenhower Park (A6), 610-E to McCarty exit; east on McCarty (which becomes old US 90) to C.E. King Parkway; left onto C.E. King, which becomes S. Lake Houston Parkway until it Ts into Acqueduct; turn left, go about 1.5 miles to park entrance); 456-0973. *NCH.* This is a 1005-acre park with hiking, fishing, restrooms, picnic, cookers. Alcoholic beverages permitted but no glass containers. No hunting or firearms.

Houston Campgrounds, 710 State Highway 6 South; 493-2391. *I.* Features: tents permitted, convenience store, R-V supplies and hook-ups, pool. Facilities: picnic tables, playground equipment, restrooms, water, paved roads. No open fires, loose pets, or firearms.

Houston Leisure RV Park (C6), 1601 South Main in Highlands; turn north off I-10 East at exit 787, just a short distance on the right after turn; in Highlands, TX; 426-3576. *I.* Water, electric, sewer, toilet, hot shower. Also laundry, L-P gas, convenience store, R-V parts, pool, playground. Weekly and monthly specials available. Recreation room and tent sites.

KOA-Houston Central, 1620 Peachleaf near Aldine-Westfield Rd., between I-45 and U.S. 59 north; 442-3700. *I.* Tents permitted. R-V hook-ups. Facilities: restrooms, lighting, picnic, barbecue grills, playground, pool, laundry, store, recreation room. No ground fires, firearms, or loose pets. After first week's stay special long-term rates available.

Stephen F. Austin Park, about 50 miles west of Houston, take San Felipe exit off I-10 west, in San Felipe, TX; 1-409-885-3613. *I.* Features: a state park with museum and historical area, and hiking trails. Facilities: tent and trailer camping, 18-hole golf course, pool, picnic area, recreation hall, playground, and shelter. No public consumption of alcohol.

Resorts

April Sound, Highway 105 West in Conroe, TX. Take I-45 north to 105 exit; 350-1173. *M.* This beautiful 1,000-acre private resort on the shores of Lake Conroe offers two types of accommodations. There are villa-type cluster homes and condos with one, two, and three bedrooms. Features include 27-hole golf, 17 tennis courts, four pools—one olympic size and another a whirlpool. Also boat launch. The property has several packages such as tennis clinic, golf, and honeymoon. For business travelers and corporate groups there are ample facilities with fully equipped meeting rooms. Arrangements available for fishing, boating, and water skiing. Offers 24-hour security.

Camp Manison (F5), 201 W. Parkwood, Friendswood; 482-1251. *I.* This rustic resort just minutes south of Houston has accommodations for 175 in bunkhouse- or motel-style rooms. Both European Plan and the American Plan available. Caters to youth groups internationally and is open by reservation only for two-, four-, and six-week sessions for children ages six to sixteen. Special group rates. Can cater for up to 10,000 with barbecue, hayrides, and campfires. *FL.*

Columbia Lakes Resort & Conference Center, 188 Freeman Blvd., in West Columbia, TX, about 50 miles from Houston, out Highway 288 to County Road 521, turn right, then eight miles just across the Brazos River. *M to E.* Two- and four-bedroom cottages with parlor and duplexes with kitchenettes. Wet bar in four bedroom units. A conference hall, restaurant, lounge, and club house with locker rooms for men and women, saunas, an 18-hole championship golf course, four lighted tennis courts, two fishing lakes, and a private marina with boat rentals. Also swimming pool, jogging track, and bike rentals. Helicopters available for groups. Catering for private parties. Reservations: 1-409-345-5151 or 1-800-231-1030.

The Houstonian Hotel and Conference Center (C1), 111 N. Post Oak Lane; 680-2626; from outside Texas, 1-800-231-2759. E. In the heart of Houston is this modern retreat where the hustle and noise of city life is softened by a buffer zone of heavy wooded acreage meandering along Buffalo Bayou. This hotel/club/conference center features three restaurants, two lounges, two swimming pools (one heated), many tennis, racquetball, basketball, and volleyball facilities, and an indoor/outdoor track plus spa and workout room. The business man and woman and conference groups find this property ideal with its 29 fully equipped meeting rooms and five private dining rooms.

Walden on Lake Conroe, 14001 Walden Road, in Montgomery, TX; 353-9737. E. Located 54 miles north of Houston. Take I-45 North to FM 105 exit in Conroe, turn left and go 12 miles to Walden Road, turn right and proceed 2fi miles to the Walden entrance. This lush lakeside environment provides the ideal setting for business meetings or pleasure. With one- and two-bedroom condominiums, 14,000 square feet of conference space, a championship 18-hole golf course, 16 tennis courts, and a full service marina, Walden offers the finest for both groups and individuals.

The Woodlands Executive Conference Center & Resort, 2301 N. Millbend Dr.; 367-1100; in Texas, call 1-800-533-3052; outside Texas call 1-800-433-2624. E. This famous resort caters to the business traveler and corporate groups in an idyllic setting, with resort atmosphere and fine recreational outlets—all just 25 minutes from downtown Houston via I-45 North to The Woodlands' 25,000 acres of forests, fine homes, and great weekend resort activities. This is the home of the world-famous "Houston Open" and there are three championship golf courses on the premises plus a health club, 24 indoor/outdoor racquet courts, and bike trails. Arrangements available for water sports, including boating and fishing at nearby lake. Helicopter charters from Hobby and Intercontinental plus auto rentals and assistance with airline reservations. Meeting rooms and about 270 guest rooms.

The Galvez of Galveston Island

Dale Young

DINING

Decisions! Decisions! If dining out in Houston poses a problem, making a decision is it. Six thousand eating establishments, plus scores of different cuisines and culinary styles, can make making a choice overwhelming. Fun. Delightful. But overwhelming.

Our aim herein is to assist the traveler, the newcomer, and even the long-time denizen in sorting out what's available, what to expect, and where to find it.

With our proximity to the Gulf of Mexico and Galveston Bay, seafood and fish of every description naturally top many menus. Since history has stirred Texas and Mexico together so thoroughly, our kitchens continue to share many influences, loading plates with food specialties ranging from pure Mexican to the happy hybrid called Tex-Mex.

Harris County has a long history as cattle country, and today it still ranks near the top in Texas in cattle production. So, completing a visit to what you might call the cow-pital of Harris County—Houston—means corraling a dee-licious, nutritious, Texas-size steak. To eat more exotically, enjoy the world of ethnic and foreign influences evident in the great variety of cafes, restaurants, and other establishments, large and small, plain and fancy, throughout the city.

Houston continues its phenomenal growth as a dining-out town and readily seems to absorb all comers and newcomers.

But here we must serve a cautionary entremet.

While many establishments grow into local institutions, the restaurant business can be as fickle in Houston as anywhere else. Some come, some go. Specialties and menus change periodically, and so do entire themes. Even restaurants categorized by specialties tend to mix menus, such as seafood and steaks, or Italian and American, or Vietnamese and Chinese.

Prices are volatile and subject to frequent, unpredictable change. They can make an unwitting liar of the most diligent guidebook.

We have done our best to make this chapter as accurate and timely as possible, while at the same time informative. Still, the nature of this type of information, coupled with a lot of necessarily subjective judgment, requires us to remind you to consider it as guideline, not gospel. Our cost categories based on an appetizer, entree, and dessert remain:

E—Expensive, more than $20 per person.
M—Moderate, $10-$20 per person.
I—Inexpensive, less than $10 per person.

The following compendium should give you not only a good idea of the huge variety Houston offers restaurant-goers, but also lots of specific ideas about where to satisfy your appetite and your curiosity.

So, take your pick. Have a seat. And enjoy!

RESTAURANTS BY AREA

DOWNTOWN

Benihana of Tokyo, Japanese, *M-E.*
Charley's 517, Continental, *E.*
China Garden, Oriental/Chinese, *I.*
DeVille in the Four Seasons Hotel, Continental, *E.*
Ducks & Co., Hyatt Regency Houston Hotel, American, *M-E.*
James Coney Island, American, *I.*
Longhorn Cafe, Texan, *I.*
The Melange Tea Room in Sam Houston Park, Etcetera, *I.*
The Spaghetti Warehouse, Italian, *I.*
This Is It, Soul Food, *I.*
Treebeard's, Cajun, *I.*
Kim Son, Vietnamese/Chinese, *I-M.*

THE GALLERIA/POST OAK

Beck's Prime, Hamburgers, *I.*
Delmonico's, Westin Galleria Hotel, Continental, *E.*
Grotto, Italian, *M-E.*
Houston's, American, *I.*
La Reserve, Inn on the Park, Continental, *E.*
The NM Cafe, Neiman Marcus store, American/Southwestern, *I.*
Pappadeaux, Cajun/Seafood, *M-E.*
Post Oak Grill, American/Continental, *E.*
Swiss Chalet, Continental, *M-E.*
Tokyo Gardens, Oriental/Japanese, *M-E.*
Uncle Tai's, Oriental/Chinese, *M-E.*

HARRISBURG GULF FREEWAY-EAST END

Ballatori's, Italian, *I.*
Black-Eyed Pea, American, *I.*
Fuddrucker's, American, *I.*
Luby's, Cafeteria, *I.*
Merida, Mexican, *I-M.*
Ninfa's, Mexican, *I-M.*
Shanghai Red's/Brady's Landing, American, *M.*
Taj Mahal, Indian, *I-M.*

MEMORIAL DRIVE-I-10 WEST CORRIDOR

La Tour d'Argent, French, *E.*
Las Alamedas, Mexican, *M-E.*
Luby's, Cafeteria, *I.*
Otto's, Barbecue, *I.*
Pappadeaux, Cajun/Seafood, *M-E.*
Rainbow Lodge, Continental, *E.*
Taste of Texas, Steak/American, *M-E.*

THE MONTROSE AREA

Anthony's, Continental, *M-E.*
Brennan's, Texas Creole, *M-E.*
Butera's, Etcetera, *I.*
Cafe Adobe, Mexican, *M-E.*
Damian's Cucina Italiana, Italian, *E.*
Dong Ting, Oriental/Chinese, *M-E.*
La Colombe d'Or, Continental, *E.*
Museum of Fine Arts Cafe Express, Etcetera, *I.*

Nippon, Japanese, M.
Primo's, Mexican, I.
River Cafe, Continental, M.
Ruggles, Continental, M-E.
Star Pizza, Italian, I.

NASA-BAY AREA

Black-Eyed Pea, American, I.
Flying Dutchman, Seafood, M-E.
Fuddrucker's, American, I.
Landry's, Seafood, M-E.
Luby's, Cafeteria, I.
Pappasito's, Mexican/Tex-Mex, M-E.
Pe-Te Cajun, Cajun, I.

NORTHWEST AREA

Black-Eyed Pea, American, I.
Fuddrucker's, American, I.
James Coney Island, American, I.
Luby's Cafeteria, Cafeteria, I.
Pappadeaux, Cajun/Seafood, M-E.

PORT OF HOUSTON-
HIGHWAY 225 AREA

Athens Bar & Grill, Greek, I-M.

RIVER OAKS AREA

Andre's, Etcetera, I.
Black-Eyed Pea, American, I.
Confederate House, American, E.
Hard Rock Cafe, American, M.
Hobbit Hole, Etcetera, I.
Hunan River, Oriental/Chinese, M.
La Griglia, Continental/Italian, E.
Pappadeaux, Cajun/Seafood, M-E.

SOUTH MAIN CORRIDOR

Christie's, Seafood, M-E.
Kaphan's, Seafood, E.
Luther's, Barbecue, I.
The Mediterranean, Spanish, M.
Morningside Thai, Oriental/Thai, M-E.

SOUTHWEST FREEWAY-
ALABAMA-RICHMOND AVENUE

Cleburne Cafeteria, Cafeteria, I.
Maxim's, French, E.
Ragin' Cajun, Cajun, I.
Rivoli, Continental, E.
Ruth's Chris Steak House, American, E.

SOUTHWEST & FAR SOUTHWEST

Haveli, Indian/Tandoori, I-M.
James Coney Island, American, I.
Kim Son, Vietnamese/Chinese, I-M.
My Canh, Oriental/Chinese, I.
Pappadeaux, Cajun/Seafood, M-E.
Pappasito's, Mexican/Tex-Mex, M-E.
Pastine, Creole/Italian, M.
The Spaghetti Warehouse, Italian, I.

WESTHEIMER "RESTAURANT
ROW" AND WESTERN ENVIRONS

Adam's Mark Hotel, Continental, M-E.
Antonio's Flying Pizza, Italian, I-M.
Beck's Prime, Hamburgers, I.
Benihana of Tokyo, Oriental/Japanese,
    M-E.
Fuddrucker's, American, I.
Ginza, Oriental/Japanese, M.
Great Caruso, Continental, E.
The Great Greek, Greek, I-M.
Harlow's, American, I-M.
King Hua, Mandarin Chinese, M.
Mama's, American/Tex-Mex, I.
Old Heidelberg, German, I.
Old San Francisco Steak House, Ameri-
    can, M-E.
The Palm, Continental, E.
Pappadeaux, Cajun/Seafood, M-E.
Pappasito's, Mexican/Tex-Mex, M-E.
The Third Coast, American/Creole/Con-
    tinental, E.
Vargo's, American, E.

RESTAURANTS

American

Andre's Tea Room (see ETCETERA).

Beck's Prime, 2902 Kirby; 524-7085. 2615 Augusta off Westheimer; 266-9901. 11000 Westheimer; 952-2325. *I.* Bright and cheery, Beck's specializes in hamburgers, big, juicy, yummy, mesquite-grilled hamburgers that bump the ceiling on quality and flavor. Grilled onions make great even better at no extra charge. Choose sesame or whole wheat bun. Fries? Onion rings? Of course! And hot dogs for frank-o-philes. Big soft drinks with free refills. Try a thick shake, malt, or ice cream soda for dessert, snack, or meal substitute. Lunch, dinner every day.

The Black-Eyed Pea (C2), 2048 W. Gray, in the River Oaks Shopping Center; 523-0200. (E1), 9651 Bissonnet, across from Westwood Mall; 988-6442. 2675 Wilcrest, in Westchase Center; 266-0928. 551 Town and Country Village; 461-2006. 10903 Jones Rd. in Steeplechase Center at FM 1960; 890-6851. (A1), 249 W, Greens Rd.; 875-2606. (F5), 160 W. Bay Area Blvd.; 338-2571. (D4), 4729 Calhoun; 748-0471. Other locations. *I-M.* Consider Mom's meat loaf, juicy pot roast, and freshwater catfish. Or try tasty down-home items such as a big bowl of pinto beans with onions, terrific baked squash, fried okra, or cornbread. Very casual, all ages. Lunch, dinner seven days.

Butera's (see ETCETERA).

Confederate House, 2925 Wesleyan; 622-1936. *E.* A private club for many years catering to the discriminating River Oaks crowd, this fine restaurant has opened to the public for traditional dining. Specializing in fresh Gulf seafood, prime beef, and an extensive wine list to complement your meal. Open for lunch Mon-Fri, dinner Mon-Sat, closed Sun. Jacket and collared shirt required. Reservations.

Duck's & Co. (J9), in the Hyatt Regency Houston Hotel, 1200 Louisiana; 654-1234. *M-E.* A great location for business lunch engagements and intimate dinners. Start with the Market salad bar with a bountiful display of fresh greens and garnishes; have your choice of unique appetizers then dig in with a Texas steak, seafood specials, Rotisserie Roasted Duckling, or wild game. Lunch, dinner daily. Informal.

Fuddrucker's (D1), 3100 Chimney Rock; 780-7080. 7511 FM 1960 West; 469-6476. (A1), 403 Greens Rd.; 876-2611. (F6), 2040 Nasa Rd. 1; 333-1598. 2475 S. Kirkwood; 496-4490. 855 Normandy at I-10 East; 453-0672. *I.* The Hamburger Appreciation Society of North America has, in several years past, awarded Fuddrucker's its "greatest" citation. All meat is fresh-ground beef. Very casual atmosphere. Open 11 to 10, Sun-Thu and 11 to 11 Fri and Sat.

The Hard Rock Cafe (D2), 2801 Kirby; 520-1134. M. This massive free-standing building with a country club look is the Houston home of this famous cafe established in London in 1971. High in the sky out front is a 1963 T-bird perched on a pole. Here you'll find famous musician memorabilia including guitars and gold records, many posters and signs, plus a Harley Davidson cycle propped near the circular bar. Other than that the place is rather plain and personable with bare wood floors and matching wood tables and booths with checkered cloths. It draws a very lively crowd, all ages, for lunch and dinner to sample some of the unique offerings such as barbecued ribs in watermelon sauce, lime barbecued chicken, and shark soup. Also ordinary fare and specializing in burgers and a soda fountain for desserts. Open daily for lunch and dinner. Informal.

Harlow's Hollywood Cafe & Deli (D1), 3100 Hillcroft; 780-9500. I-M. Really a wide selection with salads, deli sandwiches, tacos, hot Greek meat balls, fried cheese, escargot, deluxe sandwich platters, rib eyes, knockwurst, burgers and bagels, steak & eggs, New Orleans bread pudding, and of course New York cheesecake. The walls are covered with photos of celebrities. Continuous service 11 am-4 am, daily; 11 am-5 am Fri & Sat.

Houston's (D1), 5888 Westheimer, near The Galleria; 975-1947. I. This one along the Westheimer "Restaurant Row" is popular with families as well as younger couples. It features Texas-size club sandwiches, burger platters, steaks, and chicken. The house dressing with hot bacon is a favorite. Informal. Food service 11 am-11 pm Sun-Thu, and until midnight Fri and Sat.

James Coney Island, 1600 Post Oak Blvd., near Galleria; 622-1584; (J10), 1142 Travis, downtown; 652-3819. Also numerous other locations throughout Houston. I. Since 1923 this has been a Houston tradition for the best-known hot dogs in town. Fast service, very casual. Besides the Coney Islands (as the hot dogs are called), you might sample a steamy bowl of James' own recipe Texas chili. Serving daily.

The Melange Tea Room (see ETCETERA).

Museum of Fine Arts Cafe Express (see ETCETERA).

Old San Francisco Steak House (D1), 8611 Westheimer; 783-5990. M. The Barbary Coast Bar is perfect for cocktails before an evening of dining in Victorian finery. See the Girl on the Red Velvet Swing while you nibble from a large block of Swiss cheese, then enjoy your choice of steak, prime rib, or seafood. Open for lunch Mon-Fri, dinner seven nights.

Rotisserie for Beef & Bird, 2200 Wilcrest; 977-9524. E. One of Houston's culinary institutions almost since the day owner-chef Joe Mannke opened it, American food with continental flair predominates a menu of excellent beef, poultry, and game dishes. Poultry entrees include roast meaty cackle bird (an originally female capon), mesquite-grilled partridge, hickory smoked duckling, and, from the rotisserie, roast duckling with orange sauce. Beef items include black angus steaks (sirloin strip, bone-in sirloin, rib, filet mignon, or T-bone), brochette (cubed beef skewered with onions, peppers, and mushrooms) and tournedos topped with mushrooms and seasoned with fine armagnac. Alternatives range from fresh seafood (red snapper, shrimp, scallops, Maine lobster) to wild game (axis deer, wild boar, quail) to other meats (mesquite-broiled spring lamb and butter-sauteed Wienerschnitzel). Do-it-now desserts include Jack Daniels chocolate chip ice cream with sticky pecans, hot bread pudding with whiskey sauce, and hot apple pie a la mode. Lunch 11:30-2 Mon-Fri; dinner 6-10:30 Mon-Sat; closed Sun. Elegant casual to dressy.

Ruth's Chris Steak House (D1), 6213 Richmond; 789-2333. *E.* Of Louisiana fame, Ruth's Chris specializes in legendary, corn-fed U.S. Prime beef, and offers as well select seafoods, veal, chicken, and U.S. Prime lamb. Steaks served sizzle in butter (optional), cut and cooked to your preference. Petite filet, filet, ribeye, New York Strip, Porterhouse, or t-bone. From the list of nine spud options, select potatoes lyonnaise sauteed with onions or mashed with a touch of roasted garlic. Periodic specials may include 24-ounce-plus Texas-style prime rib. Atmosphere is urban club—wood paneling, candle-lit tables/booths, upscale furnishings. Classy casual attire. Serving dinner only from 5 p.m. daily except Thanksgiving and Christmas days.

Shanghai Red's and **Brady's Landing** are right next to each other in the middle of the Houston Ship Channel on Brady Island; (D5), 8501 Cypress St. off Broadway in Harrisburg; 926-6666 (Shanghai Red's) and 928-9921 (Brady's). *M.* The Shanghai is in a rusty, mineshaft-looking building with junk Model-T cars in front. Enjoy cocktails in the dance-hall section overlooking the banks of the Ship Channel. Many cozy seating areas tucked away on different levels, all overlooking the water. Features seafood. Open daily. Casual. The newer sister restaurant, Brady's, is more contemporary with floor-to-ceiling fireplaces, a sunken dining room, and a music bar. Brady's is popular with the business crowd and features beef, prime rib, and steaks. Also banquet facilities. Lunch Mon-Fri, dinner daily. Sunday brunch at 10:30. Casual.

Third Coast, 6540 San Felipe; 783-6540. *M-E.* Unequivocally one of Houston's best restaurants. This upscale, yet casual creation by the folks who bring you Brennan's may be a bit noisy, a bit crowded, and a bit hard to get into at times, but do not let such trifles stop you. To twist an old Woody Allen quip, the food at the Third Coast is superb—and in such huge portions! The quintessence of the finest culinary quality and creativity fills plates with chili fried onion rings or grilled Gulf crab cakes as appetizers; rotisserie roasted orange duck or herbed chicken, angel-hair pasta with blackened shrimp in roasted Roma tomato sauce, or Sarge's Meatloaf (USMC-style with onions, garlic, celery, and green pepper, SIR!) as entrees; and garlic mashed potatoes and various vegetables prepared with description-defying deliciousness as accompaniments. You must have dessert, even if you have to rent a truck to take it home. All ice creams, cakes, pies, and other desserts are made on premises. The white chocolate bread pudding with dark chocolate sauce is to live for. Ditto the carrot cake. And the "Heart Attack Parfait" built from four scoops of Rocky Road ice cream. And the creme brulee. You've just got to try it all to believe how good it is. And even then you won't believe it. Lunch 11-3 Mon-Sat; brunch 11-2 Sun; dinner seven nights.

Vargo's (C1), 2401 Fondren Road; 782-3888. *E.* Just off the bright and bustling Westheimer, you come to a winding drive with a white picket fence— follow it to the end to an unbelievably serene, country-club setting. Printed menu has replaced the verbal menu of earlier days, but at lunch, dinner, and Sunday brunch, the tradition of serving vegetables family style and a complimentary relish tray continues. Traditional steak and seafood favorites now share the much broader menu with such offerings as roasted boneless Long Island duck breast with orange sauce, roasted capon breast with wild mushrooms and white grapes, and crabmeat and melon salad. To finish, there is a sorbet trio (passion fruit, pear, and blackberry) served on raspberry sauce with frosted grapes, or Triple Chocolate cake "for those with a need." After your meal, waddle out to the swinging bridge over the lagoon leading to trails along Lake Vargo for a little exercise. Coat and tie preferred, but not required. Lunch and dinner Mon-Fri; dinner only Sat; brunch only Sun.

Barbecue

Goode Company Texas Barbecue, 5109 Kirby, 522-2530; 8911 Katy Fwy., 464-1901. *I-M.* In terms of flavor and quality, Goode Company arguably smokes up some of the best and most interesting barbecue in Houston, and maybe even in all of Texas. Standards such as beef (sliced brisket or chopped), chicken, ribs, pork, and link sausage are all gloriously available, but so, too, are such succulent innovations as a special, spicy barbecued pork, yummy barbecued sweetwater duck, and a spectacular jalapeno sausage. Marvelous tangy-sweet sauce. Outstanding barbecue beans (some of the best anywhere ever). And portions that could give you a hernia. Continuous service lunch through dinner seven days.

Luther's (E2), 8777 S. Main; 432-1107. *I.* More than a dozen other locations throughout the Houston area. In a hurry? Here you can drive through for orders such as burgers and barbecued sandwiches (heavy aged beef, pork ribs, links, and chicken), all hickory smoked. Inside the rustic dining hall try cole slaw with a combination plate of barbecued meats, beans, and onion rings. Place your order at the counter. Strangely, and fortunately, the quality and consistency seem to have improved as the chain and menu have expanded. Continuous service 11 am-10 pm, Sun-Thu; 11 am-11 pm, Fri-Sat.

Old Hickory Inn Barbeque, 8338 Southwest Fwy. at S. Gessner; 271-8610. 5427 S. Braeswood at Chimney Rock; 723-8908. *I.* Very good and very reasonably priced barbecue beef, chicken, ribs, and sausage. Good side dishes include tasty barbecue beans and a sweet-sour, vinegar-dressed (no mayonnaise) cole slaw. Very simple and very casual. Freeway inn open 11-9 Mon-Sat; Braeswood inn open 11-9 seven days.

Otto's (C2), 5502 Memorial Dr.; 864-2573. *I.* Downtown workers and West Siders descend at lunchtime on this small establishment which has become a tradition for hamburgers and for barbecue ribs, links, ham, or beef. This the Otto's that gained fame as the preferred purveyor of barbecue for former President George Bush. Orders to go. Food service 11 am-9 pm, Mon-Sat. Casual.

Cajun

Sonny's Crazy Cajun Food Factory, 2825 NASA Road 1, Seabrook, Texas; M-E. A noisy, crowded, rollicking, easy-going place to feed your face and weld your innards with some right tasty Cajun cooking—gumbos, shrimp, andouille sausage ("So good," brags the menu, "it'll brang tears to a glass eye!"), boudin, etouffees, crab, crawfish (in season), even alligator. A few things can be a little salty, but the flavors are good. Great people working here, too. Open 11 am-11 pm seven says a week.

Pappadeaux Seafood Kitchen, 12711 Southwest Freeway at Corporate; 240-5533. 2525 South Loop West near the Astrodome; 665-3155. Five other Houston-area locations. M-E. It is very difficult to talk, or even think, about Pappadeaux without drooling. High on the list of favorite fooderies, this magnificent member of the Pappas family's family of remarkable restaurants epitomizes the philosophy of pleasantly and efficiently providing great food in huge portions at reasonable prices. A large menu almost bows with options, starring fresh fish and seafood expertly prepared with Louisiana-Cajun spices, authenticity and panache. And if fresh boiled shrimp with a dynamite red sauce, spicy fried shrimp, soft-shell crab fried or blackened, huge and savory stuffed shrimp, superb shrimp creole, and incendiary boiled crawfish (served by the pound with corn and potatoes) don't jump-start your appetite, surely at least one of the dozens of other selections—etouffee (shrimp or crawfish), gumbo (seafood with/without andouille sausage, or shrimp), red beans and rice, or a belly-busting Pappadeaux platter of fried shrimp, fried oysters, fried catfish fillet, stuffed shrimp, stuffed crab, fried crawfish tails AND French fried potatoes will. Off-menu specials always. If you want something done a bit differently, just ask. Nothing ever seems to be a problem for Pappadeaux people. At least as far as Cajun seafood is concerned, when "les bon temps rouler," this is where they go. Lunch and dinner served continuously every day.

Pe-Te Cajun BBQ (E5), 11902 Highway 3 (Old Galveston Road); 481-8736. I. You can't miss this bright purple and orange facade across the street from Ellington Field. This is an authentic Acadian honky-tonk with dancing to the music of live Zydeco bands. Here you'll find homemade hog cracklins, boudin, spiced gumbo, crawfish etouffee, beans and rice, and tangy barbecue sandwiches and mixed plates. From the picnic tables at the front to the back of the dance hall, the walls are covered with old license plates, vintage NASA photos, and junk. A small gift shop offers Cajun and Zydeco CDs, tapes, and musical instruments, plus NASA souvenirs. Step up to the counter for your order. Open 9 am-7 pm, Mon-Thu; 9 am-8 pm, Fri; and 10:30 am-6:30 pm Sat. Closed Sun.

Ragin' Cajun (F1), 4302 Richmond; 623-6321. I. Never mind the location or the looks; just set yourself down and enjoy some of the best Cajun cookin' this side of Port Arthur. Here you find Louisiana and Texas Cajuns come together to talk about who's got the best boudin and who makes the hottest gumbo. While they argue in their dialect you can be putting away some fine etouffee, crawfish pie, Opelousas-style red beans and rice with sausage, poorboy sandwiches (oyster, shrimp, catfish, seafood, or boudin), fried softshell crabs, BBQ hard-shell crabs, boiled shrimp, boiled crawfish (in season), and more. This is a get-down, funky cafe, walls covered with customer biz cards, Cajun-pride banners, neon beer signs, and a juke box wailing the likes of "Choate" and "Roger"—Cajun French songs. This Cajun caters when you get tired of the Texas barbecue bit at parties. Serving 10:30 am-9 pm, Mon-Sat. Casual.

Treebeard's (H10), 315 Travis, on Old Market Sq., downtown; 225-2160. I. Sitting at the tables along the sidewalk at this popular spot facing historic Market Square you can enjoy a heaping platter of tangy jambalaya or a big bowl of piquant red beans and rice with sausage, tasty fresh vegetables, spicy gumbo. Lunch Mon-Fri; dinner Thu-Sat; closed Sun. Casual.

Continental

Adam's Mark Hotel, 2900 Briarpark Drive at Westheimer; 978-7400. M-E. Even as Pelican Publishing was remodeling this book, a multimillion-dollar remodeling of the Adam's Mark Hotel and its restaurant areas hammered forward. Meanwhile the famous 50-item Sunday brunch buffet continued, as did live entertainment and a policy of casual attire. Check for days and hours during and after renovations.

Anthony's, 4007 Westheimer in Highland Village; 961-0552. M-E. This is a smaller, more casual version of the late, world-famous Tony's on Post Oak with an incredibly creative menu, emphasizing Italian/Continental specialties that could spur even a confirmed anorexic down the road to temptation. Linguine with crawfish and shrimp, mushrooms, scallions, roasted pearl onions, and lobster cognac sauce. Crab, shrimp, and smoked salmon salad with tangerine and mint vinaigrette. Sliced beefsteak tomatoes, crumbled roquefort drizzled with a cabernet vinaigrette. A peppered chateaubriand of tuna for two. Whole hearth-roasted duckling with wild rice and mango-apricot or fresh raspberry sauce. Get the picture? Elegantly casual to dressy attire here suggested but not required. Reservations. Lunch Mon-Fri; dinner Mon-Sat; closed Sun.

Brennan's (F3), 3300 Smith St., on the edge of The Montrose and close to downtown; 522-9711. M-E. Relax in this old New Orleans garden atmosphere in the Brennan's tradition in this wonderful, treasured restaurant. Gas lights, louvered windows, lattice, and palms set the right Old South mood for exquisite dining with your choice of famous Brennan's recipes, some of them American culinary classics. Brunch, stretching the tradition of breakfast at Brennan's across the solar meridian, can start with a long-time favorite turtle soup with sherry, continue with poached eggs Creole or eggs scrambled with beef tenderloin, roasted peppers, and cheese, then finish with Creole bread pudding or Brennan's classic Bananas Foster. Dinner can begin auspiciously with Gulf of Mexico crab cakes or Texas Creole barbecue shrimp, proceed to Soups 1-1-1 (demitasse of turtle soup, gumbo, and soup du jour), one of several salads, continue with grilled filet of beef finished with a raisin peppercorn sauce or grilled shrimp and lump crabmeat with champagne sauce and fresh fennel pasta, then cap the whole experience with a slab of peanut butter fudge pie or a praline parfait. Fantastic food aside, the special touch on Saturdays and Sundays is that Brennan's brunch is a "Jazz Brunch" featuring a live, New Orleans jazz band. Brunch is served only on Sat and Sun.; lunch and dinner daily. Jacket required and tie requested.

Charley's 517 (I10), 517 Louisiana, downtown in the heart of the civic and cultural center; 224-4438. E. This establishment restaurant has long been a favorite for business luncheons and intimate dinners for conventioneers and theater-goers, with comfortable upholstered furnishings, soft lighting, quiet entertainment, and a dressy atmosphere. Charley's features a comprehensive menu together with after-theater suggestions. Lunch and dinner Mon-Fri; dinner only Sat; closed Sun. Jacket recommended at lunch, required at dinner. Charley's 517 had a five-alarm fire April 24, 1995, but has already re-opened.

Delmonico's (F1), 5060 W. Alabama; 960-8100. E. This is the Westin Galleria Hotel's gourmet dining room, named after New York's landmark restaurant. For the discriminating diner, a full range of entrees is offered, created by the gold medal-winning chef. Also fine vintage wines. Lunch weekdays, dinner nightly.

DeVille in the Four Seasons Hotel (J11), downtown, 1300 Lamar; 650-1619. E. American regional specialties accented with Italian nuances bold and subtle flavor the offerings of the DeVille, one of downtown Houston's culinary landmarks. Meredith Long & Co., local art dealers, provide a rotating visual milieu of artworks among which to enjoy such culinary masterpieces as gulf shrimp and snapper broth with tomato, fennel, and saffron; cavatappi with wild mushrooms, garlic, tomato, and parmesan; Maine lobster stew with sweet potato, yellow tomatoes, and rosemary; roast guinea hen with black olives, grapes, and lemon zest; and marinated veal chop on melting onion polenta with balsamic sauce. Winner of many fine dining awards, DeVille is open for breakfast Sun-Fri; brunch Sun only; lunch Mon-Fri; dinner Mon-Sat.

The Great Caruso (see NIGHTLIFE Supper Clubs).

La Colombe d'Or (F2), 3410 Montrose Blvd. in the heart of The Montrose; 524-7999. E. One of Houston's all-time finest restaurants set in perhaps the city's smallest, most unusual luxury hotel. Everything about this erstwhile mansion has been lovingly restored by active proprietor Stephen Zimmerman, who has catalyzed and supervised the menus since he opened La Colombe d'Or in 1980. Thanks to Zimmerman, executive chef Olivier Ciesielski, chef de cuisine Fabrice Beaudoin, and their dedicated colleagues, guests, and other patrons dine on a refreshingly different menu based on the finest and freshest of seafoods, meats, poultry, and vegetables. Culinary artistry includes sauteed lump crabmeat and wild mushrooms with red wine sauce; fresh Maine lobster served with ravioli and dill-flavored vegetables; roasted pheasant breast on a bed of calvados caramelized green apples; sauteed soft-shelled crab topped with roasted pecans; pate of duck and pistachio nuts served with onion marmalade; and home-smoked shrimp with angel hair pasta. The cozy library offers an outstanding collection of vintage ports, cognacs, and armagnacs. While La Colombe d'Or is casual and relaxing, gentlemen should don a coat and tie for dinner. Lunch weekdays, dinner seven nights. Private functions for up to 500.

La Griglia, 2002 W. Gray; 526-4700. E. Is this Tony Vallone creation Italian with Continental stripes, or Continental with Italian stripes? Well, *non importa*—it makes no difference—as long as the kitchen keeps turning out such glories as Crab Claws Fra Diavolo sauteed with tomatoes, wine and garlic; linguine Marinara (with shrimp and crabmeat in rich, flavorsome tomato sauce) or La Griglia (with sauteed chicken, black olives, mushrooms, chopped tomato, garlic, and pinot grigio); Grilled Salmon Sorrento (with ruby red grapefruit, lemon, and white wine); or Peking pizza (with rotisserie duck, shiitake mushrooms, and plum sauce). Take lots of money and a big appetite. Fantastic. Lunch Mon-Fri; dinner every evening.

La Reserve, in the Omni Hotel (C1), Four Riverway, near The Galleria; 871-8181. E. This is the formal dining room in the deluxe Four Seasons Inn on the city's fashionable West Side. An unforgettable gourmet dining experience where French chefs present six courses chosen nightly for your enjoyment. Serving lunch Mon-Fri, and dinner Mon-Sat. Sunday brunch and Friday night seafood buffet in the Cafe on the Green. Coat and tie required for dinner.

NM Cafe, in the Neiman Marcus store (F1), 2600 Post Oak Road, at the eastern end of The Galleria; 621-7100. I. A delightful and memorable lunch break in this world-famous store. Soft gray walls with floral seats and filtered sunlight give the cafe an open, airy look. Fresh flowers on all tables. Seasonal light menus available. Try the chili con queso soup, NM's signature orange souffle with white meat of chicken salad, or an open-face sandwich of seasoned crab cakes, lettuce, pico de gallo, and mustard sauce on a French roll. Lunch only Mon-Sat. Occasionally there are walk-through models when there is a special fashion show. Casual.

The Palm (D1), 6100 Westheimer, on "Restaurant Row"; 977-2544. E. This is The Palm of restaurant fame in New York, Washington, D.C., and Beverly Hills. A bright, happy, casual lunch and dinner spot, and a great place to entertain that very special business client. Don't look for an intimate corner, or relaxing quiet dinner atmosphere—typically New York, this place can get cracking at a brisk clip. Famous for lobster and New York steaks. Lunch weekdays, dinner daily. Casual.

Pastine, 5300 N. Braeswood just west of Chimney Rock; 723-6434. I-M. Creative, eclectic combinations with Creole/Italian accents prevail on brunch (see Brunch section), lunch, and dinner menus of this pleasant new restaurant overlooking Brays Bayou. Try the jumbo shrimp diablo grilled in a spicy marinara sauce, the ginger-marinated seafood grilled and served with tomatillo, jicama, and black beans tossed with angel hair pasta, or the Pastine special pizza topped with sundried tomato, calamata olives, spinach, and feta. Grilled eggplant marinated in balsamic vinegar and herbed olive oil served with fresh roma tomatoes and onions makes an exciting appetizer. Very accommodating about adjusting menu items to individual tastes, so, go ahead and enjoy that big bowl of linguine marinara even if it's not exactly on the menu. Open for brunch and dinner Sun, lunch and dinner Mon-Fri, and dinner only on Sat.

Post Oak Grill, 1415 S. Post Oak Lane just north of San Felipe near the Galleria; 993-9966. E. Presented by one of Houston's best and best-known restaurateurs, Manfred Jachmich, this high-profile and high-quality American-Continental restaurant entices fashionable diners with such creative offerings as spicy grilled shrimp with black beans, roasted red peppers, and tomatillo sauces; warm grilled chicken salad with mixed greens, apples, pecans, grapes, and Roquefort; medallions of pork loin with cinnamon apple fritters; herb-crusted red snapper in pepper sauce; or roasted garlic chicken with fresh bowtie pasta in marinara sauce. Save room for dessert. Reservations. Dressy casual to dressy. Lunch and dinner seven days.

Rainbow Lodge (C2), #1 Birdsall, just off Memorial Drive, near downtown; 861-8666. E. On the banks of Buffalo Bayou, this wonderful old 1935 house was converted to a convincingly authentic hunting lodge resort complete with trophies, and huge plate-glass windows overlooking natural rustic woods and formally landscaped grounds. Specialties include numerous game dishes. Taste of the Wild offers a daily selection of wild games as an appetizer. Hunter quesadillas are made of fire-roasted pheasant and duck with jalapeno pepper, Chihuahua cheese, and red onion pico de gallo. Wild game entrees include a mixed grill of axis venison, wild boar sausage, blackbuck antelope, and quail. Vegetarians can enjoy tomato peppercorn fettucine tossed with roma tomato, mushrooms, artichoke hearts, baby corn, basil, garlic, olive oil, and parmesan. Lunch Tue-Fri and Sun; dinner Tue-Sun. Sunday brunch from menu 10:30 am-4 pm. Casual.

River Cafe (F3), 3615 Montrose; 529-0088. M. A fashionably elegant dining room overlooking Montrose Blvd. with sidewalk cafe tables so popular along this street. The menu features pastas, veal, chicken, steak, and seafood specialties. Appetizers are equally as varied with chicken and sausage gumbo, crab cakes, ceviche, or black bean cake. The brick walls are lined with changing exhibits of paintings by local artists—all on sale. Lunch: Mon-Fri 11:30 am-2:30 pm. Brunch: Sat-Sun 11 am-4 pm. Dinner: Sun-Thu 6 pm-11 pm.; Fri-Sat 6 pm-midnite. Select from a lighter, after-hours menu Mon-Thu 2:30 pm-6 pm; Sun-Thu 11 pm-midnight; Fri-Sat midnight-1 am.

The Rivoli (D1), 5636 Richmond Ave; 789-1900. E. The recipient of many awards for food and service, this classy East Coast-style restaurant is on the Houston celebrity circuit. Divided into several different intimate and richly appointed dining areas by lattice work and planters. The Rivoli boasts an extensive wine list and at tableside you have a selection of five flambees. Lunch weekdays, dinner seven days. Coat and tie requested for dinner.

Ruggles Grill (F3), 903 Westheimer, on "The Strip"; 524-3839. M *to* E. Ruggles is a familiar name among theater-going Houstonians since the Westheimer location not only serves consistently fine food but is one of relatively few places catering to late-night crowds. Menu includes a number of vegetarian specialties. Casual atmosphere, easy listening live jazz next door evenings, and serving fine entrees. Lunch Tue-Fri, dinner Tue-Sun, brunch Sun, closed Mondays. Casual.

Swiss Chalet (C1), 511 S. Post Oak Lane just off Woodway, near The Galleria; 621-3333. M *to* E. An extremely popular haunt hidden away along the bayou trail behind the booming Galleria/Post Oak center. Long famous for serving fine fowl, meat, and seafood. For dessert try the Swiss Chocolate Fondue for two. Some live entertainment. Happy Hour 3-7 pm weekdays. Lunch, dinner Mon-Sat. Closed Sun. Dress code.

Tony's. Tony Vallone closed this culinary landmark for the rich and famous in mid-1994; re-opening was planned for late summer 1995. Meanwhile, satisfy cravings for flavors a la Vallone at his other establishments—all superb—including La Griglia, Anthony's, and the Grotto.

Vendome (C2), Lincoln Post Oak Hotel, 2001 Post Oak Blvd.; 961-9300.

French

La Tour d'Argent (B2), 2011 Ella Blvd.; 864-9864. *E.* In an unlikely setting in an early log cabin, La Tour d'Argent offers excellent French cuisine, and a superior wine list. The service is excellent. Coat & tie required. Open for lunch 11:30 am-2 pm Mon-Fri; dinner 6 pm-10 pm Mon-Thu, 6 pm-11 pm Fri-Sat. Closed Sun.

Maxim's (F1), 3755 Richmond in Greenway Plaza; 877-8899. *E.* This is another of Houston's most famous, award-winning restaurants with a long tradition of great dining and fine French cuisine. Owner Camille Berman and son Ron's impressive establishment features a very large central dining room with fine paintings, Italian glass chandelier, marble floors, and perfect place settings, inviting you to a memorable experience. Friendly, expert waiters attend to your every need. Don't miss the lamb shank at lunch . . . otherwise you can count on their recommendations— the fresh Gulf seafood is excellent and Chicken Camille is exceptional, with the Creme Brulee a perfect finishing touch. Coat and tie recommended for lunch and dinner. Continuous service 11:30 am-10:30 pm Mon-Fri. Dinner only (5:30-10:30) on Sat. Closed Sun.

German

Old Heidelberg Inn (C1), 1810 Fountain View at San Felipe; 781-3581. *I-M.* Heavy, high-beamed ceilings, stained glass, and a piano bar accordionist playing all kinds of music, including old-time German favorites, create the right atmosphere for some robust, fun dancing, and hearty eating, where German cuisine is the specialty. Serving several different kinds of German beer, whetting your appetite for Wienerschnitzel, Rouladen, or smoked pork with German fried potatoes and sauerkraut. Lunch Mon-Fri, and dinner Mon-Sat. Closed Sun. Casual.

Greek

Athens Bar & Grill (see NIGHTLIFE Supper Clubs).

The Great Greek (C1), 80 Woodlake Square at Westheimer and Gessner; 783-5100. *I-M*. A spin-off of a famous Hollywood hot spot, this Greek haunt has dancing waiters serving authentic dishes. A live Greek band sets the tempo for an exciting evening of casual fun. Open seven days, seven nights.

Italian

Antonio's Flying Pizza & Italian Restaurant, 2920 Hillcroft; 783-6080. *M*. Either despite or because of its whimsical name, this delightful, friendly little place has for many years been preparing and serving some of the best Italian food Houston has ever known. The thick-crusted pizzas are terrific; the generous hot sandwiches (sausage and peppers; veal parmigiana; egglant parmigiana) on crusty, chewy Italian bread are terrific; the pastas (especially linguine with red clam sauce and the spaghetti with marinara sauce) are terrific; and nearly all the other stuff (such as shrimp scampi with lots of garlic or miglia-high lasagne) is terrific. A long-established favorite. Lunch and dinner Tue-Sun; closed Mon.

Ballatori Italian Restaurant (D4), 4215 Leeland; 224-9556. *I*. The Ballatoris appeased Roman appetites for more than 40 years before the family moved lock, stock, and barrel to this old Eastside bank building, which has become a popular lunch and dinner spot for Houstonians in the know. This typically Roman restaurant offers nothing but the finest meats, vegetables, and pastas in the full range of Italian specialties. Items specially prepared in advance include meat stuffed with olives fried, and veal stuffed with boiled eggs and ham. Lunch 11 am-2 pm Mon-Fri; dinner Mon-Sat; closed Sun.

Damian's Cucina Italiana (C3), 3011 Smith between the Montrose and Downtown; 522-0439. *E*. Step into the warm and aromatic dining room for a true Italian feast of antipasto, pasta, soup and salad, and an intriguing entree. The pasta list is especially pleasing with a range of linguine, fettuccine, tortellini, and cannelloni. Entrees vary from fish and seafood to chicken breast stuffed with sausage and spinach. Lunch, Mon-Fri; dinner, Mon-Sat; closed Sun.

The Spaghetti Warehouse (G10), 901 Commerce at Travis in downtown; 229-9715. Two other locations. *I-M*. On the banks of Buffalo Bayou in historic downtown, this massive former warehouse was given a million-dollar look with beveled and antique stained glass, huge crystal chandelier, mammoth carved wood stairs, and antiques throughout. A large lounge with old tonsorial chairs and full bar allows relaxation before dinner in the Gazebo or upstairs. Made-from-scratch spaghetti sauces. Open daily. Casual. Lunch and dinner.

Star Pizza (F2), 2111 Norfolk, on the edge of The Montrose just off Farnham near Shepherd; 523-0800. *I*. A casual dining room and front porch tables—nothing to brag about here except really great pizzas, all hand-made to order. And you can do your own thing and create your pizza fantasy with over 20 different extras from anchovies to fresh garlic to jalapenos to zucchini. They make their own sauce and dough (from unbleached, untreated flour) fresh daily. Other items on the menu include Italian sausage sandwich, antipasto salad, and several pastas. Beer/wine and soft drinks. Restaurant open 11-11 Sun-Thu; 11 am-midnight Fri-Sat. Deliveries end 30 minutes before closing.

Mexican

Cafe Adobe (F2), 2111 Westheimer; 528-1468. *M-E*. Truly a tropical oasis on this busy street, the pink adobe two-story structure is surrounded by palms, banana trees, and Mexican pottery. There are several pleasant surprises—the popular Acapulco Bar upstairs overlooking the traffic scene below, the beautiful tiled fountain forming the center of an outdoor dining patio, and the indoor facilities with brightly painted floral design ceilings and walls augmented by colorful tiles, tropical foliage, and costumed personnel. Now, about the food . . . this is true Tex-Mex with some original creations on the vast menu. Try the Mexican Bread topped with broiled cheese and pico de gallo hot sauce. Open daily for lunch and dinner.

Las Alamedas (B1), 8615 Katy Freeway at Voss Rd.; 461-1503. *M to E*. In a beautiful 19th-century-style hacienda, filled with gorgeous Mexican antiques, this sybaritic retreat offers unusual Mexican dishes. The menu also provides for local Mexican favorites as well. Lunch 11 am-2 pm Mon-Fri; dinner 6 pm-10 pm Mon-Thu, 6 pm-11 pm Fri and Sat; and Sun brunch 11:30 am-9:30 pm. Live entertainment Tue-Sun. Happy Hour 4-8 pm Mon-Thu, 4-7 pm Fri.

Merida Restaurant (C4), 2509 Navigation; 227-0260. *I-M*. Authentic Mexican-American surroundings at a large, bright, colorful, clean establishment, with menu offering traditional Mexican and Tex-Mex dishes, but highlighting Yucatecan specialties (Merida, the restaurant's namesake, is the capital of the Mexican State of Yucatan). Mexican breakfasts are *especialamente* worth trying—especially the huevos a la mexicana (eggs coarsely scrambled with chopped onion, tomato, and serrano pepper). For lunch or dinner, try cochinita pibil, Yucatecan-style marinated roast pork, served with black beans, rice, marinated onions, and tortillas. Or you may try the Merida Special to sample a bit of nearly everything. Casual. Open seven days.

Ninfa's (C4), 2704 Navigation; 228-1175. Other locations. *I to M*. This is the original location of this burgeoning chain that now includes a dozen or more restaurants plus a catering business. Specializing in char-broiled meats and upscale Mexican food, Ninfa's keeps bringing back its legion of regulars, who include former U.S. president George Bush. Try a Ninfarita, the house version of a Margarita. Open daily for lunch and dinner.

Pappasito's Cantina, 6445 Richmond Ave.; 784-5253. And a dozen or so other locations. *I-M*. This miracle of Mexican meals is Greek to most folks who know that the Pappas family knows what it is doing in nearly every kind of kitchen. In any language, in any cuisine, as in all their other restaurants, Pappas family magic translates Pappasito's as superior Mexican food delightfully served in enormous portions at reasonable prices. Clock your arrival before or after peak feeding hours to avoid waits that can stretch from just a few minutes to more than an hour. Fajitas of beef, chicken, or both; frijoles a la charra; agujas (pork ribs); spicy camarones diablos (spiced-up, sizzling shrimp); an exciting queso fundido (cheese with Mexican sausage, onions, peppers, mushrooms); tamales; tacos (soft or crispy); enchiladas; crispy corn tortilla chips; and addictive salsa are just a few of the mucho gustos at Pappasito's. Lunch and dinner seven days.

Indian/Pakistani

Indian

Haveli Indian Tandoori Restaurant, 9817 Bissonnet (just west of Westwood Mall); 776-0702. *I to M*. A pleasant, cheerful restaurant in an unpretentious strip shopping center, Haveli prepares astoundingly tasty dishes with all the exotic, often incendiary nuances the Indian subcontinent can inspire. A full and exciting dinner menu of tandoori specialties (chicken tikka, tandoori shrimp, seekh kabab), vegetable specialties (mushroom bhaji, mixed vegetables Kashmiri korma), and more chicken, lamb, fish, shrimp, and rice dishes, plus baked-to-order Tandoori breads (Peshawari naan, stuffed with nuts and dried fruit, or onion kulcha), awaits all alimentary adventurers. Sneak a preview of some items at the daily lunch buffet. The midday array features tandoori chicken and curried chicken; arguably the best saag paneer (creamed spinach and a special, tofu-like cheese that together yield a delicate, nutlike flavor) anywhere; sliced, marinated raw onion (very spicy, very addictive); subtly flavored rice (superb when basmati is used); a rotating assortment of great vegetable dishes; tandoor-baked naan bread; and a loose, but very flavorful rice pudding. Taste why regulars have been regulars for more than a decade. Lunch and dinner seven days.

Taj Mahal (E5), 8328 Gulf Freeway at Bellfort exit; 649-2818. *I to M*. This fascinating restaurant is richly decorated with tapestries, rugs, brass trays, and lamps. A glassed-in main dining area allows guests to watch the process of charcoal broiling various meats on skewers in the barrel-shaped pit-ovens called tandoors. This restaurant in particular takes heed of the American taste and serves mild Indian dishes. Lunch and dinner Tue-Sun. Casual.

Oriental

Chinese

China Garden (K11), 1602 Leeland, near China Town; 652-0745. *I*. One of Houston's most popular, well rounded Chinese menus printed both in Chinese and in English, and offering an unbelievable array of 85 different dishes ranging from Cantonese to Sichuan to Mandarin. Here you will find your favorite vegetables with chicken, sirloin, pork, shrimp, squid, or just plain. For a party of six or more you may give 24-hours' notice for the special Chinese Gourmet Dinner. Lunch weekdays; dinner nightly. Casual.

Dong Ting (F3), 611 Stuart; 527-0005. M *to* E. This promises the finest and most authentic Hunan Province specialties in town. Dishes include Spicy Squids and Hot Sauce Shrimp or you can try other delicacies such as Steamed Fish. The most personable owner, San Hwang, comes from a family of Hunan cuisine experts who can come up with at least 50 ways to cook a chicken. A small, modestly decorated, Chinese country-home atmosphere, relaxing and rewarding. Serving lunch and dinner daily. Casual.

Hunan River (C2), 2015 W. Gray; 527-0200. M. A modern presentation of fine Chinese country cooking. This small, serene dining room brings the best in Hunan to fashionable River Oaks. No preservatives, artificial ingredients, or frozen foods go into these more than 75 entrees. The owners trace their recipes back to the classical form of cooking for Chinese dynasties. Hunan is synonymous with hot, but here the chef prepares your choice to the degree of spice you tolerate. Open 11:15 am-10:15 pm Mon-Thu; 11:15 am-11:15 Fri; noon-11:15 pm Sat; noon-10:15 Sun.

King Hua, 9600 Westheimer just east of Gessner; 780-9119. M. This charming, pleasantly low-key restaurant is owned and operated by the Wei family who, more than 20 years ago, pioneered introducing Houstonians to the range of Chinese cuisines beyond the familiar Cantonese. Everyone gets warm smiles and cheery greetings, automatic candidates for membership in the legion of regular customers welcomed with more smiles, hugs, and tableside chatter. And, naturally, everyone has access to such wondrous culinary glories as some of the world's best hot-and-sour soup, sweet-and-spicy Sichuan-style shrimp, chao ma mien (noodles with shrimp, pork, and vegetables in spicy broth), snow-white chicken and, by advance special order, perfectly roasted Peking duck. Lunch and dinner Tue-Sun; closed Mon.

My Canh, 10600 Bellaire Blvd. west of the Sam Houston Tollway; 530-6789. *I*. This is just one of many Chinese restaurants serving an all-you-can-eat noon buffet at unbelievably low prices, as well as bit pricier a la carte lunches and dinners off a menu the size of a telephone directory. But what makes My Canh a favorite is its astounding array of dim sum, which Chinese friends euphemistically understate as "to have tea." Stuff yourself silly on what the Chinese, in another euphemism of moderation, call "snacks": steamed shrimp, pork or beef dumplings; char siu pao (steamed bun stuffed with Chinese barbecued pork); chicken feet (delicious! honest!); Chinese broccoli with oyster sauce; pork ribs with garlicky black bean sauce; seafood-stuffed green bell pepper; spring rolls; and much more, nearly beyond counting. All these dim-sum, whether sweet or savory, are set out on carts rolled tableside for your inspection and selection. Dim sum is served 9 am to 3 pm every delicious day. Lunch buffet weekdays only. A la carte lunch, dinner daily.

Uncle Tai's Hunan Yuan (F1), 1980 Post Oak Blvd.; close to The Galleria; 960-8000. M to E. This is a classy, dressy establishment offering scores of hot and spicy dishes of Hunan Province. Many of the offerings were introduced to Houston by Uncle Tai who made his first claim to fame in New York before moving his family to Houston. He consistently puts out great specialties such as Sliced Duck with Ginger Roots, and Chunked Rabbit with Orange. Lunch daily except Sun, dinner every evening.

Japanese

Benihana of Tokyo (J9), 1318 Louisiana; 659-8231. (D1), 9707 Westheimer; 789-4962. M-E. Japanese showchefship at its sharpest as knife-wielding whizzes put sizzle into steak, chicken, shrimp, scallops, or lobster together with fresh vegetables. Soft music and oriental decor conducive to conversation, whether on business or pleasure. Lunch and dinner.

Ginza Benkay (C1), 5868 San Felipe, near The Galleria; 785-0332. M-E. This sushi bar is usually packed. Small seating area at the bar, where you can watch sushi chefs ceremoniously prepare your favorite raw fish, seafood, and rice rolled in seaweed. Also serving traditional Japanese dishes. Casual but neat dress. Lunch and dinner Mon-Fri, dinner only Sat. Closed Sun.

Nippon (F3), 3939 Montrose; 523-3939. M. This bright, modern, two-level sushi house is family run with great taste. The interior is accented with original art of warriors and geishas. Upstairs is devoted to a teppanyaki grill while downstairs is the sushi bar. Appetizers include aged tofu, softshell crab, and octopus vinegared salad. Entrees include sushi or sashimi with tuna, salmon, octopus, and yellow tail, or you may prefer a substantial shrimp tempura or sukiyaki, or traditional beef and chicken preparations such as shabu-shabu and Chicken Teriyaki. Also soups, desserts, and beverages. Open for lunch and dinner seven days.

Tokyo Gardens (F1), 4701 Westheimer, near The Galleria; 622-7886. M to E. A beautiful and authentic Japanese restaurant constructed in the traditional manner. The large, open but partitioned seating areas, around a stream stocked with carp, permit guests to see the classical Japanese dances performed nightly. Western seating also. A fine feast from a varied menu featuring all-time favorites, but also introducing uncommon items. Also a large Sushi Bar. Japanese beer, hot sake, and mixed drinks available. Casual but neat attire. Lunch Mon-Fri, and dinner seven nights. Banquet facilities available.

Thai

Morningside Thai (D2), 6710 Morningside at Holcombe; 661-4400. M-E. In a former home in this residential area, you'll feel right at home with friendly attentive service willing to assist with your perusal of the menu. Tiny finger-size freshly cooked egg rolls are good starters. Another great appetizer is Shrimp Toast or sample the variety tray. Seafood is the specialty, but there are also meats. Especially delicious is Whole Snapper in Plum Sauce. Reservations suggested. Open for lunch and dinner seven days. Casual.

Vietnamese

Kim Son, 8200 Wilcrest at Beechnut; 498-7841, downtown 2001 Jefferson; 224-2461. I to M. Houston has one of the largest Vietnamese communities in the country, and, therefore, enjoys the wealth of authentic dining establishments that come with it. Perhaps the best known of them, in a large strip shopping center at the hub of a heavily Vietnamese sector of southwest Houston, is Kim Son. From mid-morning until the wee hours, patrons can feast on Vietnamese, Chinese, or hybrid specialties, including various noodles, rices, and other dishes that either fit or defy nearly any description. Many items come served with fresh cilantro, mint, and bean sprouts as standard issue. Fresh gulf crabs, prepared with either black pepper sauce or ginger and green onion, are more than delicious enough to justify the mess they generate. Soup noodles with duck or pork, or rice noodles with charcoaled beef or pork palatize more pleasure. Don't let these few examples fool you. If you laid all the items on Kim Son's enormous menu end to end, they'd probably just about reach to Vietnam. Whether for its inexpensive buffet lunch or the more exotic repertoire of its 26-volume (just kidding) menu, Kim Son is popular with lots and lots of all kinds of people. The enlarged, improved original Kim Son still packs 'em in downtown, but this one is more convenient to lodgings in the west and southwest parts of Houston. Open daily. Casual.

Seafood

Christie's (E2), 9200 S. Main; 667-1833. Two other locations. M-E. Since 1917 this family chain of seafood restaurants has been a traditional dinner spot for Houstonians. Fresh Gulf fish and seafood include whole flounder, trout, snapper, oysters, shrimp, crabs, and squid. Also crawfish (in season), frog legs, and gumbo. Separated from the main dining room is an oyster bar and lounge. Open 11 am-10 pm Mon-Wed, 11 am-2 am Thu-Sun. Casual.

The Flying Dutchman (F6), 505 2nd, in Kemah, TX, on Galveston Bay; 334-7575. M-E. A very casual, nautical theme, massive two-story oyster bar and restaurant at the junction of Clear Creek and Galveston Bay where diners delight in weekend parades of pleasure craft and shrimp boats constantly plying these waters. The best seat in the house is on the outer deck for boat watching and feasting on oysters on the half shell (in season). Huge wooden poles support the heavy cedar beams downstairs where dining is more casual. The more formal room upstairs is open evenings. The lunch and dinner menus together offer an extremely varied selection from alligator bisque to red snapper topped with creamy seafood and mushroom sauce. Also scrumptious salads, sandwiches, and cold boiled seafoods. Open for lunch and dinner daily.

Kaphan's (E2), 7900 South Main, several blocks from Astrodomain; 668-0491. *M-E*. Another highly reputable, traditionally great, long-time favorite seafood restaurant serving the discerning taste of fish lovers. A gracious dining room plus a garden room and banquet facilities. Kaphan's (pronounced kuh-PANZ) features a very large dinner menu including stuffed crab (100% lump backfin crabmeat), whole Texas flounder, fish throats, filet of redfish steak Pontchartrain, plus beef, chicken, and steaks char-broiled favorites. Continuing a delicious and endearing seasonal tradition, Kaphan's, with its compliments, passes around a chafing dish of oysters sauteed in a wonderful sauce of sherry and spices. Open for lunch and dinner Thu-Tue. Closed Wed. Casual.

Landry's Seafood Inn & Oyster Bar (F6), 201 Kipp, in Kemah, TX, on Galveston Bay at the Clear Lake channel; 334-2513. *M to E*. Landry's, formerly the landmark Jimmie Walker's, affords a grandstand view of a parade of pleasure craft plying the channel waters. You can drive up or sail up for good Gulf Coast dining on fresh oysters, shrimp, swordfish, snapper, flounder, and hot spicy seafood gumbo. Also prime rib and hearty salads. Expect long lines at prime time on Saturday. Upstairs slightly different menu, slightly higher prices, but shorter wait (if any). The third level is for private parties. Open seven days, lunch and dinner.

Soul Food

This Is It (C3), 239 W. Gray; 523-5319. *I*. Situated at the edge of downtown, this place is usually packed with denizens of the historic old, predominantly black Fourth Ward, together with weekday visits by downtown business types. Arrive hungry and be prepared for Texas-size portions of soul food from the steam table. Your choice of ox tails, hocks, chitterlings, baked chicken, smothered steak, cabbage, cornbread dressing, yams, peas, rice, and pintos, plus other down-home dishes. Most items daily; others rotate. No alcoholic beverages. A plain and simple place with good eats. Open 6:30 am-8 pm, Mon-Thu; 6 am-10 pm, Fri and Sat; 6:30 am-6 pm, Sun.

Spanish

Mediterranean Restaurant & Bar (D2), 2425 W. Holcombe Blvd.; 662-8302. *M-E*. The house specialty in this small house near the Medical Center off S. Main is Paella, a traditional Spanish feast of mixed meats and seafood over a bed of saffron rice. To begin try a Tapa, Spanish appetizers ranging from kidneys with sherry, ox liver and onions, and saucy tongue to squid rings, Spanish cheese, and red sausages. Other recommendations are the seafood casserole, filet of Hake, and grilled filet of tenderloin. Also serving Sangria. Open 11 am-10:30 pm daily. Casual.

Texana

Longhorn Cafe (I10), 509 Louisiana, downtown; 225-1015. *I*. Wood floors, brass foot rail at the bar, neon beer signs, boots 'n jeans and a wailin', twangin' jukebox let you know in a hurry this is authentic Texas country. The menu explains the makin's of a Chicken Fried Steak. All "Frieds" served with home-made cream gravy. Then there's regular steak and chicken fingers, Texas three-alarm chili, deep-fried potato skins, and a South Texas salad bowl. Serving lunch-dinner 11 am-9 pm Mon-Fri; lunch only 11 am-3 pm Sat; closed Sun.

Mama's Cafe (C1), 6019 Westheimer, "Restaurant Row"; 266-8514. *I-M*. Also in Baybrook Mall. This place . . . looks like an old-timey Sinclair filling station with art-deco tiles and benches out front, concrete floor, enamel-painted walls and shelves lined with license plates, vintage Texas postcards, and hundreds of local and imported beer cans, plus country antiques and plants. Whether for full meals or a proverbial bite, extremely popular with all kindsa folks. Huge weekend crowds for breakfast, especially southwest Texas country-style breakfast combinations; lunch and dinner crowds usually more navigable. Daily specials announced on blackboard. Excellent steak and eggs for breakfast become outstanding when the steak is blackened with cajun spices. Refried beans are some of the city's tastiest. Gargantuan lemonades made from freshly-squozen, not frozen. Everything else tried here has been good to very good or better, especially chili and other Tex-Mex items. Homemade pies and cakes. Serving Mon-Thu 6:30 am-2 am; Fri 6:30 am-4 am; Sat 8 am-4 am; and Sun 8 am-2 am.

Taste of Texas, 10505 Katy Freeway; 932-6901. *M-E*. Owners Edd and Nina Hendee, along with special deputies, feverishly patrol their superior, superb, and otherwise superlative steakhouse to make absolutely sure everything is to everybody's satisfaction. They needn't worry, although, perhaps because they do, satisfaction rules. Said satisfaction sizzles to juicy perfection in 100% Certified Angus steaks, from the petite filet mignon to the 32-ounce porterhouse. En route to the salad bar, customers select steaks (or whole lobsters) from a huge working display case. If you don't see a steak you want, more are cheerfully and voluntarily produced. Each steak gets a number, each customer a matching tag. Taste of Texas is so meticulous about quality, they will replace a steak and/or knock it off a bill without being asked—and occasionally even after being asked not to. Unless you eat very early or very late, very long lines are inevitable, but ameliorated with complimentary chips, salsa, and soft drinks in a waiting lounge. Most of all, those long lines are justified by the flavor and quality of the entire Taste of Texas repertoire. Special cinnamon coffee complimentary after dinner. For many reasons, an absolute must for at least one meal in Houston. Lunch and dinner Mon-Fri; dinner only Sat-Sun.

ETCETERA

Andre's Tea Room (F2), 2515 River Oaks Blvd. in Lamar River Oaks Shopping Center; 524-3863. *I*. This is an enormously popular lunch spot and shopping stop. Andre's ambiance is convincingly Swiss mountain cabin with natural woods and Alpine bells constituting a casual, intimate, but still lively atmosphere. The luncheons change daily, but a typical meal would include a choice of three entrees, a salad, buerli (chewy, Swiss hardrolls), a beverage, and a freshly baked pastry. Lunch only, Mon-Sat, 11-2:30. Casual.

Butera's (F3), 4621 Montrose Blvd. close to the Museum/Garden Circle in The Montrose Area; 523-0722. *I*. Artists, young professionals, students, museum patrons, and construction workers alike line up here daily to sample a vast variety of deli treats and a host of wines, ales, and other beverages from around the world. Instead of sweets you may enjoy any one of many fine imported cheeses for dessert. Seating both indoors and on the sidewalk. Open 10:30 am-10 pm, Mon-Fri; 9 am-10 pm, Sat; and 9 am-8 pm, Sun.

The Hobbit Hole (C2), 1715 S. Shepherd; 528-3418. *I*. Probably the oldest nutrition center cafe in Houston, the Hole is a house with both indoor and outdoor dining. Specials may include grilled fish and stir-fried vegetables over brown rice, spiced chicken with vegetables over vermicelli, a variety of vegetarian sandwiches on homemade bread, and quiches and salads. Continuous service 11 to 11, Mon-Thu; until midnight, Fri and Sat; 11:30 am-10 pm, Sun.

The Melange downtown in Sam Houston Historical Park (J8), 1100 Bagby; 655-8514. *I*. In back of this quaint little emporium of gifts and historical mementoes, Melange is a welcome addition to the tours and peaceful surroundings of this park on the edge of bustling downtown. The Melange serves soup, salad, sandwiches, and one hot entree in the Town Hall Tea Room of this replica of The Long Row, Houston's first commercial building. Lunch 11 am-2 pm Mon-Fri.

Museum of Fine Arts Cafe Express (D3), 1001 Bissonnet, in the Museums/Garden Circle at the Mecom Fountain on Main; 639-7370. *I*. A perfect way to cap off a day at the Museum in the street-level cafe, Tue-Sat. 11 am-3 pm; closed Sun-Mon. The menu changes daily with soups (black bean is a big favorite), sandwiches, salads, desserts. Casual.

CAFETERIAS

Cleburne Cafeteria (D2), 3606 Bissonnet; 667-2386. *I*. One of Houston's oldest family-owned cafeterias. Fresh vegetables and no pre-prepared mixes. Lunch and dinner Sun-Fri; closed Sat.

Luby's Cafeterias. *I*. There are 30-plus locations in just about every key area of town and in malls such as Town & Country and Baybrook. All open 10:45 am-2:30 pm and 4-8:30 pm seven days.

BRUNCHES

We have selected a sampling of brunch spots across the city, but counsel you to double check with any listed here or elsewhere before rushing out. Main reason: Brunch formats change frequently. Some establishments have buffet brunches. Others offer brunch from a special menu or based on their regular menu. Still others may offer brunch simply by extending the hours of breakfast service into early or late afternoon. Brunch may be an established tradition at some restaurants, an experiment at others. What is here today may be completely gone tomorrow. Correspondingly, today's impossible dream may emerge as tomorrow's tangible, edible reality. One effective approach is simply to select a restaurant in which you would like to have brunch, then call and ask whether it is served. Check, however, for any possible changes in time or format.

Brennan's (F3), 3300 Smith St.; 522-9711. This famous restaurant peppers its weekend brunches with live New Orleans jazz on both Saturday and Sunday. Texas Creole, American foods with French accents. Reservations. Jackets required.

DeVille in the Four Seasons Hotel (J10-11), 1300 Lamar; 650-1619. E. A very snazzy jazz brunch includes complimentary glass of Roederer Estate Champagne. Sip while you contemplate an omelette made-to-order at the omelette station. Or while you decide which of the vast assortment of salads, seafoods, viandes, entrees, and desserts to devour first. Reservations recommended. Sundays 10:30 am-2 pm.

Nassau Bay Hilton (E5), 3000 NASA Rd. 1; 333-9300. M. A perfect spot to take friends and relatives for a relaxing Sunday brunch overlooking the Hilton Marina on Clear Lake. The seafood station is loaded with cold boiled shrimp, plus whole salmon. Also waffles, eggs, and other breakfast items and off-the-menu lunch dishes. Hours are 11 am-2 pm. Casual.

Pastine 5300 N. Braeswood just west of Chimney Rock; 723-6434. I-M. Creative, eclectic combinations with Creole/Italian accents prevail on the brunch menu of this pleasant new restaurant overlooking Brays Bayou. Shrimp crepe blends vegetables and cream cheese with a guajillo sauce. Breakfast burrito wraps scrambled eggs, roasted poblano pepper, melted cheese, and a garlic-tomato sauce in a tortilla. Nice seasonal fruit plate, too. Different menu for lunch, dinner.

Pepper's Restaurant in the Ramada Inn Hotel Northwest, 12801 Northwest Fwy. (A1); 462-9977. Champagne starts you off with a pre-toast toast to a hearty brunch buffet with many selections such as roast beef, vegetables, cheese board, eggs, sausage, and much more. Reservations if four or more in group. Sundays 11:30 am-2:30 pm.

Rainbow Lodge (C1), #1 Birdsall; 861-8666. While away the hours casually in this hunting-lodge atmosphere overlooking landscaped gardens on peaceful Buffalo Bayou. Imaginative Sunday brunch selections off a special menu of salads, sandwiches, egg entrees (including mixed grill of game or crabmeat

Niels Esperson Building in front of Pennzoil Place   Dale Young

omelette), pasta, chicken, seafood, and, of course, dessert. Reservations. 10:30 am-4 pm.

Ruggles Grill (F3), 903 Westheimer; 524-3839. Eggs Provencal and Benedict, trout, steak sandwiches, and pasta are among the items in this bright, stylish atmosphere. 11 am-3 pm.

Shanghai Red's (D5), 8501 Cypress St.; 926-6666. Select from an attractive buffet. Great view from Brady Island overlooking the Houston Ship Channel. Reservations. 11 am-3 pm.

Vargo's (C1), 2401 Fondren Rd.; 782-3888. *I-M*. Here you are seated and order from a brunch menu. The view is spectacular, for the entire dining room overlooks the famous Vargo gardens with winding brook and small lake where small wild animals and tame peacocks meander. There is a mix of choices from breakfast to luncheon items. Dressy casual. Sun. 11 am-2:30 pm.

THE PERFORMING ARTS

There rarely is a dark night on Houston stages, where scores of local performing arts groups delight audiences with every conceivable form of entertainment.

This is one of the few cities in the nation to boast major professional resident performing arts companies plus its own Broadway musical production group. The big four—Houston Grand Opera, Houston Ballet, Houston Symphony, and the Alley Theatre—combined are currently presenting over 1,000 performances a year, here and all over the world.

Visitors not only have a choice from among an impressive slate of events in the fall and winter, but are treated to stellar outdoor performances in the spring and summer as well. An added bonus is that many of the latter are free.

Thus the visitor and newcomer are promised bountiful opportunities to witness a wide range of programs from traditional to contemporary theater, from folkloric dance to full classical ballet, and from Bach to pop.

Check with the local paper for details on current performances, especially the Sunday amusement section and pre-weekend arts and entertainment preview sections for most complete coverage.

DANCE

Many Houstonians traditionally are as enthusiastic about the dance as they are about their favorite sports teams. And to satisfy this demand there are no fewer than twelve dance companies.

The **Houston Ballet** leads this list; 523-6300. Started in 1968, it has already reached a widely proclaimed pinnacle of success, both in the U.S. and abroad. While it enjoys a fine reputation as a classical company, it is equally aggressive in developing a blend of contemporary works. It ranks as the nation's fourth largest dance company, with 50 dancers, 13 soloists, and eight principals. Its backup is drawn from an enrollment of some 400 students in the Houston Ballet Academy.

Of a total of about 60 performances a year, most are at home and the rest on tour. The company has performed in Spain, Italy, France, Luxembourg, Switzerland, Monaco, Indonesia, and Scandinavia.

The Ballet performs its regular season in Wortham Theater Center (I9), 501 Texas, from September to June. It also does a major program at Miller Outdoor Theatre (D3), Concert Drive, in Hermann Park, in June. *NCH.*

Greater Houston Civic Ballet, 468-3670. Chartered in 1958, this company presents four major programs a year in Blaffer Auditorium at the Kinkaid School, 201 Kinkaid School Dr., 782-1640, and in the Music Hall, Bagby at Walker downtown. It maintains a well-rounded repertory of classical, contemporary, and some original works.

Allegro Ballet of Houston 1570 S. Dairy Ashford; 496-4670. Primarily a classic and neo-classic company performing at many locations here and out-of-town, including public schools, libraries, in city parks, and at the Kinkaid School.

Southwest Jazz Ballet Co.,; 686-6299. A professional group of fifteen dancers active year-round with performances here and around the world. They perform in the Music Hall and do a summer program at Miller Outdoor Theatre, in Hermann Park on Concert Drive. *NCH.*

There are a number of other student and adult dance groups throughout the city such as the **Concert Dancers** at the High School for the Performing and Visual Arts, 4001 Stanford, 522-7811; and the **Dance Collective** at the University of Houston Clear Lake, 2700 Bay Area Blvd., 283-7600.

In addition, there are about fifty ethnic dance companies, excluding those from Latin America, which keep Houston's toes tapping to the many rhythmic forms expressed in the dance all year 'round.

MUSIC

Classical Music

Since 1913 Houston has sought out symphony, even when it was performed in a vaudeville house.

The city did provide more suitable surroundings in its City Auditorium where early Houstonians flocked to see such illustrious immortals as Paderewski, Caruso, and others. Years later this hallowed old structure gave way to the beautiful new home for the city's symphony, **Jones Hall for the Performing Arts** (I10), 615 Louisiana. The $7fi-million-dollar Continental-style hall is a multi-purpose, multi-form facility with four separate seating arrangements, ranging from the capacity 3,000 to 1,800 for more intimate audiences.

The **Houston Symphony Orchestra,** 224-4240, presents its full season of concerts from September to May and the Exxon Pop series May to July.

Out of the total 200-plus concerts a year, 50 are during the main season, 21 make up the Satellite Series and pop concerts, 34 are in front of student groups, and the remainder are on tours in the United States and abroad.

Strongly dedicated to civic educational efforts, the 94-piece Symphony has performed annual summer series of concerts in Miller Outdoor Theatre, NCH, and for several years has participated in The Houston Festival. The Symphony has recorded for Pro Art and has had several compact discs reach the top 30 list.

Some designated rehearsals in Jones Hall may be open to the public. NCH. Check to be sure.

Other classical music groups, both on and off campuses, complement the symphony programs with city-wide concerts almost year 'round. They include the **Houston Civic Symphony,** which plays in churches, schools, museums, and also tours.

Houston Friends of Music brings outstanding chamber ensembles to Houston from around the world to perform in Hamman Hall at Rice University (D3), on campus. Information; 285-5400. CH.

The **Shepherd String Quartet,** 527-4854, is a faculty ensemble at Rice University and performs in the spring and fall at Hamman Hall. Most of the performances are open to the public, NCH.

The **University of Houston** (D4), 743-1000, has a large number of student and faculty music groups including the *Symphony Orchestra, Symphony Brass Quintet,* the *Lyric Art Quartet,* the *Wind Ensemble, U of H Concert Band, Woodwinds of Houston,* and others which play on campus in Cullen Auditorium and Dudley Recital Hall. NCH & CH.

The **University of St. Thomas,** 522-7911, has several musical groups including the *Classic Guitar Ensemble* and a *Flute Ensemble,* which give concerts in Cullen Hall on campus. NCH.

Opera

Interfaced with the long list of music ensembles in Houston is an equally large and varied list of choral groups ranging from barber-shop quartets to Gregorian, and from gospel to grand opera. The latter is the granddaddy of them all.

Houston Grand Opera, 546-0200, has achieved meteoric fame and has been widely acclaimed for its broad innovative repertoire. It is the winner of several major awards including a "Tony" for the best revival of an American musical, *Porgy and Bess,* and subsequently a "Grammy" for a recording of the same.

The Opera performs its regular season in Wortham Theater Center from October into July. It also does three special performances in Miller Outdoor Theatre in May during the annual Spring Opera Festival. NCH.

While it has an outstanding reputation for its staging of traditional operas in their original languages plus English-language programs, the company also performs many works by American composers. Among its U.S. and world premieres, it has gained greatest renown for its revisionist treatment of such works as *Tremonisha* and *The Lady of the Lake,* which, until the HGO revived it in 1981, had not been seen in 150 years. Other innovative productions have been *Seagull* and the 1981 world premiere of *Willie Stark* by Carlisle Floyd.

Rated as one of the top six opera companies in America, the Association has two other branches working in conjunction with the main company. They are the **Texas Opera Theatre** and **Houston Opera Studio,** together they present 250 performances a year, here, in the United States, and abroad.

Texas Opera Theatre, 546-0200. Founded in 1974 as a touring and educational subsidiary of Houston Grand Opera, this organization has two groups, the main company that does full-length works, and a resident troop that performs one-act operas and does introductory workshops in conjunction with the national organization called Young Audiences.

The Theatre does four double-bill performances each year in January and March in Wortham Theater at the University of Houston, and also performs an annual student matinee of comic opera.

Gilbert & Sullivan Society, 627-3570. This group performs light opera in an annual series in July in Wortham Theater Center.

Specialty Music

Apart from the many ethnic musical groups, there is a growing number of jazz ensembles, new music groups, and a lot of the oldies-oriented talent still around.

City of Houston Parks & Recreation Department, 845-1111. Concerts run from early May to mid-August. There are numerous open-air concerts in parks throughout the city. *NCH.* The variety of sounds is as great as the number of programs, which range from pulsating Latin beats to martial music and from ballads to blues.

These band concerts may be heard in most municipal neighborhood parks as well as in major locations such as Hermann Park, Sam Houston Park, and Hermann Square in front of City Hall, all convenient for visitors.

Texas Southern University; 527-7011. The TSU **Jazz Ensemble** is a 26-piece band, which plays several major open park concerts a year.

Vocal Music

Bay Area Chorus. This group has performed for 17 years in the area doing traditional choral music. They usually give two regular concerts a year, one at Christmas in the NASA LBJ Space Center Theatre, and the other in spring, at the Bayou Building Auditorium, University of Houston Clear Lake.

Concert Chorale of Houston: A professional choral organization with 34 singers. The group performs a broad scope of music from the 16th century to modern day. Occasionally they invite internationally known soloists and conductors to perform with them. The regular season is September-May in Wortham Center.

The University of Houston Concert Chorale, and the **University Chorus** are student groups at the University of Houston Central campus. Information: 743-3009 (UH School of Music).

The first is an auditioned select mixed choir, which performs at times with the Houston Symphony Orchestra and Houston Ballet; and the second group is the larger of the two and does major works. Both the Chorale and the Chorus groups give fall and spring concerts on the University campus. *NCH.*

THEATER

Cinema

A cross-section of theaters in Houston are as follows: **Almeda Square AMC Theatres** (E5), I-45 at Almeda-Genoa, 941-3444; **Galleria Cinema I,II, III & IV** (F1), 1390 Galleria Post Oak, 626-4011; **Galleria Cinema II & IV**, 5085 Westheimer, 626-0140; **Cineplex Odeon Sharpstown** (D1), Sharpstown Shopping Center, 995-9696; **Greenspoint Cinema** (A1), 430 Greenspoint Mall, 874-9558; **Greenway 3 Theatres** (F1), Five Plaza East, 626-0402; **Gulfgate Cinema** (E5), 7400 S. Loop East, 644-3806; **AMC Meyer Park 14,** S. Post Oak Road at W. Bellfort, 721-0140; **Long Point Cinema** (B1), 10016 Long Point, 468-7948; **Meyerland Cinema** (E1), 4848 Jackwood, 666-0735; **Northline Cinema** (A3), 700 Northline Mall, 692-4487; **Spectrum 9 Theaters,** 2660 Augusta off Westheimer, 781-3233; **River Oaks Theatre** (C2), 2009 West Gray, 524-2175; **Willowbrook Cinema,** 7925 W. FM 1960, 890-0245; and **Dollar Cinema Briargrove,** 6100 Westheimer, 780-1869.

Professional and Semi-Professional Theater

There is such an abundance of new talent on the boards in Houston that even many of the locals are not fully aware of the array of theatrical events available.

The anchor establishment has been and is today the world-famous **Alley Theatre** (I9-10), 615 Texas Ave.; 228-8421, one of the oldest resident theaters in the United States.

Since its humble beginnings in 1947 in an 87-seat theater converted from a dance studio at the end of an alley (hence the name), this center has emerged as one of the leading theatrical production and training facilities in the world.

Regular season is from October through June, and the Alley enjoys strong support from a subscription audience of more than 30,000.

It is Houston's only professional resident repertory theater and has attracted guest directors from New York, Canada, and the former USSR. The Alley does hundreds of performances a year, divided between the regular season and summer productions, plus such special productions and programs as children's plays. The Alley has two theaters: one is a proscenium arch stage with seating for more than 800, and the other is a Neuhaus Arena for 300.

Dancing Girl in front of Jones Hall facing the Alley Theatre

Dale Young

This theater is dedicated to plays of literary merit and brings to Houston a broad spectrum of both classical and contemporary works by world-famous playwrights. The Alley staff conducts interesting tours. CH (nominal).

The Arena Theater (D1), 7324 Southwest Freeway at Fondren; 988-1020. The Arena is a professional theater bringing top stars and musicals to Houston year 'round. It has been totally remodeled for sound, lighting, and decor. Seating around a revolving stage allows a full house of 2,800 unobstructed viewing from any position. Tickets are available at the Arena Box Office or at Ticketmaster, 629-3700.

The **Ensemble** (F3), 3535 Main; 520-0055. This 100-seat theater primarily features productions by black playwrights. The full season from September to August offers six productions, each lasting five weeks with a one-week preview. There also is a supporting program of children's theater throughout the summer. This professional company's productions range from comedy to mystery, from musicals to drama.

Main Street Theatre (D2), 2540 Times Blvd. in the Village; 524-7998. Founded in 1975, this theater has moved to an arena stage. It features works of intellectual appeal as well as pure entertainment.

Stages (C3), 3201 Allen Parkway; 527-8243. This is a repertory theater and the second largest in Houston. It is home of the Texas Playwright's Festival and the Early Stages Children's Theatre. Presently the concentration is on contemporary plays, musicals, and new and innovative works. There are two stages, the larger seating 250 and a more intimate one for 195. The large resident professional company rounds out its season with a revival of an American masterpiece of a world classic in the mainstream of theater. Ticket information, 527-8243.

Theatre Under the Stars, 622-1626. This is Houston's own Broadway musical production company, which has staged world premieres of original Houston productions. From October through April, TUTS performances are in the Music Hall (I9), Walker at Bagby. Tickets, 622-8887.

In July of each year TUTS produces an extravaganza musical open to the public in the magnificent Miller Outdoor Theatre (D3), Concert Drive, in Hermann Park. NCH. With 1,700-plus seats, this is one of the largest amphitheaters in the nation. Miller has outdoor air conditioning for approximately half of the permanent seating area. The grassy hill behind the seats accommodates overflow crowds that swell into the thousands. Seat tickets are distributed at the theater at noon, first-come first-served, NCH, for TUTS performances as well as for all other events at Miller.

Cynthia Woods Mitchell Pavilion, 363-3300, provides a lushly, forest-enveloped amphitheater that serves as summer home for the Houston Symphony and delightful venue for other top performers at The Woodlands, 25 miles north of downtown.

University and Amateur Theaters ——————

Surprisingly good productions are found throughout the city in campus theaters and neighborhood little theaters.

Among them are several major university and high school drama department companies such as the **High School for the Performing and Visual Arts**, 522-7811; the **University of Houston**, 743-1000; and the **University of St. Thomas**, 522-7911. While it does not have a drama department, Rice University is the home of the **Rice Players**, the city's oldest collegiate theatrical company. Rice University; 527-4040.

Little Theater groups include the **Country Playhouse** in Town & Country, 12802 Queensbury, 467-4497; **Theatre Southwest**, 3750 S. Gessner, 977-6028; and **Theatre Suburbia**, 1410 West 43rd, 682-3525.

Shakespeare Festival, Miller Outdoor Theatre, Hermann Park; 520-3292. This festival is under the direction of University of Houston drama professors, who produce Shakespeare plays open to the public during the summer. *NCH.*

CALENDARS OF EVENTS

For printed calendars listing performing arts events contact the **Greater Houston Convention & Visitors Bureau,** 801 Congress.

For ticket agencies see MATTERS OF FACT.

NIGHTLIFE

With a strong shot of adrenalin and plenty of stamina, one can nightclub hop across Houston, mixing it up with a little bit of country, jazz, opera, rock, reggae, and salsa all in one night. You could go out every evening of the year and never backtrack in this swinging metropolis of thousands of watering holes.

At many places, the scene begins with happy hour and usually doesn't let up until 2 am; some clubs may stay open later but can't serve alcohol after hours. Some neighborhood bars are open and jumping by 8 am, and others save their big bash for Sunday jam sessions, brunches, and tea dances.

No matter what your mood, you can find the right setting here, where the dress codes run the gamut from extremely casual to ball gowns. One restriction is that you can't enter a place where food is served without shoes and shirt, and Texas law says you must be 21 to belly up to the bar. If you are underage you can enter a bar only if accompanied by parent or legal guardian. Most supper clubs require coat and tie, which a few may lend unsuspecting patrons.

BARS

Black Swan (C1), Omni Hotel (lower level), Four Riverway; 871-8181. Could be your own den atmosphere here but with British ditties, some oldies, and pop to liven up the most intimate corners and booths on different levels throughout. Live entertainment Friday and Saturday nights.

Cadillac Bar (C2), 1802 Shepherd; 862-2020. You don't need a Cadillac, but it helps if you want to be one of the "in folks" at this funky bar that packs 'em in from downtown after five. For years Houstonians have headed for the famous Cadillac Bar in Nuevo Laredo, Mexico, but now they've got one in their own backyard. This place is totally unpretentious, but the "margaritas" and nachos are fine. Mexican beer with lime and lots of lively chatter, mostly in English, mix well here with Mexican melodies on stereo. Open seven days.

Cattle Guard (F3), 2800 Milam; 520-5400. Just on the outskirts of downtown you can sit on the front porch of this Western-style watering hole and enjoy while you watch the rest of the world hit the freeways. A fun stop for chips and dips during Happy Hour. Leave the coat and tie in the trunk, this is casual.

Grif's Shillelagh Inn (F3), 3416 Roseland; 528-9912. If you are a sports celeb, sports buff, or just looking for happy times in a get-down indoor-outdoor atmosphere, this Montrose neighborhood bar is it.

A long-established Houston sports boosters' crowd dwells here, win or lose. The club features bus trips to our pro games, and for those left behind there're two TVs. Draft beer is served from 4 to 6 pm, frequent parties are held in the patio, and pipers and Irish dancers may pop in on Fridays. The downtown office crowd descends here in hopes of meeting some of the sports celebrities. How about a Rockets or Oilers T-shirt and green tie for dress code?

La Carafe (H10), 813 Congress; 229-9399. This is the best of what's left of Old Town, downtown. Hardly the Ritz; in fact, only wine, beer, and champagne are served, but it's heavy on nostalgia. This is all that's left of Houston's oldest commercial building on its original site. Among its early uses were a stagecoach inn where Sam Houston is supposed to have slept, and an Indian trading post. Be sure to peek at the petite patio at the rear and check out the upstairs bar weekends. The walls are covered with memorabilia and the old juke has the most curious selection of disc offerings including opera, Piaf, old Broadway tunes, and other collectibles. It's one of a kind, folks are casual and friendly, and you might even meet a native Houstonian here.

Marfreless (C2), 2006 Peden (entrance on McDuffie); 528-0083. Every town has a neat bar tucked away from the roar of the crowd, but this one is so tucked there are no signs and the entrance could dub for deliveries. This is a surprise pub, usually packed in spite of its secrecy, with mostly youngish to older college crowds rapping away in the good vibes atmosphere with low-key classical background music. Soft and easy, very intimate on two levels, and the kind of neighborhood bar everyone likes to discover. Open nightly.

Shucker's Sports Bar (F1), second level between Westin Oaks Hotel and The Galleria mall, 5011 Westheimer; 960-8100. Tired of shopping? Too many meetings, charts, and lectures? Then this is the spot to unwind. A large bar but subdued atmosphere and masculine decor with accents in leather, and wood paneling. Highly respectable drinks, TV news and sports if you care to watch, and a good place to contemplate the day. Happy Hour features hot and cold hors d'oeuvres.

Spindletop (J9), at the top of the Hyatt Regency Houston Hotel, 1200 Louisiana; 654-1234. While the world turns below on the frenzied "Spaghetti Bowl" traffic circles, you may enjoy a turn around downtown in this revolving club with soft stereo music for your relaxation. Lunch and dinner served. A splendid view of the city and one of the few from this level. No jeans or sneakers please.

T.G.I. Friday's, 9550 Bissonnet; 988-7179. Several other locations, too. No self-respecting city would be caught without its Friday's, and this West Side club has the typical Happy Hour madness with hot 'n' cold nibbles and happy crowds, mostly singles. Lunches offer burger varieties, Texas chicken fried steaks, croissant sandwiches, and other items. **Closed in 1995.**

CABARETS AND SUPPER CLUBS

Athens Bar & Grill (C5), 8037 Clinton Dr.; 675-1644. You don't need a ticket to Greece to get a taste of the resinated spirits, tasty cuisine, and exotic music and dance common to that Aegean paradise.

Simply step off Houston's ship channel waterfront and into this cave-like club, and you'll be transported into another world of non-stop entertainment direct from Greece. The belly dancer whips the crowds into frenzies with shouts of "Opa! Opa!" The Greek sailors do their own show with athletic gyrations and balancing acts. The owner's private recipes are something to write home about. Try the spinach pie.

Cody's (F2), 3400 Montrose Blvd.; 522-9747. This penthouse supper club is very upbeat. Stylish patrons enjoy fine food while listening to some of the greatest big jazz sounds anywhere. Cody's has the most spectacular unobstructed view of Houston's three commercial centers. Casual but no jeans, sneakers, thongs, or cut-offs. Outdoor seating (weather permitting).

Great Caruso, 10001 Westheimer; 780-4900. The only other place like this is the Petite Caruso in Paris. A great showplace with an array of continuous entertainment. Opera, Broadway tunes, and popular ballads brighten the atmosphere while you dine on gourmet cuisine in an Old-World opera house setting. An invaluable collection of European antiquities makes up the decor in this sensational club. Try not to miss this one. Dress code.

Howard Johnson Lodge (D1), 6855 Southwest Freeway; 771-0641. Asian-style karaoke entertainment is belted out at The Rama Room here. Nightly 8 pm-2 am.

Magic Island (D2), 2215 Southwest Freeway at Greenbriar; 526-2442. It's not often one finds a massive Egyptian monument on the side of a busy freeway but . . . shazam . . . there's Magic Island. This beautiful modern Egyptian edifice is a $3-million replica of ancient desert splendor with many rooms to explore and to wonder at the hocus pocus going on inside. Each room features different acts of magic, stand-up comedy, room for dancing, and regal dining. Continental cuisine and a romantic lounge for a quiet interlude. Open Mon-Sat. Dress code.

Marina Via Club (F6), 3000 NASA Rd. 1; 333-9300. Hear the band on the lake by the pool bar on the Marina level. Also food, swimming, volleyball, and dancing. Sundays from 2-7 pm. At the Nassau Bay Hilton & Marina overlooking Clear Lake.

Laff Stop (C2), 1952 A West Gray; 524-2333. Brings professional stand-up comedians direct from New York, Vegas, and Hollywood with a new show every week. Great cabaret in the heart of the River Oaks center.

River Cafe (F3), 3615 Montrose; 529-0088. Fine Continental dining, together with live music (Tue, Fri, & Sat).

MUSIC FOR LISTENING AND DANCING

El Caballero (D1), 5322 Glenmont off Chimney Rock at Southwest Freeway; 665-6241. This Latin nightclub features popular bands with the full range of rhythms. Hot Salsa dance contests for cash prizes. Two dance floors. Weekend cover.

Fitzgerald's (B3), 2706 White Oak; 862-7580. In the Heights near downtown, this club features a wide variety of name entertainment from rhythm and blues to Latin jazz. Seating is concert-style and tables around the dance floor. Casual or dressy. Cocktails. Recommend reservations. Cover.

Melody Lane Ballroom (D1), 3027 Crossview; 785-5301. On most days of the month there is some type of activity here, from ballroom dancing with live orchestras to dance classes to theme nights. Join the Parents Without Partners Dance, attend Singles Nites for buffets and dance classes, or go Country & Western Sundays. For reservations and information call the above number.

Pe-Te Cajun (E5), 11902 Galveston Road; 481-8736. The Cajun influence has swept Houston with dozens of cafes dishing up spicy, exotic foods, and together with the Cajun craze comes zydeco. This is Louisiana French swamp music and the traditional band includes accordion and washboard among other pieces. This music is not only foot-tapping good, it's contagious and will drive you to the big dance floor at Pe-Te. Bands scheduled Saturday afternoons and on the evening of the third Saturday of the month. Work up an appetite and try some of the light orders of Cajun cooking here.

Quincy's (D1), 2900 Briar Park Dr.; 978-7400. Located in the Adam's Mark Hotel, this very popular dance club features live entertainment.

Rockefeller's-The Night Club (C3), 3620 Washington Avenue; 861-9365. Formerly the old Heights State Bank Building, this nightspot is one of the hottest in town with a brilliant array of star singers and musicians. Try jazz, rock, zydeco (Cajun swamp music), rhythm and blues, soul, Brazil beat—you name it, they'll eventually book it, and it's the best. Usually these are one- or two-night gigs, so make your reservations right away.

The Roof (D1) in Westin Oaks Hotel, 5011 Westheimer; 960-8100. High above The Galleria, enjoy a breathtaking view and dance to the music of popular bands. A favorite stop for the chic, dressy crowd. Open nightly. Call for reservations.

HAPPY HOURS

Numerous hotels and restaurants throughout Houston compete for this expanding lucrative business, offering drink specials, complimentary hors d'oeuvres, and at times entertainment. Here is a selection. Happy Hours generally are featured Mon-Fri.

Birraporetti's (C2), 1997 W. Gray; 529-9191 (plus several other locations). This spacious club has enough old signs on the walls to compete with I-45 North. Very lively crowd. Hours 4-7 pm.

Cody's Jazz Bar & Grill (F2), 3400 Montrose; 522-9747. The best penthouse view in all of Houston. Very happy crowds at the bar and on the open terrace (weather permitting).

Omni Hotel (C1), 4 Riverway; 871-8181. The Black Swan features hot and cold buffet from 5-7 pm. Music and dancing.

Sheraton Grand Hotel (F1), 2525 W. Loop South; 961-3000. The Buckingham (sports bar) serves hot hors d'oeuvres plus chips and dips. Open 5-7 pm.

SIGHTS

Most newcomers and first-time visitors don't think of Houston in typical touristic terms. With an image of smoke-belching refineries, trade, and high finance, many think of this as a severe business-only town with little time for frivolity. But you will find it does have a surprising number of both manmade and natural tourist attractions, some yet to be discovered even by many Houstonians.

The biggest surprise is the variety of things to see and do that are either free or nominally priced. Some of these sights and happenings will be mentioned in other chapters on visual art, sports, and special events. Here, we will discuss only the points of general interest to the tourist.

Consider the wide range of choices: a celestial show or a visit to a medical museum; a day of family fun at an amusement park or an excursion down a ship channel; a serene stroll through a forest preserve or joining thousands of fans cheering their home team in a covered sports palace.

Houston is one of the few Southwestern cities that boasts several candidates for the *Guinness Book of World Records,* including the world's tallest monumental column. And perhaps the world's tallest bank building at 75 floors, or 1,049 feet.

However brief your visit or whatever the season, there is always a changing slate of things to do.

Armand Bayou Nature Center (E6 & F6), 8600 Bay Area Blvd.; 474-2551. NCH. In early days this was a dwelling site for the Karankawa Indians, a small but vicious, cannibalistic Gulf Coast tribe. It is situated on nearly 2,000 acres at a point where three ecological systems merge, and it affords the visitor an exceptional view of the upper Texas coast as it was before the French and Spanish explorers arrived. There is a mix of native plants and animals reflecting Houston's curious blend of sub-tropical and continental elements.

Start at the main building where there are displays of the plant and animal life, then follow the trails that lead into the heart of the preserve. Among the animals you might encounter are deer, armadillos, nutria and mink, cottontails, and with any luck, you may spot an alligator. Open to the public is an authentic turn-of-the-century ranch, which offers a glimpse of life as it was among the pioneers who eked out a living raising figs, citrus, sugar cane, and cattle.

Guided tours of the trails are available weekends at 11 and 1. Farm tours are at 10 and 2. The Center is open 9 am-5 pm daily.

Astrodome—Harris County Domed Stadium (E2), Kirby at I-610 Loop; 799-9544. *CH*. This is one star in the Houston galaxy of attractions that needs little introduction. Of all the developments in the city's tourist industry, none has had greater impact than the Astrodome. Not only have many millions come from around the world to see the tremendous variety of events here, but it has been a magnet for visitors who pay a nominal fee just to take a look at an empty building.

Of course the best way to see the Astrodome is when it's in action with crowds up to 66,000 cheering for their team or enjoying one of the many other events such as auto thrill shows, jazz concerts, and rodeos.

Tours are at 11, 1, and 3 daily, except when there is a matinee. Games or events can pre-empt tours. Tours last 75 minutes and may include a video presentation.

Six Flags AstroWorld Theme Park (E2), I-610 at Kirby; 799-1234. *CH*. AstroWorld brings the Six Flags family brand of amusement, fun, and games to Houston's Astrodomain. Situated over marsh land that once was inhospitable to anything but mesquite, sage, and jack rabbits, this 75-acre park has been converted to a veritable garden land complete with fountains, streams, and a lagoon, plus many species of tropical flora.

There are more than 100 rides, live shows, and games for all ages, divided among eight major venues. A unique feature is the Thunder River ride, the first man-made rapids allowing a free float down a mock river.

The Tidal Wave is billed as the wettest ride in the park, while the Texas Cyclone roller coaster is deemed a park "icon." AstroWorld and adjacent Six Flags WaterWorld offer a full selection of rides, adventures, concerts, games, and performances. Special seasonal events, too. Police Academy stunt show added in summer of 1994 is among the many kinds of shows, music, and other entertainment that can become a perennial favorite or change season to season.

Open daily late May-early September, mid-March and late December; weekends only late March-mid-May, mid-November-mid-December. Variable days and hours at other times of year. Call to check in advance. Also inquire about the various discount admissions and passes.

American Funeral Museum, 415 Barren Springs; 876-3063. Since Houston is home of Service Corp. International, the first funeral service company to have its stock traded on the New York Stock Exchange, what more logical locale for the giant firm's collection of historic funeral service memorabilia and artifacts? Learn about funerals of the famous and the history of embalming. See antique hearses and ornate coffins. Open daily.

Battleship Texas (D6). See San Jacinto Battleground State Historical Park below.

Bay Area Park (F6). You can't miss the park, it is approximately in the 7800 block of Bay Area Blvd.; 474-4891. *NCH*. This delightful Harris county park faces a confluence of three bayous and is shaded by beautiful old oaks with Spanish moss. There are flocks of geese and ducks to feed and the chance of sighting one of the many water birds in the area such as egrets and the great blue heron. Open daily 7 am-10 pm.

Burke Baker Planetarium (D3). See Hermann Park below.

Children's Museum of Houston, 1500 Binz; 522-1138. Spectacular, new, and bright yellow, bursting with hands-on exhibits for children. Includes a KID-TV studio, computer technology, a mini-market, and other areas of interest for the young. Open 9 am-5 pm, Tue-Sat; noon-5 pm Sun. CH. Free family nights Thursdays.

Fun-plex, 13700 Beechnut; 530-7777. One of Houston's largest indoor recreation complexes for the family. Features include bowling, miniature golf, skating, movies and arcade, rides and games, eateries, nursery where little ones play safely. Also a gift shop with toys, gifts, candy, and souvenirs. Open daily year 'round. Parking and admission NCH. You pay only for games and attractions you choose.

Glenwood Cemetery, 2525 Washington; 864-7886. NCH. It is estimated that this founders cemetery goes back some 150 to 175 years. Unusual for pancake-flat Houston, this 65-acre park-like setting is on hilly terrain overlooking Buffalo Bayou and the downtown skyline. At the center is a caretaker's office, which in itself is an attraction, a petite German "gingerbread"-style house commonly found in older sections of the city such as The Heights. Many of Houston's rich and famous are buried here including the late billionaire, Howard Hughes, Jr. Hours 7 am-5 pm, daily.

The Heritage Society (J8). See Sam Houston Historical Park below.

Hermann Park (D3), bounded by Fannin, Almeda, Hermann Dr., and N. MacGregor; 845-1000. CH for some individual attractions.

One can spend days and evenings in this beautiful municipal park enjoying a host of activities, visiting museums and a zoo, and participating in recreational diversions including golf and tennis. Principal points of interest are a zoological garden, children's zoo, aquarium, planetarium, museums of medical and natural science, an amphitheater, and a garden center.

The Kipp Aquarium, NCH, is situated at the zoo's entrance. Its collection represents a sampling of salt and fresh water fish and invertebrates from around the world. Open 9:30 am. Closes at 5 pm in the winter and 8 pm in the summer.

Houston Zoological Gardens, has an outstanding collection of rare albino snakes and vampire bats. Feeding time for the bats is 2:30, a bit gory but interesting. Other features include a 2.2-acre rain forest and primate habitat, a hippo-dome, white rhino pen, and a tropical bird house resembling an Asian rain forest. At the entrance to the main zoo is the *Kipp Aquarium* with a variety of rare and bizarre species.

The *Children's Zoo, NCH,* is accessible via an Aqua-tunnel with Gulf Coast marine life swimming overhead. Especially educational are the animal nursery and children's theater with scheduled shows.

The Houston Zoological Gardens are open daily year-round. Nominal admission, but free on City of Houston holidays.

Next to the zoo is a *miniature train ride* through the woods and around a small fishing lake for youngsters. CH (except children under three *NCH*).

Nearby is one of the city's fine *golf courses*.

At the center of the park is a manmade grassy knoll used for seating at *Miller Outdoor Theatre, NCH*. From May through November there are events ranging from grand opera to Broadway musicals; 520-3292.

The *Museum of Natural Science, CH,* is the fourth most-visited museum in the United States. It frequently stages outstanding traveling international exhibitions of art and artifacts from Egypt, Peru, and other fascinating parts of the globe. Permanent exhibits include cavernous halls of dinosaurs, petroleum and space science, the hall of the American Indians, and sections devoted to gems and minerals, and energy. The huge and growing facility also comprises an IMAX theater and a rain forest-butterfly habitat with a 40-foot waterfall.

The *Museum of Medical Science* facility, CH, temporarily closed while a new venue is being built. Keep asking.

In *Burke Baker Planetarium* are year-round celestial shows, star shows, and laser-rock shows with several stunning 45-minute presentations. CH. Shows daily.

The museums are open 9 am-6 pm daily; noon-6 pm Sunday.

Across the street is the *Houston Garden Center, NCH,* with 5,000 species of roses. Offers a six-month schedule of flower and bulb shows; 529-5371.

Next to the Center is a colorful pavilion, a gift to Houston from its oldest "Sister City," Taipei.

There are objects of art throughout the park plus a children's playground, picnic facilities, and snack bars.

Houston Garden Center (D3). See Hermann Park above.

Houston Zoological Gardens and Children's Zoo (D3). See Hermann Park above.

Kipp Aquarium (D3). See Hermann Park above.

Museum of Medical Science (D3). See Hermann Park above.

Museum of Natural Science (D3). See Hermann Park above.

Museum of Printing History and Graphic Arts (C3), 1324 West Clay; 522-4652. *NCH*. Printing has long been a major industry here, and this museum spotlights this fascinating pursuit. It boasts some of the oldest known examples of printing pieces and rare documents. A feature is the world's oldest printed example of a temple scroll dating back to A.D. 764. Old printing equipment is exampled by an Albion Press introduced in England in 1817. The gift shop offers both new and old samples of wood types and other authentic pieces. Open Tue-Sat 9 am-5 pm; closed Sun, Mon, holidays. Admission free, but donations encouraged.

NASA Lyndon B. Johnson Space Center (F6), 2101 NASA Rd. 1; 483-4321. About 25 minutes from downtown. *NCH*. Known the world over, the space complex is frequently called the nerve center of the nation's space

An exhibit at NASA LBJ Space Center   Greater Houston Convention
& Visitors Bureau

program. It is here that the astronauts receive their training, where man and machine undergo testing for endurance in outer space environment, and where all space flights are monitored. It is now the pivotal point for the newest NASA program, the development of a permanent space station.

The LBJ Space Center is no longer open to unescorted tours or visits by the general public. All such visitor functions have shifted to the new Space Center Houston complex. Details follow.

Observation Deck (I10), Texas Commerce Tower. Facing the corner of Milam and Capitol is the 75-story Texas Commerce Tower, Houston's tallest skyscraper with an observation deck on the 60th floor, providing a panoramic view of Downtown, Uptown, and the South Main Corridor. Open 8 am-5:30 pm, weekdays. *NCH*.

The Orange Show (D4), 2401 Munger off I-45 South; 926-6368. This is a multi-level, folkloric sculpture to walk through. It is dedicated to health and nutrition derived from oranges. It is truly one-of-a-kind and was built with countless found objects transformed into elaborate sculptures, displays, portals, gates, and railings. Days, times vary. CH.

Port of Houston (C5), Gate 8 off Clinton Dr.; 670-2416. NCH. This port has one of the heaviest concentrations of industry and ships anywhere in the world. Ships making the 50-mile channel voyage upstream from Galveston to the Turning Basin must do a round-house turn at the deadend with the aid of tugs for the return trip to sea. A two-story observation deck is a good lookout point to observe this action.

A short distance away is the Sam Houston inspection boat, its popular narrated tour lasting about 90 minutes and affording a close-up look at the mighty industries and ships lining the channel. The boat offers tours daily, except Mondays and holidays. Make reservations well in advance.

Sam Houston Historical Park (J8), 1100 Bagby; 655-1912. CH for tours only. This is the oldest municipal park in Houston, a small green oasis and peaceful retreat from the frenetic pace of downtown Houston. A project of the Harris County Heritage Society, the park reflects the city's lifestyle during its early years. There are eight principal structures including the *Kellum-Noble House,* the city's oldest house on its original site; the *Nichols-Rice-Cherry House,* a Greek Revival house built in about 1845-50; the *San Felipe Cottage,* which is a simple six-room house typical of the 1870s; the *Pillot House,* built in 1868 and featuring what is believed to have been the first indoor kitchen in Houston; the *Old Place* cabin; and St. John Church, Houston's oldest church, moved to the park from its original spot in a former colony built by German settlers.

The *Texas Gallery* houses a permanent exhibit of Texas history. Open daily.

The *Long Row,* a reconstruction of Houston's first business building, facing Bagby, contains the *Yesteryear Souvenir Shop, the Tour Office,* and the *Tea Room,* a delightful place to have lunch, Mon-Fri, 11 am-2:30 pm. (See NEW RESI-DENTS.) Also featured is the 1905 Queen Anne-style Staiti house.

Tours begin on the hour: 10 am-3 pm, Tue-Sat; and 1-4 pm, Sun. The last tour begins one hour before closing. CH.

Sam Houston Race Park, 7575 N. Sam Houston Parkway W.; 807-8700. Texas' first pari-mutuel race track opened in the spring of 1994, an $84-million complex showcasing thoroughbred and quarter horse racing with an annual purse running around $20 million. The park can accommodate up to 30,000 spectators and stable up to 1,000 horses.

Space Center Houston, 1601 NASA Road 1, occupies the southwest corner of the Johnson Space Center, three miles east of I-45 about 20 miles south of downtown; 244-2105 or 1-800-972-0369. This $70-million, 183,000-square-foot, state-of-the-art concentration of educational and entertainment facilities now functions as the Johnson Space Center visitor center as well as an attraction in its own right. The project of the non-profit Manned Space Flight Education

Foundation, Inc., the center features a walk-in vault containing the earth's largest display of moon rocks (including one you can touch), escorted tram tours of the JSC, and appearances by active astronauts. Many of the exhibits and artifacts that were on display at JSC are now at Space Center Houston, along with videos, hi-tech interactive exhibits, space activity demonstrations, and opportunities for visitors to simulate space flight experiences. Open daily except Christmas. Admission $11.95 adults; $8.50 children under 12; $10.75 seniors over 65. Group discounts, annual passes available. *10-7 weekends $14.95 adults $13.95*

Gulf Greyhound Park, I-45 South, exit 15 at LaMarque; 1-409-986-9500. Billed as the world's largest parimutuel greyhound racing complex, the 315,000-square-foot facility operates six days every week. Full service dining. More than 300 teller windows. Extremely popular.

San Jacinto Battleground State Historical Park (D6), 3800 Park Road #1836 off Hwy. 225 on State Highway 134, at La Porte, TX, and flanked by the Houston Ship Channel; 479-2421. CH for some attractions. This park marks the site where Texas won its independence from Mexico in 1836. It holds several major attractions, plus granite markers throughout relating the details of this famous battle. Picnic facilities are available, but no camping is permitted. You may fish along the river banks.

The *San Jacinto Monument* is the world's tallest at 570 feet. At the base is the museum featuring regional history, NCH, from the time of the Indian civilization to Texas as a state of the Union. Near the top is an observation deck, CH, for a good view of the surrounding marsh lands. The monument foyer and observation deck are open seven days.

Nearby in permanent berth is the recently restored *Battleship TEXAS*, the only remaining dreadnought of its class. The battleship fought in two world wars and several skirmishes. Visitors can tour the ship from the bilges to the wheelhouse, and aboard are several specially dedicated museums and a Ship's Store for souvenirs. Open Wed-Sun, 10 am-5 pm. Information 479-4414. CH (children under six NCH).

Texas Medical Center (D3), bounded by Fannin, Holcombe, N. MacGregor, and Braeswood; 797-0100. NCH. This vast center is made up of 32 different institutions and hospitals and is still expanding. It is a magnet for students, patients, doctors, and scientists from around the world. Many know this center for care and treatment of childhood diseases, cancer, and open-heart surgery, as well as other areas of specialization.

An Assistance Center, on the ground floor of Parking #II at 1155 Holcombe (D3), offers free 75-minute bus tours through the complex. NCH. Call 790-1136. Tours are 10 am and 1 pm, Mon-Wed, and 10 am only Thu and Fri. The information center is open weekdays 10 am-4 pm.

Waterworld (E2), I-610 at Kirby; 799-1234. CH. Six Flags' 15-acre water park is located next to the 75-acre Six Flags Astroworld theme park. Ride a four-foot wave, slide down a watery course at 40 m.p.h., shoot the rapids in an inner tube, or dine in a restaurant surrounded by water. These are among the more

San Jacinto Battleground and Monument   *Texas Highway Dept.*

adult activities. There is a water playground for kids. Open daily in summer, weekends only in May and September. Variable opening for occasional seasonal or special events during off-season. One-day tickets are available or a two-day pass to both Waterworld and Astroworld.

Wortham Theater Center (I9), 501 Texas; tour office, 237-1439. Tour Houston's $70-million monument to opera and ballet. Tours available by advance arrangement. *NCH.*

HISTORIC CHURCHES
(Open daily)

Annunciation Catholic Church (I11), 1618 Texas Ave.; 222-2289. Built in the style of the great European churches, Annunciation was begun in 1867 by the Rev. Joseph Querot, a French missionary in Texas who was a canon of the Cathedral of Lyons. The most important feature of the church is the steeple. Its architectural style is Norman Romanesque. The Texas Historical Survey Committee has placed a historical medallion at the front of this church which is open for masses daily.

Christ Church Cathedral (I10), 1117 Texas Ave.; 222-2593. This was the second Episcopal parish in the Republic of Texas, established in 1839 by William Fairfax Gray. The initial structure was erected in 1845 and a second was added in 1859. The present structure was built in 1893 and is Gothic Revival in style. The interior is especially beautiful with handsome wood carving throughout and one Tiffany stained-glass window among others. The church is open daily for service at 12 noon and there is a public chapel open for masses daily. Tours by reservation.

St. John's Church. See Sam Houston Park above.

INDUSTRIAL AND CAMPUS TOURS

There are numerous special interest tours available ranging from college campuses to newspapers, and from an oil refinery to food processing plants.

A typical side interest attraction is the first and only remaining sugar mill in Texas, **Imperial Sugar**. This gives a very good insight on the refining process, from bulk sugar to boxing for supermarket shelves. Also, the **Anheuser Busch** tour offers a first-hand view of their brewing process and free samples at the conclusion. The **Greater Houston Convention & Visitors Bureau**, 801 Congress, 227-3100, has a list of such industrial tours. Most of the companies require advance notice. Check the list for details. All tours *NCH.*

Downtown Tunnel System (see SELF-GUIDED CITY TOURS).

St. John's Church, Sam Houston Park   *Dale Young*

VISUAL ARTS

A city continuously in the making, Houston is in itself an abstract of many designs, forms, hues, and dimensions, changing daily as architects, landscape artists, and designers create a new city profile with a strikingly distinct identity.

With this growth a new art consciousness is evolving, as corporate leaders, city and county fathers, and others in decision-making positions become mindful of the need to provide aesthetic oases for the revitalization of the human spirit. The burgeoning arts scene in Houston attracts new talent and is the impetus for new gallery openings and an enlarged focus on Houston as a lively center for the arts.

A long list of museums, galleries, schools of art, and art happenings promises the visitor a wide spectrum of artistic outlets throughout the city. Space does not permit a complete roster, but herein we offer a varied selection. For more information on the medley of arts organizations, schools, museums, and galleries in Houston contact the **Cultural Arts Council**; 527-9330. For a monthly calendar of events stop by the **Greater Houston Convention & Visitors Bureau**, 801 Congress.

PRINCIPAL MUSEUMS

Bayou Bend (C2), #1 Westcott; 520-2600. NCH. Bayou Bend is part of the Museum of Fine Arts Collection and houses one of the finest assortments of American art, artifacts, and furnishings in the nation. It provides a wonderful opportunity to view pure Americana in paintings, silver, ceramics, and other accessories rarely found anywhere else.

The museum is located on 14 acres of beautiful gardens and woodlands overlooking Buffalo Bayou. Following its recent $7.5-million renovation, it is again open for guided or self-guided tours by reservation and during an "Open House" once a month. A garden tour is included in the house tour or is possible separately at a lower fee.

Allow one to 1fi hours for tours. Usually closed the entire month of August.

The "Open House" tours with limited viewing are 1-5 pm on the third Sunday of each month. Guided tour *CH*. Open house *NCH*.

Contemporary Arts Museum (F2), 5216 Montrose Blvd.; 526-3129. Housed in a striking stainless-steel structure, this museum enjoys national acclaim, making bold statements in new directions. What better place than this futuristic city to indulge in the avant garde. Featured is post-1945 American art with changing exhibitions. Events include concerts, dance programs, lectures, and films.

Open Tue-Sun. Closed Mondays and holidays. *NCH*.

The Museum of Fine Arts (D3), 1001 Bissonnet; 639-7300; hearing impaired call TDD/ITY line 639-7390. *NCH*. This museum makes an important statement, both in the classics and in contemporary art. The simplistic form of the most recent addition reflects the museum's contemporary slant, in juxtaposition with the classic facade of the original structure.

Across the street is the new Glassell School of Art, an exciting glass-brick, art-deco building, which is perhaps the largest museum-affiliated school in the Southwest. The two are joined by the Lillie and Hugh Roy Cullen Sculpture Garden designed by the architect-artist, Isamu Noguchi. The original sculpture garden on the south side of the museum already features a number of fine pieces, including a Chillida.

The permanent collections at this museum include Spanish and Italian High Renaissance works, Indian art of the Southwest, a classical collection of pieces from Greece, Rome, and Egypt, and pre-Columbian art. The museum boasts one of the finest collections of Frederic Remington Westerns and an impressive list of the old masters. Also important to the collection are impressionist and post-impressionist paintings, post-1945 American works, the Glassell collection of African gold, and a fine photographic collection.

Throughout the year the museum features events of interest such as films, concerts, and lectures, and, with fair regularity, a major traveling exhibit of wide interest. Guides conduct tours at 1:30 and 2 pm on Wed and Sun, September-May. *CH*. Thursdays *NCH*. Closed Mondays and holidays. Call for hours.

The Menil Collection (F2), 1515 Sul Ross; 525-9400. What is acclaimed as one of the world's most outstanding private collections has found a home in Houston's new Menil museum in the Montrose. Hotly pursued by Paris and New York, the collection consists of over 10,000 pieces with emphasis on primitive art and sculpture, Byzantine and Medieval art, Cubism, Surrealism, Pop art, contemporary Minimalism, mid-century New York School, and contemporary work from Europe. The museum building made up of several galleries was designed by the famous architect Renzo Piano, co-creator of the Pompidou Art Center of Paris. Open from 11:30 am to 7:30 pm, daily. *NCH*.

The Rothko Chapel (F2), 3900 Yupon at Sul Ross; 524-9839. *NCH*. The last works of the late Mark Rothko are housed in this simple octagonal building located behind the University of St. Thomas campus.

Rothko's 14 monumental paintings are complemented by sculptor Barnett Newman's *Broken Obelisk* in its own reflection pool at the front of the building.

These huge canvasses emphasize color and scale and are effectively illumed by natural light emanating from strategically placed skylights.

Apart from the Rothko experience, the chapel is also the scene of rare ethnic performances such as the Bhutan Dancers and Whirling Dervishes. And it has served as a venue for such visiting speakers as the Dalai Lama and Nelson Mandela.

It is open from 10 am to 6 pm, daily.

MUSEUMS AND GALLERIES

Blaffer Gallery (D4), University of Houston Central campus, Entrance #16 off Cullen Boulevard; 749-1320. *NCH*. This museum's exhibits range from the old masters to the leading contemporaries plus an annual spring exhibition of student works. Regular hours are 10 am-5 pm, Tue-Fri; 1-5 pm, Sat-Sun. Closed Mondays.

High School for the Performing and Visual Arts (F3), 4001 Stanford; 522-7811. *NCH*. This was the first school in the United States to provide a concentrated arts program with regular academics. To qualify for certification, students must present a thesis in their special field; thus there are continuous exhibitions in the school's Gallery of Art. Open Mon-Fri.

Lowell Collins School of Art and Gallery (F1), 2903 Saint; 622-6962. *NCH*. This gallery specializes in ethnic art from Africa, the Middle East, and the Far East; Russian and Greek orthodox icons; pre-Columbian and oceanic art; and Greco-Roman glass. Open from 9 am to 5 pm, Mon-Sat.

Museum of American Architecture and Decorative Arts (E1), Houston Baptist University, 7502 Fondren; 995-3311. *NCH*. A fascinating permanent collection and changing exhibitions. Permanent items include unusual early 19th-century dolls used by artists to design murals such as Jacques-Louis David's mural of the *Coronation of Josephine by Napoleon*. Open Tue-Sun, September-May. Closed all summer.

Texas Southern University Arts Center (D3), 527-7326. *NCH*. This center houses a large collection of student works in the main lobby and central corridor. Call for days, hours, directions. Closed holidays and summer months.

COMMERCIAL GALLERIES

As may be expected in a city with several art museums and schools, and a growing appreciative audience with the means to support them, galleries are spread throughout the city. They usually congregate in the affluent areas or around professional centers of artistic endeavor.

There is sufficient variety to suit all interests as well as most budgets. While we would like to present a full list, we must limit the discussion to the following, most of which are members of the Houston Art Dealers Association and which have long established reputations in the city.

DuBose Rein Galleries (F2), 1700 Bissonnet; 526-4916. Under new ownership, this gallery generally features American contemporaries. It represents a number of well-known artists such as Sally Anderson and James Busby. There is a minimum of one show per month. Open Mon-Sat.

Harris Gallery (D3), 1100 Bissonnet; 522-9116. One of the features of this gallery is contemporary landscape, but exhibits cover a wide spectrum. Featured artists have included Joe Almyda and Glen Whitehead.

Hooks-Epstein Gallery, 2631 Colquitt; 522-0718. This gallery represents eight beginning and middle-career artists in changing exhibitions about every six weeks. It also shows works by some 30 masters. Open 10 am-5:30 pm, Tue-Fri; 11-5 Sat.

Jack Meier Gallery (F2), 2310 Bissonnet; 526-2983. Representing about fifteen artists, a good number of whom have been nationally recognized, such as Rosemary Mahoney, Jose Perez, and Peter Shu, watercolorist. Open Mon-Sat.

Janie C. Lee Gallery (F2), 1209 Berthea; 523-7306. The Lee Gallery represents about 25 internationally known artists. They feature 20th-century American and European paintings, drawings, and sculpture. Shows change about every six weeks. Open Tue-Sat.

Meredith Long & Co. (C2), 2323 San Felipe; 523-6671. Long known throughout the nation for selling the best in American art, this gallery features all types of works on paper, oils on canvas, and sculpture. They show from the American School of Artists in a totally remodeled gallery. Exhibits change frequently during the fall and winter and about every two months in the summer. Open 10 am-6 pm, Tue-Sat.

Millioud Gallery (F1), 4041 Richmond Ave. at Weslayan; 621-3330. This is one of the largest collections of masters in Houston with more than 2,000 original prints by realistic, abstract, and surrealist contemporary artists. Among the many great masters in the collection are Goya, Gauguin, Cezanne, Pissarro, Lautrec, Renoir, Matisse, Chagall, Miro, Dali, Picasso, and others. Open 11:30 am-4 pm, Tue-Fri; 11-5 Sat.

Robinson Galleries (F1), 3514 Lake; 521-9221. This gallery features late 19th- and early 20th-century American and Latin American art, international contemporary art, and has represented popular art in the Americas, also art tribal studies programs. Viewing 10 am-5:30 pm, Tue-Fri; 11 am-4 pm Sat; at other times by appointment.

ART IN PUBLIC PLACES

There is growing momentum in Houston to bring quality art to public buildings, plazas, parks, and campuses. We have selected some of the distinguished examples of works by resident, national, and international artists. For the convenience of the viewer we have put these works in groups by region.

Downtown ────────────────────────────

Ballet Dancer, bronze by Marcello Mascherini. Jones Hall for the Performing Arts (I10), 615 Louisiana.

Central Public Library, 500 McKinney (J9). *NCH.* The Library features monthly exhibits ranging from art objects to antique dolls.

The Family of Man, by Barbara Hepworth, on South Plaza of First City Tower (J10), 1001 Fannin.

First City National Bank (J10), 1001 Main; **First City Tower** (J10), 1001 Fannin; **First City East Building** (J10), 1111 Fannin. All three have on-going lobby exhibitions of important art by well-known artists.

Frozen Laces-One, by Louise Nevelson, on Four Allen Center plaza (K9), corner of Smith and Andrews.

Gemini Two, sculpture by Richard Lippold, in the Grand Lobby of Jones Hall for the Performing Arts (I10), 615 Louisiana. Except during performances, you can only see this through the glass over the marquee; it is suspended from the ceiling.

Geometric Mouse X, sculpture by Claes Oldenburg, Central Public Library Plaza (J9), 500 McKinney.

High Plains Drifter, sculpture by Peter Reginato, Allen Center (J9), on Polk between Smith and Bagby streets.

Houston Lighting & Power Company Building (I9), 611 Walker. The lobby of this building features continuous art exhibitions.

Julia Ideson Library and Archives (J9), corner of McKinney and Smith streets. A treasure trove of permanent art plus temporary exhibitions. Included are bronze and marble busts, portrait paintings, stone sculpture, steel engravings, and a number of Spanish murals of special interest. Also interesting is the intricately carved and painted ceiling in the rotunda.

Large Spindle Piece, sculpture by the famous British artist, Henry Moore, between downtown and the Montrose area across Allen Parkway from the defunct Jeff Davis Hospital (C3).

Monument au Fantome, by Jean Dubuffet, on Interfirst Bank Plaza (J9).

Music Hall (I9), Bagby at Walker. Several works by famous artists are in the lobby. They are *The Banjo,* a sculpture by Carroll H. Simms, which can be seen from Bagby Street; *Lily Pads,* a painting by John Alexander; and *Quilting Bee,* a mural by Dr. John Biggers, director of the school of art at Texas Southern University.

Pair of Horses, sculpture by Robert Fowler, in Lower Lobby at entrance to Jones Hall for the Performing Arts (I10), 615 Louisiana.

Personage and Birds, a 55-foot sculpture by the world-renowned Spanish artist, Joan Miro, on United Energy Plaza in front of Texas Commerce Tower (I10), corner of Milam and Capitol.

Reclining Figure, by Henry Moore, in South Lobby of First City Tower (J10), 1001 Fannin.

Spirit of the Confederacy, sculpture by L. Amateis, in Sam Houston Historical Park (J8). Can be seen from Lamar Avenue.

Texas Commerce Tower (I10), Milam at Capitol. In the lobby is a 40-foot tapestry of *Six Flags Over Texas,* by Swedish artist, Helena Hernmark.

Two Houston Center (J10), corner of Fannin and McKinney. At this entrance, lobby levels P2 and P3 feature on-going exhibitions brought in from private collections and galleries around the nation.

Virtuoso, by David Adickes. Designed with its own system to play music throughout the day. On plaza of the Lyric Centre building (I10), 404 Louisiana.

Wortham Theater Center (I9), 501 Texas. The eight, 28'-tall Albert Paley sculptures may be seen from the plaza in front of the 90' glass archway of this grand structure. It is the largest such contemporary project in the United States and is a mix of steel monuments to the movement of life, setting the mood for patrons of the arts.

Montrose Area

Broken Obelisk, sculpture in pool by Barnett Newman, in front of the Rothko Chapel (F2), Yupon at Sul Ross, behind the University of St. Thomas campus.

Passages, sculpture by Hannah Stewart, on the University of St. Thomas campus (F2), can be seen from Mr. Vernon Street.

Pueblo Bonito, sculpture by Charles Ginnever at Heights Boulevard; Waugh Drive, and Feagan Street (C3), across Buffalo Bayou from the Montrose district.

South Main Corridor

Abesti Gorgora V, sculpture by Spanish artist Eduardo Chillida, South Main Sculpture Garden, Museum of Fine Arts (D3), between Main and Montrose.

Adam 1889, bronze by Emile-Antoine Bourdelle, Cullen Sculpture Garden (D3), Bissonnet at Montrose.

Atropos Key, sculpture by Hannah Stewart, on top of the hill overlooking Miller Outdoor Theatre (D3), on Concert Drive in Hermann Park.

Backs I, II, III, IV, bronze by Henri Matisse, Cullen Sculpture Garden (D3), Bissonnet at Montrose.

The Crab, sculpture by Alexander Calder, Cullen Sculpture Garden, Museum of Fine Arts (D3), Main at Montrose.

The Elephant, sculpture by Robert Fowler, in front of the Houston Zoological Gardens in Hermann Park (D3).

The Gorilla, sculpture by Robert Fowler, in front of the Gorilla Habitat (D3), in the Zoological Gardens.

Hercules Upholding the Heavens, sculpture by Paul Manship, South Main Sculpture Garden, Museum of Fine Arts (D3), Main at Montrose.

Bob Fowler's The Elephant *outside Houston Zoological Gardens*   *Dale Young*

Houston Triptych, bronze by Ellsworth Kelly, Cullen Sculpture Garden (D3), Bissonnet at Montrose.

Magari, steel sculpture by Suvero, Museum of Fine Arts (D3), Bissonnet at Montrose.

Manila Palm, sculpture by Mel Chin, Contemporary Arts Museum (D3), 5216 Montrose.

Pieta, sculpture by Charles Umlauf, Museum of Fine Arts (D3), Main at Montrose.

Portable Trojan Bear, sculpture by Jim Love, Hermann Park (D3).

Pranath Yama, Kinetic sculpture, by Mark diSuvero. McCollum Plaza (D3), Texas Medical Center.

Sam Houston Equestrian Statue, sculpture on arch by Enrico Cerracchio, main entrance to Hermann Park (D3), Fannin at Montrose.

The Walking Man, sculpture by Auguste Rodin, Cullen Sculpture Garden, Museum of Fine Arts (D3), Main at Montrose. Also other works in Cullen Garden.

Airport

Perhaps the last place you might expect to find a delightful sculpture is outside an airport terminal, but that is just where Jay Baker's *Light Spikes* brightens arrivals and departures. Aluminum trusses and fluorescent lighting, just outside the new Mickey Leland International Airlines Building at Houston Intercontinental Airport, depict the flags of eight major industrialized nations.

Campuses

There are numerous works of art on college campuses, especially at the University of Houston Central (D4), and Texas Southern University (D3).

Some of the titles of interest are *African Queen Mother*, and *Jonah & The Whale*, sculptures by Carroll H. Simms, Texas Southern University. *Round-A-Bout*, sculpture by Linda Howard, *Tower of the Cheyenne*, sculpture by Peter Forakis, and *Troika*, sculpture by Charles Ginnever are just a few of the many outdoor pieces at the University of Houston.

SELECTED SCULPTURE STUDIOS

Of all the sculptors in Houston we have selected one with a number of works in public places for easy viewing. The artist is different in style and form in what she has to say, and she enjoys a wide reputation.

Hannah Stewart came to Texas by way of Alabama. Studies in the United States, Mexico and Sweden were followed by teaching appointments in Houston and Florida.

Twenty solo exhibitions in the United States and dozens of selective group shows all over the nation, including a Smithsonian Institution traveling show that toured the United States and Europe, are among her accomplishments. Her commissions have been equally as impressive and widespread throughout the United States and Mexico.

Even works that dwarf the human being exhibit great serenity in their form. Her work teems with universal symbols of positive cosmic energy.

The sculpture, *Passages* at the University of St. Thomas, though on a smaller scale than her usual works, best addresses to this subject in style.

Among her other pieces in public places here is the *Atropos Key* in Hermann Park.

SHOPPING

With its myriad shops of every description, Houston resembles a Southwestern Hong Kong aglitter with everything the buyer could possibly need or imagine. The city has a reputation as a land of opulence, and the world's merchants seem to have gotten the message.

Many of the leading names in retail are here, plus thousands of lesser-known shopkeepers yet to be discovered by you. In Houston you can find that one-of-a-kind item with a price tag to match, but you may also delight in your own clandestine discoveries in flea markets, resale shops, and discount stores.

It's all scattered over miles of urban sprawl, so we will orient you first to the various key regional centers before we define what's available by category of merchandise.

MAJOR SHOPPING DISTRICTS

Downtown

Houston's original center of commerce gleams with its brightest new sparkle: **The Park.** This two-block long, three-story atrium mall has more than 70 shops and eateries plus a number of other services. For dining you'll find everything from fast foods to upbeat pubs and sidewalk-style restaurants. Specialty shops abound and there's an assortment of jewelry, apparel, books, and sporting goods stores. The center attraction is a pipe sculpture with cascading fountains. The mall is connected to Houston Center buildings via skywalks.

Most of the household names in retail took their first steps in early downtown Houston before joining the march to the suburbs. About half of them, however, held on to a semblance of their original roots, including Foley's and Oshman's, and, while the buyer profile has changed considerably, there remains a strong work force that still confirms downtown as a good shopping stop.

It's easy to get around on foot downtown and major retailers there cluster in close proximity along Main, Travis, and Milam. Some have burrowed underground along the pedestrian tunnel system.

Galleria/Post Oak (F1)

In a high density area, which tends to more trendy clothes than the career-conscious downtown district, you will find store owners who had their start downtown, lined up with many new emporiums from the four corners of the globe that attract numerous visitors from out of town and abroad.

A visit to **The Galleria** is truly exciting since it offers one of Texas' most colorful parades of stores, with supreme pageantry in display, and anchored by Neiman-Marcus, Lord & Taylor, Marshall Field's, and Macy's.

The **Galleria-Post Oak** area is known locally as the "Magic Circle," and indeed it is when one considers this "haute couture" circle grew from farmlands and cow pastures to featuring Saks Fifth Avenue.

5015 Westheimer.

Greenspoint (A1)

It used to be that anyone who built anything miles from the center of town was thought to be a bit foolish, but along came Greenspoint, and everybody—from Beaumont to Brownsville, from the Midwest to Mexico—came to gawk at the new flash in the pan. Overnight Greenspoint grew to become one of the city's largest malls with nearly 200 outlets including Foley's.

I-45 North at Greens Rd.

Sharpstown (D1)

The Southwest Freeway is the most heavily traveled in Houston, at least in part because it is the route to Sharpstown, the center of one of the greatest influxes of newcomers to Houston. This is one of the busiest shopping centers in town, Houston's first air-conditioned, covered mall—still on the grow, having added a second level, nearly 90 new stores, and expansions of existing stores.

Most of the famous names found downtown and in other malls are also here, such as Foley's, J.C. Penney, and Victoria's Secret, together with numerous newcomers to Houston's trade channels.

Southwest Freeway at Bellaire Blvd.

Town and Country Village Mall

At first impression there seems to be an inordinate number of shoe stores here. But considering the size of the area, the number of shops, and no less than five major anchor stores, a new pair of walking shoes might not be a bad idea!

A covered mall houses more than 150 stores, services, and a fast food island for those on the go. The village is uniquely designed with earth-tone stucco and red-tile roofs. Most stores are free-standing with shaded corridors while the mall is a massive high-tech structure with arched canopy atrium throughout.

T & C has numerous food outlets, too.

I-10 West (Katy Freeway) at West Belt Drive.

MINI CENTERS

China Town

Just at the fringe of the George R. Brown Convention Center is this growing concentration of oriental—mainly Chinese and Vietnamese—shops, jewelers, boutiques, food markets, and cafes. Exotic offerings range from fungus to herbal medicines. Also fine jewels, tapestries, architectural pieces, furniture, clothing, plants, oriental wines, carvings, paintings, souvenirs, and, of course, oriental foods.

Covering a large area downtown, but primarily bounded by St. Emanuel, Chartres, Rusk, and Lamar.

Lamar River Oaks (F2)

Probably the most prestigious corner in Houston and one of the oldest small shopping centers in town, next door to River Oaks. It is the home of an incomparable gift shop where (many) debutante brides are registered; there is a marvelous small smart shop for ladies wear; and there is a guaranteed non-dietetic sensational Swiss tea room here (see DINING).

Westheimer at River Oaks Blvd.

Old Town Spring

This picturesque section surrounding a long abandoned railroad center features a potpourri of shops and cafes in restored buildings reminiscent of the early 1900s. Old Town has more than 100 shops ranging from antiques to crafts plus assorted eateries. In October, Spring celebrates its heritage with entertainment including German, Western, and Indian song and dance.

Open Tue-Sun.

Take the Spring/Cypress exit off I-45 North on to Main St., 1½ miles to the railroad tracks. Information: 353-2317.

Rice Village (D2)

This is almost like being in a time warp, where people seem to stroll more and hustle less, with more options to eat, drink, and people watch alfresco. You'll find a pleasant blend of medical center professionals, students, and faculty from nearby Rice University, some old-time homesteaders, and a few European expatriates.

Here you see neighborhood pubs, galleries, Mexican bistros, European gourmet shops, college clothing stores, American Indian artifacts, arts and crafts, and fascinating bookstores.

Morningside, University, Kirby, and Bolsover.

River Oaks Center (C2)

Tall stately palms along West Gray mark the perimeter of one of the oldest shopping centers in the city. Another area that caters to the River Oaks district, with a new mix of shops, dining, and entertainment for the young newcomers moving into the vicinity. Here there is an antique shop next to a homemade pasta place, a deli cafe across from avant-garde movies, and many other specialty shops, superb restaurants, galleries, and service centers.

West Gray at Shepherd.

Westbury Square (E1)

In the middle of contemporary Houston sits a surprising old-world village with narrow, winding streets leading to a central plaza complete with a fountain, carillon clock tower, and gas lights. Most of the retailers here offer imported goods ranging from Holland to China. It is enhanced with a touch of fine foods.

Chimney Rock at W. Bellfort.

SPECIAL STREETS

There certainly are many streets that could be singled out for interesting shopping but we will point out several in close proximity, yet diametrically different from each other.

Ferndale Place and Bammel Lane (F2)

A quaint and charming array of shops doing business in former homes along these neat, tree-lined neighborhood streets. Some of Houston's best antiques may be found here. Shop owners are friendly and know how to make the shopper feel special, almost a lost art in so many places today.

Ferndale and Bammel are two blocks apart between Westheimer and West Alabama.

Montrose Boulevard (F2-3)

Montrose Boulevard was once the street early Houstonians toured on

Sundays to see majestic palms and gardens gracing fashionable homes. The Link-Lee mansion, now headquarters for the University of St. Thomas, is a reminder of those times. More recently the boulevard has been revitalized with plantings, restorations and conversions, creating a variety of things to see and do. Beginning at the crossroad of Westheimer, Montrose is punctuated with new and unusual shopping centers, sidewalk cafes, and points of interest all along the way to the junction of the Mecom Fountains on S. Main, which we refer to as the Museums/Park Circle. Two mini centers are especially inviting. One is in front of the St. Thomas campus at West Alabama and the other, Chelsea Center, is at the corner of Chelsea. Both offer a mix of boutiques, specialty stores, fine dining, and outdoor cafes. Interspersed are shops ranging from cards and gifts to African art. Points of interest include the Consulate General of the People's Republic of China with its exhibits, one of the world's smallest luxury hotels, museums of art, and a pleasant mini-park for respite along the way.

Westheimer—The Strip (F3-2)

From Ferndale back toward town on Westheimer is The Strip, where good dining and entertainment spots intersperse with some of the city's more bizarre curiosities. Here you may find fantasy accessories next to a tattooed ladies shop; wine tasting just a stone's throw from tarot card reading; gourmet dining to just plain spuds; and Broadway musicals and amateur night at a topless bar—all in a row.

OTHER MAJOR MALLS

Almeda Mall (E5), 12200 Gulf Freeway.
Baybrook Mall (F5), I-45 South at Bay Area Blvd.
Carillon Shopping Center, 10001 Westheimer.
Champions Village, 5505 W. FM 1960.
Deerbrook Mall, FM 1960 at U.S. 59 North.
Gulfgate (E5), I-45 South at I-610 Loop.
Memorial City Shopping Center (B1), Katy Freeway at Gessner.
Meyerland Plaza (E1), Beechnut at I-610 South.
Northline Mall (A3), I-45 North at Crosstimbers.
Northwest Mall (B1), Highway 290 at I-610.
Weslayan Plaza Shopping Center (D2), 5564 Weslayan.
Westchase Mall, 10863 Westheimer.
West Oaks Mall, Hwy. 6 at Westheimer.
Westwood Fashion Mall (E1), Bissonnet at Southwest Fwy.
Willowbrook Mall, FM 1960 at Hwy. 149.
Windsor Plaza Shopping Center (F1), 4901 Richmond Ave.

MAJOR DEPARTMENT STORES

Most malls boast one or more of the following as anchor stores among their numerous boutiques and specialty shops.

Foley's. This is the largest in Houston with headquarters downtown at 1110 Main (J10) plus numerous branches in shopping centers throughout Houston and Pasadena.

Dillard's. Born in San Antonio and now a well-established large chain of Dillard's stores, the main store is at 4925 Westheimer (F1). In addition, there are several branches in Houston and Pasadena.

J. C. Penney Co. Locations in malls throughout Houston.

Macy's. Several locations in Willowbrook, Baybrook, and Deerbrook malls, plus an anchor store at The Galleria.

Marshall Field's Co. (F1), 5115 Westheimer and Town and Country Mall. A specialty department store with variety merchandise ranging from top-line clothing for men, women, and children to home furnishings.

Montgomery Ward. Full-line stores at local malls include auto services, formal-wear rentals, even pest control.

Sears Roebuck & Co. (D3), 4201 S. Main and throughout Houston.

F. W. Woolworth (J10), 930 Main plus four other stores.

ANTIQUES AND AUCTION HOUSES

Antique shops abound all over Houston with the gamut of offerings from fine American and European pieces to primitives and Texana. You'll find certain areas with a heavy concentration of antique outlets such as Main Street at Holman; Westheimer from the 300 block to Shepherd; Washington Blvd. from about the 300 block to just past Shepherd; along West Gray; and along Ferndale and Bammel. For guidance, contact Houston Antiques Dealers Association at 662-4444.

Adkins Architectural Antiques (F3), 3515 Fannin; 522-6547. Houston's largest assortment of architectural embellishments in a three-story 1912 mansion crammed with decorative doors, inlaid mantels, large light standards, old Mexican masks, chandeliers, stained glass, wrought iron gates, and brass fittings.

Antique Center of Texas, 7200 Old Katy Rd., 688-4211. A major venue for antiques.

The Antique Mall, 21127 Spring Towne Dr., just west of I-45 between Houston and Conroe; 350-4557. About 100 dealers in a two-acre building.

Antique Pavilion, 2311 Westheimer; 520-9755. A major assemblage of antiques shops.

James A. Gundry Inc., 2910 Ferndale; 524-6622. Specialties include English Georgian furniture and period accessories.

Hart Galleries Antiques (C2), 2301 S. Voss; 524-2979. A long-established and highly reputable outlet dealing in fine European antiques, objets d'art, new and old oriental rugs. A major auction house in Houston.

Lloyd J. Newton Antiques, 2919 Ferndale; 520-1177.

Made in France, 2912 Ferndale; 529-7949. Specialties include country French antiques, accessories, objets d'art.

Phyllis Tucker Antiques, 2923 Ferndale; 524-0165. Specialties include antique silver.

River Oaks Antiques Center, 2119 Westheimer; 520-8238. Another significant outlet.

ART SUPPLIES

Expressing artistic creativity requires supplies purveyed by numerous outlets. Some of the most complete lines are found in several stores near the Glassell School of Art on Montrose.

Art Supply (F3), 915 Richmond Ave.; 526-2691.

Carlson Art Supply (F2), 2424 Montrose Blvd.; 524-1819.

Texas Art Supply (C3), 2001 Montrose; 526-5221; also (C1), 2237 S. Voss; 780-0440.

BOOKS

Houston reads. In fact, Houston reads a lot. Furthermore, Houston's many colleges and universities, technological industries, art schools, and the Medical Center significantly affect the city's number and range of quality bookstores, many of which are concentrated near educational centers. We have selected a cross section by location and specialization. See the discount section for other bookstores.

B. Dalton Bookseller (E5), Almeda Mall, 944-9310; 1320 Baybrook Mall (F5), 488-3327; The Galleria II (F1), 960-8191; Memorial City Shopping Center (B1), 464-2951; Deerbrook Mall, 20139 Highway 59 at FM 1960, 446-4970; Northwest Mall (B1), 686-8404; Sharpstown Center (D1), 776-1578; Town & Country Mall, 984-2465; Westwood Mall (E1), 771-0654; Willowbrook Mall, FM 1960 at Westheimer, 890-6097.

Brazos Bookstore (D2), 2421 Bissonnet; 523-0701. Literary specialties (fiction, poetry, drama, biographies, art, and architecture). Convenient to Rice University, the Medical Center, art museums.

British Isles (D2), 2366 Rice Blvd.; 522-6868. Books are a major facet of this interesting store. The best collection of maps and guides to the U.K. More than 150 titles put out by the British Tourist Authority. Also children's publications. British history, covering the Royal family.

Borders Book Shop and Cafe, 570 Meyerland Plaza; 661-2888. 9633-A West-heimer at Gessner; 782-6066. Spectacular newcomer with 100,000-plus titles.

Brown Book Shop, 1517 San Jacinto; 652-3937. Specializes in technical books catering to industry in our area. General-line store—among Houston's oldest.

Cokesbury Book Store & Church Supplies (D1), 3502 W. Alabama; 621-1755. General store with emphasis on religious publications.

Majors Scientific Books, Inc., 7905 Fannin; 799-9922. Spectacular selection of medical and technical books and featuring a large computer collection.

Milam Book Store, 1613 Richmond; 528-0050. One of the largest dealers in town for used novels. Buying and trading here for 18 years. Lots of science fiction, war stories, mysteries, and comics.

Murder by the Book, 2342 Bissonnet; 524-8597. Far more than the usual round-up of suspects, this trove of mysteries, detective fiction, police procedurals, and similar writings—in volumes both new and pre-read—is (dare we say it?) to die for!

Museum of Fine Arts Bookstore & Shop (D3), 1001 Bissonnet; 639-7365. Fine art books and magazine offerings.

Rand McNally Map & Travel Store, Galleria I, 960-9846. A whole, wide world of excellent, up-to-date travel guides, maps, atlases and travel-related tools and novelties.

River Oaks Book Store, 3270 Westheimer; 520-0061. Complete line. Special and telephone orders. Gift wrap.

Sam Houston Book Shop (F1), Galleria Mall (lower level); 626-1243. A full-line bookstore.

University of Houston Bookstores (D4), 4800 Calhoun; 748-0923. **Houston Community College Bookstore,** (E1), 7535 Bissonnet; 778-9511. **Houston Community College Bookstore,** (B2), 1749 W. 34th; 681-7117. **Houston Community College Bookstore,** 1452 Wilcrest; 784-0190. New and used textbooks in all subjects at the Calhoun store; books geared to Houston Community College classes at the other locations.

Waldenbooks, Almeda Mall, 944-7465; Baybrook Mall (F5), 488-2330; The Park in Houston Center (J10), 951-0041; 12,300 North Fwy. (A1), 875-0381; Memorial City Center (B1), 468-7142; Sharpstown Center (D1), 771-3200; Westwood Mall (E1), 777-5196. One of the largest chains in the city—general line stores.

CLOTHING

Clothing Accessories

Pick Pocket (F1), 3292 Galleria Mall; 622-2507. Very large selection of purses from budget to expensive. Also umbrellas, scarves, hats, costume jewelry, wallets, and sunglasses.

Wormser Hat Stores (I10), 816 Travis; 222-9371. The men's hat store since 1894. Carries Stetsons, English-made hats, and Panama straws which are very popular in Houston.

Clothing, Men's

Al's Formal Wear (J10), 7807 S. Main, Downtown, plus many other Houston locations; 791-1885. Instant tuxedo rentals.

Brooks Brothers (J10), 1200 McKinney; 659-4000. Since 1818, selling fine traditional clothing and accessories. Also a women's section.

Custom Shop Shirtmakers (I10), Houston Center (downtown), 655-8858; (F1), The Galleria, 621-7631; and in Town and Country Mall; 932-8055. Since 1937, the best in custom-and-ready-made shirts.

Harold's Menswear (B3), 350 W. 19th St. in the Heights; 864-2647. The clothier of the stars—sportswear, suits 36 short to 60 extra long.

Leopold Price & Rolle (J9), The Galleria, 626-5350; and in other locations, throughout Houston. Features Hart Shaffner & Marx clothes.

Norton Ditto Company (J10), 910 Travis, 688-9800; (F1), 2019 Post Oak Rd., 688-9800. Since 1908, one of Houston's most reputable quality clothiers.

Shudde Bros. (C3), 905 Trinity; 223-2191. Houston hatters since 1907. All Western and casual clothing.

Walter Pye's, Meyerland Plaza, 664-5501 and in other centers. Also on the island (see GALVESTON). Fifty-plus years in Houston selling men's suits, sports clothes, and accessories—medium-priced to high-fashion clothes.

Clothing, Men's Large and Tall

Zindler's (F1), 3111 S. Post Oak; 629-0663. Since 1892, one of Houston's oldest traditional clothiers and the South's largest specialty store for big and tall men.

Clothing, Teens to Tots

There are children's, juniors, and misses sections in department stores, but many shops cater exclusively to the young with jeans and things, plus clothing for children and newborns.

Children's Collection (F1), 1717 Post Oak Blvd.; 622-4415.

Clothes for Kids resale shop, 14520 Memorial; 558-1793.

County Seat Clothing Store, outlets in Westwood, Baybrook, and other Houston-area malls.

The Gap, 11245 Fondren and at least a dozen other stores, mainly in Houston malls.

Jeans West, Sharpstown, the Galleria, and other locations in Houston.

Little People Boutique, 11980-C Westheimer; 497-1593.

Stride Rite Bootery, Baybrook Mall, 488-4547; Memorial City, 932-6031; also Sharpstown Center, Willowbrook Mall, Pasadena Town Square, Greenspoint, West Oaks, and Deerwood Mall in Humble.

Clothing, Women's

In addition to a wide assortment of clothes in department stores, we suggest the following outlets.

Craig's Ready To Wear. Branches in most Houston malls. National labels in prestige sportswear, ladies suits, lingerie, high-fashion millinery. Featuring career women's clothing.

Esther Wolf (F1), 1702 Post Oak Blvd.; 622-1331. A leading women's fashion store featuring ready-to-wear dresses, suits, sportswear, and gowns.

Everitt-Buelow Co (F1), 2315 S. Post Oak Blvd.; 622-4710. Long a leader in high-fashion clothes in Houston.

Lerner Shops of Texas (I10), The Park, 1200 McKinney (downtown); 650-8342. Also outlets in malls and centers throughout Houston and Pasadena. Known for latest fashions at moderate prices.

Lord & Taylor; 627-8100. This nationally known chain's Houston branch is a major store at The Galleria (F1). Top line accessories, and sports- and dresswear for the family.

Margo's, The Galleria; 626-1970. Also branch stores in major malls and centers. Offering fashion at regular prices. Young women and up—sportswear, dresses, and shoes.

Neiman-Marcus Co. (F1), 2600 S. Post Oak Rd. opposite The Galleria; 621-7100. 10615 Town & Country Way; 984-2100. This world-renowned store has full-line, high-fashion clothing and accessories for men, women, and children. Also fine jewelry, a gifts salon, crystal, furs, and other departments.

Palais Royal (J10), 917 Main, downtown, 658-1182; plus branch stores at numerous other locations in Houston, Baytown, and Pasadena. A household name among Houston clothiers for men, women, juniors, and children. From moderate-price to better-line clothing, and accessories.

Saks Fifth Avenue (F1), 1800 Post Oak Blvd. in Saks Fifth Avenue Pavilion; 627-0500. Saks is shopping for junior fashions or designer originals. Anchors arguably the poshest mall in Houston.

Tootsie's (D2), 4045 Westheimer; 629-9990. Exclusive designer clothes boutique with some moderate-price apparel as well.

Weiner's. With numerous stores in all sections of the city, this is Houston's family clothing store. Many bargains year 'round.

COINS AND STAMPS

For your convenience we have selected three dealers: two are in close proximity downtown and the other is in Rice Village. All are reputable firms doing business here for many years. It is advisable to check out the numismatic credentials of companies with whom you plan to trade.

Astro City Coins (F1), 6464 Westheimer; 626-8432.

Houston Numismatic Exchange (D2), 2486 Times Blvd; 528-2135.

Royal Coins, 4658 Beechnut; 664-0881.

CRAFTS

Blue Hand (D2), 2323 University Blvd; 666-2583. An extraordinary collection of arts and crafts from around the world overflowing in four showrooms, while nature's artistry comes alive in a back-room greenhouse filled with tropical plants. Pueblo Indian pottery, Texas Terlingua Indian crafts, unusual baskets, a large collection of jewelry, and an African crafts collection that is outstanding as are the Kilim rugs and Rafia pile samples from the Congo. Several Houston/Galveston artists are represented here.

Surroundings (D3), 1710 Sunset Blvd; 527-9838. Walls covered with Panamanian "molas," and masks from Mexico, Haiti, and New Guinea. This place brims with brilliant colors in unique handmade clothing, feathered headdresses, natural fiber rugs, large demon figures, and thousands of other items from around the world. Most interesting are the handmade cabinets, tables, benches, and rockers by local craftsmen.

DISCOUNT, RESALE, AND OUTLET STORES

As in other major cities, Houston has many thrift outlets, some selling at greatly reduced prices. Merchandise includes appliances, furniture, variety goods, clothing, shoes, accessories, jewelry and gifts, housewares, and even antiques and paintings.

Academy Stores specialize in sportswear and sporting goods. Many locations serving Houston.

Al Goldman's Office Store (F1), 4120 Fannin; 526-4401. Unbelievable array of merchandise, office supplies from seals to paper shredders. Deliveries.

Blue Bird Circle Shop (F3), 615 W. Alabama; 528-0470. Charity center with wide range of merchandise.

Brock's Books (D2), 6713 Stella Link; 661-7232. Offers 10% off new books and 50% on used paperbacks.

Encore (C2), 2308 Morse; 523-8936. Here you'll find Klein, Nippon, and Scaasi, gently worn and greatly reduced. Also sportswear, imported Indian cottons, some fancy beaded formal wear, pool and party wear, and some costume jewelry for starters. Clothes are on consignment.

Foley's Warehouse (D4), 4500 Gulf Freeway. Wide range of merchandise at discounted prices.

Goodwill Industries (B4), 5200 Jensen; 692-6221. As expected, bargains galore with emphasis on clothes.

The Guild Shop (C2), 2009 Dunlavy; 528-5095. Everything here on consignment or a donation—clothes, kitchenware, furniture, books.

Half Price Books (C3), 2410 Waugh; 520-1084; (D2), 2537 University Blvd.; 524-6635; other locations. Incredible collection of more than a million books, paperbacks, records, tapes, and magazines. Will buy anything printed or recorded. Open seven days.

Loehmann's (E1), 7455 Southwest Freeway; 777-0164. They guarantee one-third below regular price and 20% below discount. A large women's clothier buying from the manufacturer and offering a range from better to top-fashion merchandise.

Marshall's, 13316 Westheimer; 558-4600; (D1), 7055 Southwest Freeway, 988-3200; (B1), 9401 Katy Freeway, 465-8065; (E5), 10010 Kleck opposite Almeda Mall, 946-9192; FM 1960 & Breck, 537-1607; and other locations. Clothes for men, women, teens, and toddlers, with 30% to 50% off everyday low prices. Also carries name merchandise.

Mrs. Baird's Bakeries, 6650 N. Houston-Rosslyn Rd.; 690-3227. Also Thrift Stores at about a dozen other locations around town. Reduced prices on day-old breads, cakes, cookies, and other products from this famous Houston family bakery.

Salvation Army Thrift Store (C3), 2208 Washington; 869-3551. Everything from furniture to bicycles, jewelry, clothes, and appliances.

Sears Warehouse Store, 5901 Griggs Rd.; 844-9394. Dealing in appliances, furniture.

Super Crown Books, 11151 Westheimer, 789-6354; 1953 W. Gray, 527-8253; 5550 Weslayan, 664-7722; and other locations. Super Crown stores are discounted, offering savings from 10% to 35% off.

Catalog Showroom Stores

Stores where you go in, look at samples, order from a catalog, and walk out with the merchandise include:

Service Merchandise Co., 6900 Southwest Fwy. near Sharpstown; 783-8820; seven other locations. Broad range of brand-name general merchandise at discounted prices.

Sharper Image (I10), 1200 McKinney; 652-2507; The Galleria, 5175 Westheimer; 961-0123. Expensive toys for sophisticated grownups.

FABRICS AND LINENS

Of course, most major department stores and discount outlets feature fabrics and linens. Here is one shop specializing in this merchandise.

Southern Fabrics (F1), 1210 Galleria Mall; 626-5511. Serving Houston since 1938 with high-fashion fabrics you would find in ready-to-wear. Many fine fabrics including Thai silk, ultra suede, silk prints, stripes and solids, and a large bridal department plus beautiful evening wear goods. Unusual collection of notions such as boutique belts and buckles below boutique prices.

FLEA MARKETS

Spreads of merchandise from around the world sell side-by-side with American goods—the old and the new, fine crafts and junk, and an occasional real find at a bargain price all make flea market-hopping a fun venture.

Coles Antique Village Flea Market, 1014 N. Main in Pearland; 485-2277. On Highway 35 near Houston City limits. A Texas-size complex with more than 500 dealers spread over this 70,000 square-foot, air-conditioned village. Dealers from many states show antiques and collectibles weekends starting Fridays at 8:30 am.

Houston Flea Market (Southwest Common Market) (D1), 6616 Southwest Freeway at Westpark exit; 782-0391. One of the largest and most popular markets in Houston with nearly 14 acres of stalls, indoor shops, and covered tables plus 5½ acres of parking. Open Saturdays and Sundays.

The Market Place, 10910 Old Katy Rd.; 464-8023. Combines well-maintained, glass-partitioned booths with a maxi-mall open-area with a total of some 160 dealers selling primitives, antiques, brassware, plants, and collectibles. Open weekends.

Trade Mart, 2121 W. Sam Houston Tollway N.; 467-2508. Gigantic air-conditioned building with more than 167 dealers. Lots of parking space. A clean, bright quality mart with antiques, specialties, and collectibles. Open Fri, Sat, Sun.

Trading Fair II (E3), 5515 South Loop East; 731-1111. A unique indoor flea market featuring 400 dealers. Located near the Astrodome. Open Fri, Sat, Sun.

FLOWERS AND GIFT BASKETS

The right arrangement for any occasion in Houston or anywhere in the world may be found in the following locations.

Blanton-Niday Florists, 10651 Harwin; 999-7673. A complete range of floral services, fruit baskets. Deliveries; 24-hour hotline.

Brazos Floral Co. (E2), 3411 W. Holcombe Blvd.; 667-9101. One of Houston's oldest florists, doing business since 1926, with flowers, plants, and dried and silk designs. Situated close to the Texas Medical Center.

Galloway Florist, 5910 Rose; 621-2052. A small, well-known gift and flower shop.

Wademan's, 2143 Fairview; 526-1231. Serving Houston for more than 60 years with floral arrangements, gift baskets, plants, and special orders. Worldwide service.

FOODS

Shopping for foods can almost be as much fun as the pleasure in dining. The wonderful aroma of fresh baked bread, freshly ground coffee, and eye-tempting chocolates and cheeses, all excite the senses in anticipation of a special occasion.

Bakeries

The Acadian Bakery (F3), 604 W. Alabama; 520-1484. Breads and cakes from Cajun recipes. Boule, batard, and mini-baguette are the basic breads; also Acadian cheesecake with sour cream and other flavors.

Andre's Swiss Candies and Pastry Shop (F2), 2515 River Oaks Blvd.; 524-3863. At the front of Andre's Tea Room are display samples of Swiss breads and sweets to cause even the staunchest dieter to succumb. They carry the epitome of chocolates, truffles (of which there are some 30 varieties), tortes, quiches, cakes, cheesecakes, and hand-dipped tea cookies.

Droubi's Bakery & Delicatessen, 7333 Hillcroft; 988-5897. Pita and other Middle Eastern breads, still hot from being freshly baked on premises, combine aromas with herbs and spices of myriad other delicacies to welcome you to Droubi's delicious world of Mediterranean cuisines.

French Gourmet (C1), 12504 Memorial; 973-6900; (F2), 2250 Westheimer; 524-3744; 2484 Bolsover, 528-3647. One of the largest French bakeries in Houston established by a fourth-generation French Master Baker continuing the family tradition of award- winning gourmet pastries. "La piece de resistance" is the heavenly decadent "La Bombe" with chocolate mousse, strawberry, lemon, and vanilla all wrapped and tied in a chocolate bow. Also breads, quiche, fruit tarts, and Belgian candies, and a great gift idea of truffles in their own chocolate candy box. And quite possibly the best chocolate layer cake anywhere.

La Sultana (B3), 809 Quitman; 229-9460. A great Mexican bakery with a colorful array of cakes, sweet rolls, and breads fresh baked daily. While shopping you might try a cool glass of Tepache—homemade, fermented pineapple juice with piloncillo (Mexican sugar).

New York Bagels, 9724 Hillcroft; 723-5879. Plain, garlic, onion, sesame, ET (Every Thing), and other flavor bagels, a couple of bread specialties, and yummy bialys. Time it right in the morning, and your purchase will be hot enough to fog up your glasses. Adjacent to pleasant little coffee shop in case you can't wait to get started.

Three Brothers (E2), 4036 S. Braeswood; 666-2551. Houston's largest authentic Kosher bakery offering the finest in products since 1949. No fats, sugars, or preservatives used in rye, pumpernickel, or sourdough breads. Superb onion rolls and sourdough rye bread (with or without caraway seeds). Staff artist can reproduce anything on cakes for special occasions—simply bring in the picture you want portrayed.

Health Food Stores ────────────────

General Nutrition Center—There are many outlets of this chain throughout Houston. For convenience we single out the downtown location (I10), 809 Main; 226-7479. These stores carry a full line of natural vitamins, yogurts, juices, breads, grains, nuts, protein powder, pastries, chips, cheeses, and other items in the health food plan.

Whole Foods (F2), 2900 S. Shepherd; 520-1937; 11145 Westheimer, 784-7776. This has to be the largest health and natural food store in Houston with an unbelievable assortment of herbs and spices, vitamins, plus produce, meats, cheeses, sweets, and deli for takeout orders. Here, great groceries—great entertainment. Massages available.

International and Gourmet Foods ────────────

Shoppers have multiple choices among Houston's many foreign foods stores, and we have selected some typical markets, plus several general-line gourmet foods outlets.

Antone's (C3), 807 Taft; 526-1046. The original is now joined by nine other locations. One's sense of smell is titillated just by walking into Antone's where cheeses, spices, and deli meats combine to emit a powerfully appetizing aroma.

British Isles (D2), 2366 Rice Blvd.; 529-9889. This is the largest British products store in Houston, if not all of Texas. Here are the widest selections of famous English teas, biscuits, cakes, and sauces. Also great candies and syrups.

Diho Market, 9280 Bellaire; 988-5835. Chinese ingredients, fresh seafood, and culinary specialties from all over East and Southeast Asia predominate this supermarket. Also a good stock of Pacific Rim wines and beers, including some from the People's Republic of China, plus woks and other Oriental kitchen-ware.

House of Coffee Beans (D2), 2520 Rice Blvd. in the Village; 524-0057. Create your own special blends and flavors in the House of Coffee, prepared fresh every time you come in. There are straights, blends, extra specials, flavored and decaffeinated coffees, plus chocolate, green cardamom seeds, and cinnamon.

Jay Store (D1), 6688 Southwest Freeway; 783-0032. If you are looking for the best products of the Indian subcontinent, follow your sense of smell to this delightful store with its pungent aroma of curries and chiles. Special finds here include ghee (clarified butter), whole mustard, wonderful chutneys, and mild and hot curries, reasonably priced saffron, dal, mung, and other beans, and all the cooking ware you'll need to prepare your favorite Indian recipe.

Korea Supermarket (E1), 6427 Bissonnet; 772-6160. Like so many of the Oriental markets in Houston, this one carries a full line of imported foods from throughout Asia, but it also has the best assortment of dried fish, seaweed, and chiles in town. And what Korean store would be caught without an entire section stocked with kimchi (hot and spicy pickled cabbage)?

La Casita (D4), 7120 Canal; 926-1735. This little house in the huge, mainly Mexican-American neighborhood by the Ship Channel sells super-fresh home-made (mild) tamales, carnitas, menudo, and chicharrones.

Latina (F2), 1972 Fairview; 528-8304. Here you will see Cuban expatriates and others shopping for dried cod, kippers, smoked herring, special cheeses, herbs, and spices popular among Caribbeans. In addition the store sells Cuban records and tapes, Spanish language novels, newspapers, and toilet articles.

Markets

Doziers, 8222 FM 359 in Fulshear, Texas; 346-1411. This market is famous among Houstonians who enjoy fresh meats, peppered, smoked, and barbecued.

Farmers Market (A3), 2520 Airline; 862-8866. Here it truly is cheaper by the bushel; that is if you co-op with your neighbors. There are acres of fresh fruit and produce plus many products from both the Rio Grande Valley of South Texas and neighboring Mexico. Look around and compare prices.

Fiesta Marts—There are about 20 of these in varying sizes, including several incredibly giant markets. 8130 Kirby, 666-9260; (D4), 800 S. Wayside, 928-2854; (E4), 5600 Mykawa, 644-1611; (D1), 6200 Bellaire at Hillcroft, 270-5889; and 1005 Blalock at Katy Fwy, 461-9664.

These Fiestas really should be listed in the international and gourmet foods section, but they also offer all manner of daily needs, including clothes and accessories, music, radios, jewelry, photographs, keys, bakery, et al.

There is such an abundance of everything one wonders how it's kept fresh, but when you see the crowds picking over beans, chiles, mangos, and tiny

Manzano bananas, you have the answer. Here you can buy insurance, pick up a straw hat, and highstep it right on into this unbelievable market place, where you'll see a lot of fruit and vegetables you may not even recognize, and where, after walking from one end to another, you'll need to stop at the refreshment stand for fresh, cold watermelon, cucumber, cantaloupe, or jicama juice.

Seafood and Fresh Fish

Emery's Seafood (F6), 109 11th St. in Seabrook on Galveston Bay; 474-5620. This is it! A typical Texas Gulf Coast seafood and fish market with fresh catches of the day including Gulf tuna, snapper, trout, live crabs (in season), oysters in the shell (in season), octopus, squid, mountains of fresh shrimp, and many other delicacies from the deep. For a little extra cost they will skin or scale, and fillet your fish to suit your special needs.

FRAMERS

Allart Framing & Gallery (F2), 2635 Revere; 526-3631. Convenient to Greenway Plaza and not far from Galleria/Post Oak Center. A long-established, highly reputable frame shop.

The Picture Store (J9), 500 Dallas; 658-0027. This store is in the Tunnel system and convenient to downtown customers. Also sells posters, prints, unique ready framed items, and other gift-oriented pieces.

GIFT SHOPS AND GREETING CARDS

Of so many fascinating shops that qualify, here are a few to underscore for unusual and fine quality merchandise.

Alfred Dunhill of London (F1), 5085 Westheimer in The Galleria Mall; 961-4661. While this name connotes quality tobacco products, there is also an exclusive men's shop with imported gift items from the United Kingdom, Switzerland, and Italy. Featured are hand-painted silk ties, watches, lighters, and bar accessories. Also handsome attaches and other leather goods. ˙

Carlton House (F2), 2509 River Oaks Blvd.; 529-6148. This is the debutante registry headquarters in the small but elite Lamar River Oaks Shopping Center. It handles the finest gifts in imported china, silver, crystal, clocks, brass, oriental urns, lingerie, soaps and perfumes, unusual dolls, bath sets, linen place sets, and a limited selection of toddler's clothes.

Sportsmans Gallery (F1), 5015 Westheimer in The Galleria; 622-2662. This is an unusually fascinating place to browse, with the emphasis on Western bronzes, wood carvings, and wildlife paintings. Also a good line of nautical antiques. Most interesting are the nature paintings, a rare technique whereby the artist first paints a real fish then skillfully transfers an imprint onto canvas.

The Wooden Star (F1), 4344 Westheimer on Mid Lane; 840-8832. Gifts and souvenirs to suit any age, and to match any budget. There is even a Texas Christmas section stocked year 'round. High-quality gifts. Texas library, flags, and foods.

Yesteryear Shop (J8), 1100 Bagby in Sam Houston Historical Park downtown; 655-9114. Mainly books and decorative items in keeping with this museum shop's historical theme.

JEWELRY

Jerome Berger Jewelry, 4950 Bissonnet in Bellaire; 665-2431. Continuing a family tradition of several generations as a jeweler's jeweler, Jerome Berger himself does custom design work, repairs, even antique restoration with all precious metals—gold, platinum or silver—and setting or resetting diamonds, rubies, emeralds, and other precious and semi-precious stones. Now, at realistic prices, he offers the general public the same craftsmanship he continues to provide for some of Houston's most prestigious jewelry stores.

Cartier (F1), 1800 Post Oak in Sak's Center; 871-0177. Jewelry, watches, and gifts bearing the Cartier signature.

Fred Joaillier Inc., (F1), 5015 Westheimer; 960-9441. This exclusive design house, based in Paris, is known for its contemporary classics with the finest in precious gems. Fred's designer for the United States is in Houston.

Gordon's Jewelers, Westwood Mall, 772-3754; other locations throughout the city. This was one of the first jewelers on the stock market. It was started by a Houston family and sells a wide variety of quality jewels, fine watches, and gifts.

Quenton Elliott Co. (F2), 528-1641. Gemologist, appraiser, and fine jewels.

Sweeney & Co. Jewelers, Town & Country Village; 464-1956. Also stores at other locations. The best in jewelry, watches, china, silver, crystal, and porcelains.

Tiffany & Company (F1), 5015 Westheimer in Galleria I; 626-0220. The classic, simple pigeon-hole window displays understate the finest quality merchandise.

LEATHER

Bag 'n Baggage/Houston Trunk Factory (I10), The Park in Houston Center; 650-8236. Repair Division (D4), 3900 Polk; 223-2181. Also outlets at other locations in major malls and shopping centers. Houston's oldest, serving Houstonians, conventioneers, and visitors for nearly 100 years. Handles superior brands of luggage, trunks, briefcases, and many accessories.

Luggage & Leather Outlet, 9880 Harwin; 266-0237. Good to heavily discounted prices on brand-name luggage and accessories. Look for first-quality, discontinueds, and some factory seconds.

Mark Cross Ltd. (F1), 2210 Galleria at 5015 Westheimer; 626-4729. Another classic name in leather goods since 1845 with large variety for travel, plus many gift items such as complete desk sets, clocks, belts, manicure sets, office frames, billfolds, and jewelry boxes.

North Beach Leather (F1), Galleria I, 5015 Westheimer; 629-5880. A San Francisco tradition with all drum-tanned leather goods. Featuring high-fashion articles in leather and suede with feathers, coyote-collar jackets, lined leather pants, women's bikinis, and many other designs.

Tandy Leather Co. (F3), 3901 S. Main, 521-0477; (E1), 9647 S. Gessner; 777-6998; (B1), 1819 Bingle, 461-2109. This well-known national firm sells every kind of leather craft and supplies, plus finished goods, which include hats, belts, vests, and a large collection of buckles. New to Tandy is a Western Saddle Kit.

OFFICE SUPPLIES

For the business traveler and conventioneer, there are numerous outlets for emergency supplies and items you may have forgotten in your haste to get here.

Houston Blueprint & Stationery (K9), 1333 Louisiana, (downtown), 659-2960; (D1), 5510 Richmond, 266-1236. Full-line stores with all your office and business supplies.

Office Depot, 3401 Kirby, 522-9981; about a dozen other locations. Enormous office supply source at reasonable to amazingly discounted prices.

Office Max, 8100 S. Gessner, 772-1110; about eight other locations. Another enormous office supply source with reasonable to amazingly discounted prices.

Wilson Stationery & Printing Co. (C3), 6869 Katy Rd.; 868-8001. Wilson's is a long-established supply store selling not only office supplies, but full-line drafting materials, and stationery.

PHOTOGRAPHIC SUPPLIES

Check the following for camera sales/service/rentals, for film/supplies and/or for processing/developing.

Camera Exchange, 4014 Richmond; 621-6901. A wide range of cameras, lenses, projectors, lighting equipment, darkroom equipment, plus underwater still and movie equipment. Also buys, sells, and trades used equipment. Good prices.

Eckerd Drug Stores all over Houston.

Fox Photo Finish 1-Hour Labs. There are many walk-in and drive-up stores throughout the city. Downtown try Texas Commerce Center, 223-0547 or One Allen Center, 951-9990.

Jobar's Camera Center, 4909 Bissonnet; 668-5773. Full-line camera store with helpful, knowledgeable staff. Reasonable prices on equipment, discounting available on film in quantity.

NPL Inc., 1926 West Gray; 527-9300. Arguably Houston's best-known, most established, most versatile custom processing lab. Not cheap, but excellent work.

RECORDS AND TAPES

Among hundreds of outlets, here are two of the largest locations convenient to each other, and, because of size and variety, the most likely to stock the labels you're looking for.

Cactus Music & Video (F2), 2930 S. Shepherd; 526-9272. A large store featuring the pops plus.

Sound Warehouse (F2), 3800 Farnham; 523-2200. This one is the supermarket of records, tapes, movies, and video with numerous other locations for your convenience.

SHOES

If you follow our suggested trails around Houston, you'll be wearing your soles thin before long. We have selected several shoe outlets outside of major stores as alternate choices.

Bally of Switzerland (F1), 5015 Westheimer in The Galleria; 629-4180. One of the world's finest men's shoe stores with other items as well, including passport and briefcases, suede jackets, suede trim sweaters, and ties.

Brucal's Shoes, 2027 Post Oak Blvd.; 621-2991. Name-brand merchandise at attractively reduced prices.

Morgan Hayes (J10), The Park, 655-9077; (F1), Galleria, 5085 Westheimer, 961-0085, and several other locations. Selling men's name-brand shoes such as Bass, Adidas, Lucchese, Nunn Bush, and others.

SKIN AND BODY CARE

Institute of Cosmetology, 7011 Harwin; 783-9988. This studio takes care of nearly everything but the hair for both men and women. European-style biogenic facials, masks, manicures, and pedicures.

The Phoenix (C1), 111 N. Post Oak Lane; 680-1601. Offers a one-week full program of exercise, weight training and muscle tone, meal planning, beauty treatment including massage and facials, hair conditioning and styling, pedi- and manicure, and special evening programs on fashion and how to carry the health-care plan into the home.

SPORTS EQUIPMENT

The temperate climate in Houston enables its citizens to enjoy outdoor sports almost year 'round, creating a big demand for sporting goods, and we have selected a couple of the best-known stores in town.

Oshman's Sporting Goods (F1), 2131 S. Post Oak, 622-4940; (J10), The Park, 1200 McKinney, 650-8240. Also stores at other locations and in major malls. Started by a Houston family, this international chain offers everything you could possibly need from indoor ski ramp practice to complete freeze-dried dinners for backpackers. Also a wide selection in sportswear and accessories for men and women; alterations available. You may purchase fishing and hunting licenses here.

Whole Earth Provision Co., 2934 S. Shepherd; 526-5226. Terrific lines of outdoor clothing, equipment, travel goods, and books.

STOCK AND BOND BROKERS

Although the downtown area along Travis and Milam streets once served as Houston's little Wall Street, today brokers are more scattered, with offices convenient to nearly every major sector of the city.

Merrill Lynch, 1221 McKinney (downtown), 658-1200; (F1), 12 Greenway Plaza East, 871-9111. Also other locations.

Olde Discount Stockbrokers, 910 Travis; 759-9700.

TOYS

The Toy Maker (F1), The Galleria II, 3rd level, 5015 Westheimer; 840-1099. The Galleria store once had exact duplicates of wedding party dolls that Nancy Reagan had made for the White House.

Toys R Us (F5), W. Bay Area Blvd. opposite Baybrook Mall, 338-2915; (A3), North Freeway at Airline, 695-8873; (E5), 10220 Almeda-Genoa Rd., 941-1920; (B1), Katy Freeway at Bunker Hill Rd., 465-0087; 7323 West FM 1960; 583-7733. These supermarkets of the toy world offer acres of everything you could imagine from doll cribs to real baby beds. Aisle after aisle stacked high with party goods, sporting equipment, games, stuffed toys, bikes, gas-powered toys, radio-controlled vehicles, camping equipment, and even children's swimming pools. Look for the jolly face of "Geoffrey" the giraffe at these freeway warehouses.

WESTERN WEAR

For garb synonymous with Texas, there are dozens of Western stores in Houston, some of which are not simply keeping up with fads—they started them, as far back as 1870.

Palace Boot Shop (I11), 1212 Prairie; 224-1411. Another landmark in Western wear in Houston since 1919. The Palace people are personable and anxious to custom design and handmake a pair of boots just for you. They also have a large selection of ready-made name brands such as Tony Lama, Frye, and Texas. There is a great variety of accessories, feathers, and some clothing as well.

Stelzig's of Texas (D1), 3123 Post Oak, 629-7779; (E1), 9511 Southwest Freeway, 988-6530. This has been Houston's complete line Western store since 1870. Not only will you find a wide selection in clothing, boots, hats, and accessories but all of your needs in both Western and English saddles, stockman's supplies, veterinary equipment, and many authentically Texas gift items.

SPORTS

SPORTS TO SEE

Spectator sports of nearly every description abound in Houston. The importance they play in the community is prominently underscored by the palatial homes Houstonians have provided for their teams, and by the frequency of sellout games, both for the big leagues and the college teams. You know you have arrived in a sports-crazy town when you see a standing-room-only crowd thunderously welcoming home a team whether it wins or loses.

Of course, when Houston teams win—as when the Rockets whipped the New York Knicks for the 1994 NBA championship—Houston goes happily nuts.

Canoe Racing

An annual regatta on Buffalo Bayou draws some 500 participants for four key races including the U.S. Canoe Association, Senior Aluminum, an Unlimited, and the Novice group. The longest stretch is 16 miles upstream from downtown.

College Football

With three major university teams, Houston fans have a full schedule of college football. The **University of Houston Cougars** play their home games in the Astrodome while the **Texas Southern University Tigers** split theirs between the Astrodome and Robertson Stadium on the UH campus. The Tigers play in the Southwestern Athletic Conference.

The **Rice Owls** play in their own stadium and a much anticipated game of rivalry is when the two Southwest Conference teams, Rice and U of H, face off at home for a trophy called the Bayou Bucket.

Ticket Information for the Tigers 527-7270; the Cougars 743-9444; and the Owls 527-4068.

Golf

With its temperate climate and excellent public and private facilities Houston enjoys year-round golfing. The crowd-drawing Houston Open is the big one with some 50 top golfers in the country teeing off at The Woodlands Inn & Country Club, north of Houston in Montgomery County off I-45 North. Information, 367-1100. For a Calendar of Events, stop by the Houston Golf Association office, 1830 S. Millbend, The Woodlands; or call 367-7999.

Major Leagues

The **Houston Astros,** National Baseball League. Games from April through October, in the *Astrodome* (E2). Ticket information, 799-9555.

The **Houston Oilers,** National Football League. The regular season is from September through December. Games in the Astrodome (E2). Ticket information, 797-1000.

The **Houston Rockets,** National Basketball Association 1994 and 1995 championship team. Games from October through spring, in The Summit at Greenway Plaza (F1). Ticket information, 627-0600.

Motor Racing

Auto thrill shows, motocross, and motorcycle races are big annual crowd pleasers in the Astrodome. The "Destruction Derby" usually in January pits celebrities and men's and women's teams on collision course.

The **American Motorcycle Association** race features short track and TT Steeplechase with high jumps.

The **Annual Supercross** in February features 80 motorcyclists in head-to-head competition on a manmade course in the Astrodome.

Tennis

A Calendar of.Events and other tennis information is available at the Houston Tennis Association, P.O. Box 79341, Houston, TX 77279. Telephone 973-7636.

SPORTS TO DO

With a median age of only 30, Houstonians lead very active lives and the stress is on keeping fit with participatory and recreational activities. The range is vast with opportunities for everyone, no matter how brief your visit, how busy your schedule, or whatever your need or preference.

The Houston Astrodome

Greater Houston Convention & Visitors Bureau

Archery

You'll find your own "enchanted forest" just outside of downtown in Memorial Park (C2), where you can practice any day. *NCH.* For directions call 845-1033.

If you are only visiting and would like to rent and practice, try these private indoor-outdoor ranges.

Archer Sports Inc. (E5), 12722 Old Galveston Rd., just south of Ellington Field. Open noon-9 pm weekdays, and 10-6 Saturdays. Information 488-4504.

Hillcrest Archery Center (C1), 1422 Blalock in Spring Branch. Take I-10 west to Blalock exit, then right about six miles. They have indoor ranges plus rentals. Information 467-1577.

Bicycling

For easy riding along scenic trails, Houston's flat terrain is ideal for this excellent form of exercise. The city, in cooperation with private interests, has developed several good paths with exercise facilities and water fountains along the way.

There is a signed route through downtown, which is more enjoyable with less traffic on weekends. To avoid some of the traffic on weekdays, we suggest you start on the edge of downtown at Lamar and Bagby (J9), going west on Lamar past Sam Houston Park onto Allen Parkway. From the Sabine St. bridge you will see the hike and bike trail running along Buffalo Bayou. Continue out several miles to the Shepherd St. bridge, cross over and return to town via the Memorial Drive trail.

A much longer path is along Braes Bayou (E1), over 15 miles from South Gessner on the southwest side to the University of Houston area and then beyond into Mason Park (D5), on the east side.

Two city parks are especially oriented toward biking.

One is **Hermann Park** (D3), just off the South Main Corridor where you will find winding streets with possible stops at several points of interest such as museums, outdoor theater, rose trails, the zoo (no bikes inside), a lake, and refreshment stands.

The other is **Memorial Park** (C2), on the west side with paths between I-610 Loop and Memorial Loop Dr.

If you are visiting and would like to two-wheel it through these scenic areas, you may rent bikes.

For additional information and bike-path maps call City Parks & Recreation Dept. Public Information 845-1000.

For information on **Houston Area Bicyclist Alliance** activities call 729-9333.

The Alkek Velodrome, 19008 Saums Rd. Out I-10 West to Katy to Barker-

Cypress exit, turn right and proceed to first light, then to the left on Saums Rd., 578-0693 or Parks Dept., 845-1000. This facility is open for riding Tue-Sun. Guests need a 10- or 12-speed or track bike and helmet. Rentals. Coaches available. First-timers must attend riders sessions Sat or Sun *NCH*. Otherwise *CH* for rides.

Bowling

This is a great way to beat the heat and still get your exercise in a friendly social atmosphere. Houston has some of the largest bowling alleys in the Southwest and has been a popular stop for the big pro bowlers' tour.

If you are a member of the American Bowling Congress or women's group, and have an average on the books, you can compete in monthly tournaments at **Stadium Bowl** (E2), 8200 Braesmain near the Astrodome. This facility is open 24 hours, seven days, and has 72 lanes. Information 666-2373.

For general information try the **Houston Bowling Association** (C3), 2805 Bagby; 524-3185.

Dancing

As a form of mild exercise to music, aerobic, square and round, and even belly dancing are sweeping Houston. There is a class somewhere for nearly every age, from tots to teens to senior citizens, and for the handicapped.

The **Downtown YMCA,** which is greatly expanded and open to men and women, is convenient to visitors in downtown hotels. For a nominal one-day fee you can participate in any number of activities. It is located at 1600 Louisiana (K9), next to the Cullen Center. Information 659-8501.

The **YWCA** is limited to members only but if you have a card from your hometown location you may pay a one-day fee for their activities. It is located at 3615 Willia near Heights and Memorial Blvd. (C3). Information 868-6075.

Probably the widest variety of dance programs and other activities open to the public on a limited basis is at the **Jewish Community Center** (E1), 5601 S. Braeswood just off I-610 and not far from the South Main Corridor of hotels and motels. There they have non-member aerobic and exercise classes, plus other recreational programs which are available for a few dollars a day for adults and for children. Inquire about their passes. For information call 729-3200.

Golf

There are numerous golf courses, both public and private, and, with Houston's temperate climate, you can nearly always see golfers on the green in county and city parks and at private facilities. There are seven city parks with golf courses, the most convenient to major hotels are Hermann and Memorial parks.

City Public Parks

Brock Park (B5), 8201 John Ralston Rd.; 458-1350.
Glenbrook Park (E5), 8205 North Bayou; 649-8089.
Gus Wortham Park (D4), 311 S. Wayside; 921-3227.
Hermann Park (D3), 6201 Golf Course Dr.; 526-0077.
Melrose Golf Course, 401 E. Canino; 847-0875.
Memorial Park (C2), 6001 Memorial Park Dr.; 862-4033.
Sharpstown Park (D1), 660 Harbortown; 988-2099.

County Public Parks

Bear Creek Golf World, 16001 Clay Rd.; 859-8188. Three courses, range, cart, and club rentals.
Melrose Park Golf Center (A3), 401 Canino Rd.; 221-6447 (Precinct 4).

Miniature Golf

Malibu Castle of Houston (C1) is a small kingdom for children and adults, located at 1105 West Loop North between I-10 West and N. Post Oak. Information 688-5271.

Private Clubs Open to the Public

We recommend your checking out **World Houston Golf Course** on the H&H Ranch (A2), 4000 Greens Rd. across from Houston Intercontinental Airport. This is an 18-hole championship course. Information 449-8384.

Tour 18 reproduces famous holes from some of the most celebrated courses in the United States. Located at 3102 FM 1960 E., Humble; 540-1818.

Health Clubs

As in any other major city, there are many outlets here with varied fitness programs and equipment. We limit this discussion to features at the YMCA, YWCA, and one major health club which is affiliated with International Physical Fitness centers welcoming out-of-towners.

The **Downtown YMCA** (K9), 1600 Louisiana, admits men and women, and for a small charge per visit you may use all of their facilities, including an indoor pool, indoor/outdoor track, exercise room, sun room, sauna, steam room and whirlpool, and 23 courts for handball, racquetball, and squash. Travelers may use the courts only when they are not in use by members. Information 659-8505.

Ladies who are members of a **YWCA** somewhere else may use the Houston branch for a one-day price on all activities, which include indoor pool, exercise room, weight room, racquetball, and a bayou jogging trail. It is located at 3615 Willia (C3), near Heights and Memorial. Information 868-6075.

The **Jewish Community Center** (E1), 5601 S. Braeswood has special guest fees for the use of indoor-outdoor pools, exercise room, tennis, racquetball, track, and other recreational programs aimed at getting newcomers into the mainstream of Houston living with social outlets. Information 729-3200.

Anyone who is a member of a club anywhere that is affiliated with **International Physical Fitness** may take their pick from among some 30 health clubs here. One of the largest and best equipped is **Olympia Fitness & Racquetball Club** (E1), 8313 Southwest Freeway (U.S. 59 South), at Gessner. It is open to men and women, seven days, and has saunas, indoor pool, cold plunge, basketball, whirlpool, racquetball, billiard room, and about every kind of work-out equipment conceivable. Information 988-8787.

Hiking

The abundance of trees and park trails make hiking a pleasant form of exercise here. We recommend four possible routes convenient to the three major commercial centers.

Buffalo Bayou Park (J7), is on the edge of downtown, and its trails follow the sloping banks of the bayou several miles west, then back east on the other side into town. Start at Sam Houston Park (J9), corner of Bagby at Lamar, and follow the hike and bike trail along Allen Parkway. At the Shepherd St. bridge (C2), cross over and come back in on the path along Memorial.

Hermann Park (D3), is convenient both to downtown and to the South Main Corridor. It, too, is wooded but with more open spaces dotted with things to see along the way such as a fragrance garden, outdoor art, Chinese pavilion, museums, and refreshment stands. It is bounded by Fannin (the main entrance), N. MacGregor, Hermann Dr., and Almeda Rd.

Houston Arboretum and Nature Center (C2), is farther out west off Memorial on Woodway, at the I-610 Loop. This is convenient to those staying in hotels in The Galleria-Post Oak area. The expansive Arboretum features gardens as well as an abundance of native trees and flora. Keep your eyes peeled for small animals foraging on the rustic trails. It is located at 4501 Woodway. Information 681-8433.

Memorial Park (C2), Houston's largest, is between downtown and the Post Oak area. Besides more than 1,500 heavily wooded acres, there is a 3-mile exer-trail with workout stations, water fountains, and night lighting along Memorial Drive, which divides the park. This park is bounded by I-610, I-10, Crestwood, and Buffalo Bayou.

Horseback Riding

While you are here you may as well "Go Texan" and saddle up.

If you have your own horse, try the Hermann Park equestrian trails for a

slow and easy gait. Whether you are a visitor or a resident, try the following locations for rentals, lessons, and practice riding.

Abis Rent-A-Horse, 13250 Westheimer, has 80 acres for Western riding
only. Information 497-1630.

Hermann Park Stables (D3), 5716 Almeda, offers lessons in English riding
only. Information 529-2081.

For youth group activities and convention planning, check with the Houston
Convention and Visitors Bureau for Western hay-rides that are available at some
stables.

Hunting

The variety of game in Texas is very good and includes javelina, deer, antelope, coyote, bobcat, and exotic game. Of course bird hunting is popular seasonally as well, and includes such game fowl as geese, ducks, doves, quail, and
turkey. There are no major public lands for hunting in Texas, which means most
is done on private property, and owners require lease fees. There is often a waiting period just to secure a lease for the better ranches and lodges.

You must have a license for hunting, which is obtainable at most major sporting-goods stores such as Oshman's with several locations in town. Also the
Texas Parks & Wildlife offices here sell licenses both for fishing and hunting.

A good source of information on hunting outlets is **Glenn Slade's Executive Travel** (D1), 5373 W. Alabama; 623-4800.

For more details on hunting in Texas you may call the **Texas Parks &
Wildlife Dept.** toll-free number in Austin, 1-800-792-1112, or the Houston
office, 931-6471. They can tell you where to get a copy of their "Regulations
Handbook" on hunting.

Ice Skating

Curiously, for a town that almost never sees ice, this sport is gaining in popularity as is Little League hockey.

The most fashionable spot, and a convenient one for visitors, is the **Galleria
Ice Rink** in The Galleria mall (F1), 5015 Westheimer just off I-610 Loop. Skating lessons are alternated with public sessions. Information 621-1500.

Sharpstown Ice Center (D1), 7300 Bellerive; 784-2971. Public sessions and
lessons daily. Pro shop.

Miniature Motorcar Races

Part of a national chain, **Malibu Grand Prix** has several locations here. For your convenience, we recommend the one at 1111 W. Loop North, next to The Castle Putt Putt (C1), between I-10 West and N. Post Oak. This activity is gaining rapidly in popularity and is full of challenges to see how well you handle a car. What better place than Houston for this type of activity? Information 683-8255.

Racquetball

This is an extremely popular sport in Houston and there are numerous private and public facilities. The downtown **YMCA** (K9), 1600 Louisiana, has many courts with a one-time visit fee. Also the **Jewish Community Center** (E1), offers one-day passes to use their facilities. *CH.*

A major spa chain, **Presidents First Lady,** permits the use of their courts and other health facilities on a reciprocal basis for members of certain other spas around the country. Information 771-8395.

Rifle and Pistol Ranges

There are a number of good rifle and pistol ranges with day and night practice, indoor and outdoor ranges, skeet trap, turkey shoots, gunsmiths, boresighting, and gun and ammunition sales. One-day practice fees available. Check the Yellow Pages for outlets.

Roller Skating

Local roller rinks include:
Bear Creek Roller Rink, 5210 N. Highway 6; 463-6020.
Dairy Ashford Roller Rink, 1820 S. Dairy Ashford; 493-5651.

Running

Top trails are those already mentioned in the section on hiking.

The **YMCA** (K9), 1600 Louisiana, is a good location for the busy traveler, conventioneer, or tourist in downtown hotels. They have both indoor and outdoor track, and it is a coed facility. Information 659-8501.

There are several resort and conference center-type hotels in the area that have indoor and outdoor facilities, but of course you must be a guest. Try the **Houstonian Hotel & Conference Center** (C1), 111 N. Post Oak Lane, 680-2626; or both **Westin** hotels at The Galleria, which have access to the University Club (F1), at 5051 Westheimer, 621-4811 (club), or 960-8100 (hotels).

Skiing

We like to think Houston has it all, but here is where we may have to bite the dust. The saying "Think Snow" hasn't worked yet, any more than the maxim "if the Good Lord had intended for Texans to ski, He would have made B.S. white." Since Houston's highest hill would be a freeway slope, for this sport you'll have to join locals on treks to out-of-state resorts.

At least you can take lessons and practice on artificial belts at **Oshman's Ski Ramp** (F1), 2131 S. Post Oak near The Galleria. Both lessons and practice sessions available. Information 622-4940. Or try **Ski Houston** at 12505 Hillcroft; 721-7788.

Sky Diving

Skydive Spaceland offers skydiving lessons on Saturdays and Sundays. The Center is behind Houston Gulf Airport off I-45 South in League City. Call for directions 337-1713.

Squash

Again, the **Central YMCA** makes available a wide range of recreational activities including squash. Showers. Located at 1600 Louisiana. Call 659-8501.

Tennis

Public courts are plentiful around town, but for your comfort we suggest you locate an indoor court during the summer.

Municipal and County Courts

Bear Creek Park, War Memorial Drive between Eldridge & Clay; 496-2177.
Homer Ford Tennis Center (D4), 5225 Calhoun; 747-5466.
Memorial Tennis Center (C2), 1500 Memorial Loop in Memorial Park; 861-3765.
Southwest Tennis Center (E1), 9506 S. Gessner; 772-0296.

Other Public Courts

For information on other facilities and a Calendar of Tennis Events call the **Houston Tennis Association,** 973-7636.

Water Sports

Canoeing

There are canoe rentals for out-of-towners and if you have your own equipment the best possible sport is on **Armand Bayou** at Bay Area Blvd. (E6). On the boulevard is a bridge crossing between Bay Area Park and Armand Bayou Nature Center, which is a good point to put in. The most scenic nature-trail route is upstream. You should abide by Texas water-safety codes requiring that you have life jackets, and children 12 and under must have them on at all times.

Diving

Southwest Scuba is on the Southwest Freeway at Wilcrest; 498-3483.

The Houston Scuba Academy has two locations; 721-7788. Also check Galveston Directory. Many good spots in the Gulf of Mexico.

Fishing and Crabbing

Houston hubs a fishing paradise of lakes, rivers, bays, and the Gulf of Mexico nearby. Texas law requires that you have a current fishing license, which may be purchased at major sporting-goods stores such as Oshman's, at Texas Parks & Wildlife offices, and at most bait camps. None is required for crabbing. There is good fishing on several lakes such as Lake Houston (A6), Lake Conroe, and Lake Livingston. Galveston Bay is lined with piers at fishing camps, from La P~~ (E6), all the way south to Texas City, where there is a great facility for d night fishing called the Texas City Dike.

lf-day fishing in the Gulf of Mexico or in Galveston Bay is in big demand. For fishing party boat trips try the Judy Beth Fishing Boat. You may rent equipment and buy bait from the boat. You may catch many types of fish, but the most popular are such as trout, reds, drum, croaker, whiting, and flounder. The boat is at 1024 W. 2nd in Freeport, Texas, about 60 miles south of Houston. Information 225-1312.

Just a few miles south of Kemah is the village of San Leon (F6), which has a beautiful public pier with bait camp called Spillway Fishing Pier at Bayshore Park. Also in this area are several good private piers with equipment and boat ramps, which charge a nominal fee to put in.

Deep sea fishing at its best is with Galveston Party Boats, 1-409-763-5423, on Galveston Island, Pier Nineteen. To get there continue on Broadway over the causeway until you get to 19th Street. Turn left and go to the end of the wharf. This company has full-day trips daily starting in early morning. Everything is included. Seasonally you may catch the big snappers and groupers from about mid-December until mid-May. After May the good catches include ling, amberjack, dolphin, King mackerel, jack fish, and sharks. Big fish can be caught in September and October.

Surf fishing is also extremely popular on Galveston Island toward West Beach and farther toward the end of the island just before the San Luis Pass toll bridge.

Crabbing is a fun and easy family activity. You will find crabs during summer months along the bays, off the jetties in Galveston, on canals and river deltas.

Motor Boating

With your own equipment you would enjoy boating on **Lake Houston** (A6), **Lake Conroe,** and **Clear Lake** (F6), the latter being the closest to Houston. We suggest you call the Regional & District Law Office of the **Texas Parks & Wildlife Department** for details on safety rules required by the State: 931-6471.

Sailing

If you don't have your own boat, you may rent at **Clear Lake Park** (F6), NASA Road 1 just past the LBJ Space Center. This is Harris County's oldest park with a lake seven miles long. There are many facilities for children and adults, and you may rent sailboats, catamarans, wind surfboards, and canoes here. There are free public boat ramps and there is a free fishing pier as well.

If you own your own boat, you will find assorted marinas in this area all the way down NASA Rd. 1 to Galveston Bay at Seabrook and Kemah, on major area lakes, and, of course, at Galveston.

There are also boat and sailboard rentals and sailing lessons at **Gulf Coast Sailing Center** in Kemah, 1206 FM 2094; 334-5505.

Surfing

We don't promise to deliver the Oahu Pipeline, but there are areas along Seawall Boulevard on Galveston Island where surfing is permitted. During certain periods, especially the winter, the surf gets lively enough for an enjoyable ride. Call on the **Galveston Island Convention & Visitors Bureau,** 2106 Seawall Blvd., for the best locations, 1-409-763-4311.

Swimming

There are a few places where you are not allowed to swim, but they are the exception to the rule. Houstonians flock to Galveston during the spring and summer and even into early fall. There are 30 miles of public beaches, some with amenities for public convenience.

The most popular is **Stewart Beach Park**, Seawall at Broadway. It has cafes, a bathhouse, parking, a children's playground, a water coaster, restrooms, lifeguard stations, and clean wide sandy beaches with lounge chair and umbrella rentals, all within close proximity. It is also alcohol-free, which means no beer, booze, or other intoxicating beverage may be carried or consumed on that beach.

The City of Houston maintains dozens of swimming pools open to the public during the summer. See the **City of Houston Parks & Recreation Department Swimming Pools** list in the Business and Government Directory.

The downtown **YMCA** has an indoor heated pool for men and women as do the **Jewish Community Center** and the **YWCA.**

Many hotels and motels have pools, some indoors and heated.

Water Skiing

With your own equipment, there are numerous spots on rivers, lakes, and some bayous for this activity. Check with the **Clear Lake/NASA Area Chamber of Commerce** as one source of information, 488-7676. This area has many waterways such as **Clear Lake, Clear Creek, Dickinson Bayou,** and **Taylor Lake** where skiing is permitted. Also the **Galveston Island Convention & Visitors Bureau,** 2106 Seawall, has information on ski facilities on the island.

Team Sports and Other Recreational Activities

There are outlets for just about every known team sport. Some are private groups and others are under the auspices of the City Parks & Recreation Athletic Department. Most teams play either at municipal parks or at Houston Independent School District facilities.

Badminton, Houston Badminton Club; 482-3328.
Basketball League, Parks & Recreation Dept.; 845-1000.
Free Play Basketball, Fonde Recreation Center; 223-9106.
Physical Fitness, Fonde Recreation Center; 223-9106.
Softball, Parks & Recreation Department (seasonal); 845-1000.
Special Events for the Handicapped, Fonde Center; 223-9106.
Table Tennis, Joyce Byrd, Fonde Center; 223-9106.
Touch Football, Parks & Recreation (seasonal); 845-1000.
Tumbling, Fonde Center; 223-9106.
Volleyball, Fonde Center; 223-9106.

SPECIAL EVENTS

More than 500 events suggest that Houstonians celebrate, participate, indulge in, or observe all kinds of things, but particularly do they relish sports, the outdoors, the arts, ethnicity, and food.

We have selected events that occur on or about the same dates each year. Visitors and newcomers alike are encouraged to check out the following and join in the Houston style of fun.

As pointed out in the SIGHTS section, many activities throughout the year are free.

January

Auto Thrill Show, Astrodome (E2), Kirby at I-610 Loop; 799-9500. This is a long-standing popular "Destruction Derby" in which men, women, and celebrity groups drive head on, crashing into one another until the last one still rolling wins. *CH.*

February

Chinese New Year, downtown at St. Emanuel and McKinney, other locales. This traditional celebration features dragon dancers, spectacular fireworks, live entertainment, and food concessions. *NCH.*

Houston Antiques Dealers Association Show. Contact association for dates, times and location; 622-4444. Dealers arrive from all across the county to be in this highly lucrative marketplace, where buyers can shop for days, pondering everything from primitives to antique jewelry. *CH.*

Houston Livestock Show & Rodeo and Parade, Astrodomain (E2), Kirby at I-610; 799-9500. Parade downtown. This is arguably Houston's favorite annual tradition—from late February and into early March champion rodeo riders compete for big money. Superb specimens of some of the world's finest breeds of livestock are on view for judging and auctioning, and a galaxy of Country-Western music's brightest stars performs during the more than two weeks of "Go Texan Days" rodeos.

144

It begins with a huge one-of-a-kind parade that brings back the nostalgia of the old West. Proceeds go to help young people with scholarships. Livestock Show and Rodeo, CH. Midway and Parade, NCH.

Houston Supercross, Astrodome (E2), Kirby at I-610; 799-9500. This motocross features some 80 contestants in head-to-head competition for judging on how they handle all manner of obstacles. CH.

Mardi Gras in Galveston. The island celebrates what has grown into one of the nation's top week-long, pre-lenten festivals, culminating in a night parade. The Momus Parade features magnificent floats, giant walking heads, bands, and colorful performers from the United States and abroad. Also street bands, dances, live entertainment, and concessions along the route. And parties everywhere. For details call the Galveston Island Convention & Visitors Bureau, 1-409-763-4311. NCH.

Motorcycle Races, Astrodome (E2), Kirby at I-610, 799-9500. An American Motorcycle Association race in Houston brings short track and TT Steeplechase with daring jumps. CH.

March

Azalea Trail, River Oaks Garden Club Forum (F2), 2503 Westheimer; 523-2483. Houston is a horticulturist's dream with bouquets of club programs and flower shows almost year 'round.

This one is the granddaddy of them all and ranks as another must event. It is largely contained within the confines of Houston's most exclusive residential district, River Oaks. Visitors get a chance to see Houston's "silk-stocking" crowd in their formidable mansions.

Visitors may tour any or all of the seven sites selected each year, but if time is limited stop by Bayou Bend, the highpoint on the trail. CH (nominal).

St. Patrick's Day Parade, downtown. This is the largest such parade in the Southwest. It features floats, drill teams, bands, and marching units, plus celebrities. NCH.

April

Arabia Temple Shrine Circus, Astroarena; 664-7210. Eleven days of thrills, and daredevil stunts, clowns, garlanded performers, trained animals, and all the rest of circus fare at this event. CH.

Houston Astros Baseball, Astrodome (E2), Kirby at I-610; 799-9500. Houston's National League baseball team opens its annual season this month. CH.

Houston International Festival, located in several staging areas downtown; 654-8808. This expansive street festival draws artists and performers from across the nation featured in such realms as acting, dancing, singing, music and mime, plus crafts for two weeks of exciting entertainment, art shows, and fun. This civic festival draws hundreds of thousands for its impressive array of free public events as well as some paid indoor performances. Everyone gets into the act—opera, symphony, theater, ballet, ethnic groups. Houston restaurateurs set up booths purveying exotic foods as well as familiar favorites. Definitely a family affair. Charged admission in 1995, but complaints may force repeal.

River Oaks International Tennis Tournament. This is one of two world-class tennis pro tours. Their Houston stop is at the River Oaks Country Club (C2), 1600 River Oaks Blvd. The matches are in mid-April but ticket inquiries should be made starting January or no later than February. Information: 529-4321. CH. (Note: Dates subject to change.)

Westheimer Arts Festival, between the 100 and 1000 blocks of Westheimer (The Strip) (F2-3); 521-0133. A longtime favorite bash for artists and artisans from around the country. This show is semiannual, with the fall installment held in October. Arrive early as the crowds can swell to half a million over the weekend. This is a super event for good art buys, people-watching, entertainment, and extremely casual fun.

The staging area of lower Westheimer itself is something of an attraction with its sidewalk cafes, pubs, antique shops, specialty stores, and a variety of off-beat enterprises frequented by Houston's artist colony, the young, and sometimes bizarre individualists. NCH.

May

Shell Houston Open, The Woodlands Tournament Players Course in The Woodlands, just outside of Conroe, Texas, in Montgomery County off I-45 North; 367-7999. This is the big one with about 150 top golfers, many of them Hollywood celebrities, playing this nationally famous course for big ($1 million-plus) money. This is a week-long event in late April to early May and, weather permitting, the daily action is from 8 am to 6 pm. Spectator tickets through the Houston Golf Association, 367-7999. CH.

Pin Oak Charity Horse Show, This is the Blue Ribbon pageant of such events. It is a totally English show featuring 100 jumpers, five- and three-gaited Tennessee Walking horses, roadster ponies, and pleasure classes. Contact the Pin Oak Charity Horse Show Assn. at 464-1181 for dates, times and location. CH.

June

Houston Ballet, Miller Outdoor Theatre (D3), Concert Drive in Hermann Park; 520-3292. In the years that Houston Ballet has been a full professional company it has risen to international prominence. The Houston company was the first in the United States to work with the People's Republic of China in producing a world premier Chinese-theme ballet. This is one of many marvelous opportunities for visitors to join Houstonians at the great steel canopy of this theater for outdoor cultural highlights. Snacks and beverages sold, but many bring picnic dinners for a full evening of enjoyment. Tickets for the permanent seating area are distributed on a first-come, first-served basis at Miller box office. *NCH.* Otherwise there is space for thousands on the grassy hill behind the seating area.

July

Freedom Festival, Sam Houston Historical Park (J8-9), 1100 Bagby; and Bayou Park. An enormous and traditional Fourth of July celebration complete with martial music, flags, cotton candy, and a major fireworks display. A real family-oriented day and evening of fun and entertainment sprawl from this charming gas-lit park at the edge of downtown Houston to line the banks of Buffalo Bayou. *NCH.*

Houston Symphony Summer Festival, Miller Outdoor Theatre (D3), Concert Drive, Hermann Park; 520-3292. Another hit on the city's annual gala program of outdoor performances. Outstanding and versatile, the internationally cherished Houston Symphony has a history of great music conducted by world-famous maestros. On these summer nights, they usually feature a varied repertoire of fine music that sparkles under the stars. *NCH.*

August

Blessing of the Shrimp Fleet, Galveston Bay and Clear Creek Channel between the villages of Seabrook and Kemah on State Highway 146, just East of NASA Rd. 1; 488-7676. Events usually include a street dance, a shrimp-boil, and a carnival. *NCH.*

August/September

Houston Oilers Football, Astrodome (E2), Kirby at I-610; 797-1000. The "Luv Ya Blue" Oiler fan chant builds momentum about now as the Oilers National Football League team kicks off its annual season. *CH.*

Ice Capades, The Summit (F1), U.S. 59 South at Edloe; 961-9003. This brilliantly costumed and choreographed spectacular on ice is a great show for the whole family. *CH.*

October

The **Theta Charity Antique Show.** Usually around mid-October. Check local papers for dates and location. *CH.*

"Christmas in October." The auxiliary of the Harris County Medical Society holds a bazaar several days, usually in mid-October. All proceeds go to charitable causes in support of community health and medical research in Harris County.

The show consists of 75-100 unusual boutiques, with participants mainly from throughout Texas, selling a wide variety of merchandise. The idea is to create a venue whereby people can do their Christmas shopping early and under one roof . . . and for a good cause. For information, call the auxiliary at 794-0231. *NCH.*

Greek Festival, Annunciation Greek Orthodox Cathedral (F2), 3511 Yoakum; 526-5377. For three nights in a row, thousands line up to enter the cathedral grounds where they enjoy Greek music, song, and dance and put away thousands of pounds of Greek foods, wine, and rich pastries. One of Houston's oldest and most beloved ethnic festivals, the program includes an interesting guided tour of the cathedral for a look at the icons. *CH.*

Houston Grand Opera, Wortham Theater Center, 500 Texas Ave.; 546-0200. This world-famous opera company begins its formal season. The company has gained wide acclaim for its revisionist productions. Programs are sung both in English and in the traditional languages for which they were written. *CH.*

Houston Rockets Basketball, The Summit (F1), U.S. 59 South at Edloe; 627-0600. The Houston Rockets National Basketball Association team starts its pre-season here, in Greenway Plaza, in the very Houston sports arena in which it beat the New York Knicks to win the 1994 NBA championship. *CH.*

Texas Renaissance Festival, near Plantersville, 50 miles northwest of Houston; 1-800-458-3435. This recreation of fifteenth-century England draws hundreds of thousands of Houstonians and out-of-towners to a giant festival held every weekend in October. There are music, drama, games, contests, jugglers, mimes, dueling, horse races, and other events under the trees in a medieval country-village setting. *CH.*

Westheimer Arts Festival (see April events).

November

Thanksgiving Day Parade, downtown, 10 am. This is another of the highly popular parades that Houstonians and their families look forward to each year. Huge floats, balloon characters, bands, and drill teams plus celebrities highlight the parade, which culminates with the arrival of Santa Claus to announce the Holiday Season. *NCH.*

"Star of Christmas." Between Thanksgiving and New Year's days, the Burke Baker Planetarium stages a special show revolving around the Star of Bethlehem. Planetarium at the main entrance to Hermann Park, Fannin at Montrose Blvd. (D3). Ticket information 639-4600. *CH.*

December

Bluebonnet Bowl, Astrodome (E2), Kirby at I-610; 799-9500. The famous Houston Bluebonnet Bowl game on New Year's Eve is sponsored by the Greater Houston Bowl Association and the Greater Houston Partnership. *CH.*

Christmas Candlelight Tours, Sam Houston Historical Park (J8-J9), 1100 Bagby; 655-1912. Houston's oldest municipal park takes on a special charm during the holidays when the six historical homes and a minuscule church are decorated in the fashion of yesteryule. Refreshments add cheer to these evening tours for three nights in early December. *NCH.*

Dickens on the Strand is a popular recreation of Dickens' London of the 1800s. Costumes, live performances, food, and fun for the entire family on The Strand, one of Galveston Island's most historic streets. Information, 488-5942. *CH.*

The Nutcracker Suite. From mid-December to Jan. 2, the Houston Ballet presents Tchaikovsky's wondrous program oriented to the Christmas season. Performed at the Wortham Theater Center, 500 Texas Ave. Tickets go on sale about early November. Call Houston Ticket Center: 227-ARTS. *CH.*

A Presentation of Christmas Trees. Each year between Thanksgiving and New Year's, the Museum of Natural Science presents a display of decorated trees in the museum's Cullen Grand Entry (D3), main entrance to Hermann Park at Fannin and Montrose Blvd. Information: 639-4600. *NCH.*

SELF-GUIDED CITY TOURS

The Greater Houston area offers numerous points of varied interest. To touch on some of the highlights we recommend one downtown walking tour—above ground and underground—and one easy metro driving tour.

Dress comfortably, wear good walking shoes, and take along a compact umbrella in case of rain. It is fun to compare notes and exchange comments on such jaunts, so consider going with a companion. Certainly on the driving tour it will be a help to have someone along to follow map directions and read the legend. Many of the sights are covered in detail in the SIGHTS and VISUAL ARTS chapters.

DOWNTOWN WALKING TOUR

It is possible simply to walk across the street to pass from the shadows of pioneer days to space-age underground walks, to see Houston as it was and how it is. Along this path you begin with Houston's past and quickly move into Houston today where glass, chrome, and polished steel reflect ultra modern skyscrapers that give Houston the name, the "Future City."

This tour should last about three hours, depending on your pace. Your best starting times are about 9 am when it should be cooler or around 2 pm after the noon rush. If you take this tour on a weekday, you may finish off with your choice of refreshments high in the sky or a meal in a deli-type cafe.

We encourage you to pause, looking in on several buildings along the way. As walking tours go, this one is a little long, but on the return route we take you underground, where it is air conditioned.

Begin at Sam Houston Historical Park ———

If you have driven into downtown you will find convenient parking at the commercial lot just across the street from where you **begin at the southwest**

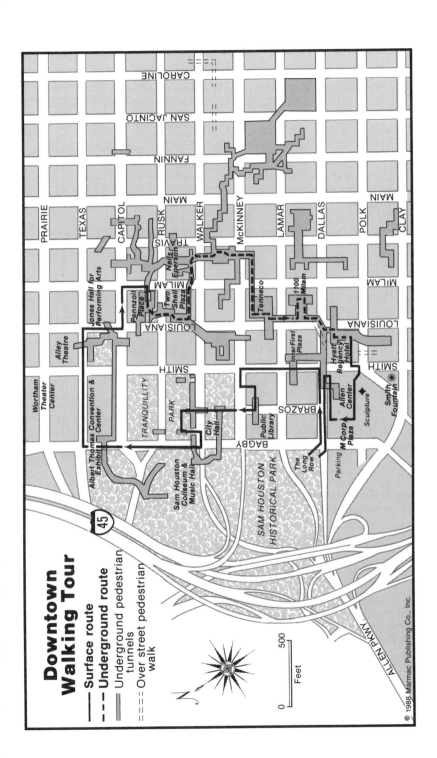

Downtown Walking Tour

— Surface route
- - - Underground route
▒ Underground pedestrian tunnels
=== Over street pedestrian walk

0   500
Feet

© 1988 Marmac Publishing Co., Inc.

corner of 1100 Bagby under the veranda of the Long Row, an exact replica of Houston's first commercial structure. This houses a "Yesteryear Shop," and the tour office of the Harris County Heritage Society. You may opt to pay a nominal charge for either a brief or extended tour of Sam Houston Historical Park, but that will add time to the estimate for our tour.

This is the city's oldest park comprising several historical structures, including Houston's earliest home on its original site, plus the city's oldest church and oldest home which have been moved to this location. Before you see the park you may want to watch a brief, free presentation that provides a good historical preface. If you have a camera, the park offers one of the best angles for shooting the downtown skyline, contrasting old against new.

Return to the Long Row on Bagby. **Go to the corner on your right then turn left and head east along Dallas.** On your right is the Doubletree Hotel. The hotel anchors one end of the Allen Center, one of several multi-million-dollar developments downtown.

Go two blocks to the corner of Dallas at Smith with the Allen Center buildings on your right. Directly across the street from that is the backside of the Hyatt Regency Houston. We will discuss this further at the conclusion of the tour.

Turn left and walk down Smith two blocks to the corner of McKinney. Across the street on the right is the 71-story, emerald-green-glass First Interstate Building. The contoured, buff-colored building across the street from that on the right is One Shell Plaza, the U.S. headquarters for that company.

Some Old-World Architecture

Turn left on McKinney. Now note the facade of the historic Julia Ideson Library and Archives on your left. Take a good look at the Spanish Renaissance style, for you won't see any more of this Old-World architecture for the remainder of the tour. This is one of the buildings we encourage you to enter, for on the first, second, and third floors are Spanish murals, changing exhibits, and an ornately carved and painted oak rotunda.

When you leave, take the side exit past the guard station on your left.

The Library and City Hall

This puts you on the plaza facing Houston's new Central Public Library, an octagonal structure with sweeping glass front and Dakota mahogany granite facing. You can't miss the large orange sculpture on the plaza. This is Claes Oldenburg's monumental piece titled *Geometric Mouse X*.

From the position of the sculpture, cross over the middle of McKinney Street to the stepped-up walk in front of City Hall.

In front of the building is Hermann Square, a popular noonday oasis for downtown workers.

You may be interested in entering this art-deco building which was remark-ably controversial for downtown when it opened in 1939. Above the cast-alu-minum doors are medallions of great lawgivers, from ancient Egypt's Akhenaten to early America's Thomas Jefferson.

As you exit, turn left and go down the steps and cross Walker Street. This puts you in the center of the approximately 20-block, multi-million-dollar Houston Civic Center. At this point you are standing over one of the Center's underground garages with parking for some 3,000 cars.

Tranquillity Park on to the Bayou

You have entered Tranquillity Park which commemorates man's moon land-ing on the Sea of Tranquillity in July 1969. In front of you there is a landscaped mound. Walk up to the left of the mound to the edge of the fountain then down the brick ramp on your left. Just ahead is a smaller grass-covered mound. Go around that to the cut-away rest area on the other side to see an authentic foot-print made from the same boot that Astronaut Neil Armstrong wore when he took that historic step onto the moon and said, "One Small Step for a Man, One Giant Leap for Mankind."

This end of the park provides another great angle for shooting the skyline, especially if the fountains are turned on and if flowering lilac and crepe myrtle are in bloom. Scanning the skyline you will see a buff-colored building with a classic cupola. This is the Niels Esperson building, Houston's first skyscraper dur-ing its first big building boom in 1927. Listen on the hour, and you may hear car-illon chimes emanating from that dome. To the left of that are the twin, trapezoidal Pennzoil Towers and, catty-corner to them, the 75-story Texas Commerce Tower.

If you walk to the other side of the park, there is a wall depicting the path of the Apollo 11 flight and the history of Tranquillity. Bronze discs embedded at the entrances to the park tell the Tranquillity story in brief in the major lan-guages of the world.

Go back to the footprint and exit up the steps leading toward the Music Hall and Sam Houston Coliseum at the corner of Walker and Bagby. Cross Bagby and go right one block past the Coliseum. On this corner between Rusk and Capitol is a small traffic island. Look to your right, and you will see a build-ing with small square windows, referred to locally as pigeon holes. This is the Federal Building, which was used during part of the filming of the life of boxer Muhammad Ali, *The Greatest*.

Move along across the street to the shade of the old oak tree just ahead to the left.

The long rectangular building you see is the Albert Thomas Convention and Exhibit Center and on this site, where the building curves, stood the old County Jail. The building was designed this way intentionally to preserve Houston's "hang-ing tree." Probably 200 years old, this tree has been the scene of several hangings.

Continue past the tree through the overhead pass on Bagby one block to the corner of Texas.

Immediately to your left is the Houston Fire Department central station, and just beyond that to the right is Houston's central U.S. Post Office. Look over the bridge railing at this corner to see Buffalo Bayou down below. This is the largest and most historical bayou in the city, for it was this waterway that prompted the city founders' idea to establish Houston for the purpose of developing a leading world port.

Now cross Bagby, turn right, and walk past the dormant Albert Thomas Hall to the corner of Smith. To your left is the Wortham Theater Center, home to both the Houston Ballet and the Houston Grand Opera. Tours available by reservation, 237-1439.

A Theater and Arts Center

On the adjacent corner to your left is the world-famous Alley Theatre, the second oldest permanent resident theater in the country. In this award-winning, fortress-looking building are two theaters, bringing the finest in professional productions to the Houston boards. Tours are available by reservation, 228-8421 or 1-800-733-SHOW.

You also get a terrific view of the Pennzoil Towers with their eight-story glass arcade in between.

Cross Smith and, continuing past the Alley, you come to the corner of Texas and Louisiana.

Across the street on the left is a beige-colored building that is the new Lancaster Hotel, one of Houston's smallest, but most luxurious. It was previously the Auditorium Hotel, housing delegates to the 1928 Democratic National Convention at which Franklin D. Roosevelt nominated Al Smith for president.

Just to the left of the Lancaster is a three-story, red-brick building that used to be the Texas Boxing Association Gymnasium, where some of our nation's greatest fighters worked out.

If you look farther down Louisiana to the left you will see a taller red-brick building with white trim, a tile rooftop, and a gazebo. This is the Hogg Building, which is named after brothers Mike and Will Hogg. The latter, together with Hugh Potter, developed the exclusive residential district, River Oaks. Miss Ima Hogg, Mike and Will's sister, had the rooftop gazebo built for entertaining friends. Miss Ima, as she was known, was one of the great ladies of Houston and a leading philanthropist. She led in forming the Houston Symphony Society, and she ultimately donated Bayou Bend, her famous River Oaks mansion, to the city as a museum of American furnishings and artifacts.

Before you leave this corner, note that Texas Avenue is somewhat wider than other downtown streets. It is 100 feet across, reportedly designed to accommodate 14 head of longhorns when cattle drives mooed through headed for market. Or to permit horse-drawn wagons to turn around without backing up. Take your pick.

Now **cross Louisiana Street** to the corner with the giant travertine marble colonnaded structure. Then **turn right and proceed down Louisiana one block to the corner of Capitol.**

This is the main entrance to the Jesse H. Jones Hall for the Performing Arts, an American Institute of Architects honorary-award winner, the home of Houston Symphony, and a venue for major touring road shows. Proceed up to the main entrance of the building and notice that it is curved; if you go inside you will see that the curve continues in the pattern of a seashell, thus the style is called "Caracol," from the Spanish for shell. At the head of stairs leading to city tunnels, parking, and offices of performing arts groups, is the bronze *Dancing Girl* by David Parsons.

If you look through the glass over the marquee, you can make out the sweeping jet stream-like sculpture called *Gemini II*. It is by artist Richard Lippold who, with the help of only one assistant, spent weeks hanging thousands of aluminum rods suspended from the ceiling on golden wires.

In the lobby below is another sculpture titled *Pair of Horses* by Robert Fowler.

On the Capitol-Louisiana corner diagonal to Jones Hall is the Western Union office surrounded by the 56-story Republic Bank Houston, which is an exciting contrast to most of the downtown buildings with its Dutch Renaissance architecture.

Turn left and walk along the Capitol Street side of Jones Hall one block to the corner of Milam.

The monumental colorful sculpture on your left is a 55-foot piece by Spanish artist Joan Miro, titled *Personage and Birds*. It enlivens the gray exterior of the Texas Commerce Tower, the tallest building in the United States outside of New York and Chicago and the world's tallest bank building. A free observation deck is on the 60th floor.

To the left behind the Texas Commerce Tower you can see the facade of the Houston Chronicle Building. The *Chronicle* is Houston's only remaining major daily paper.

Look to your right to see the original Gulf Oil Building, for years one of only two landmark skyscrapers in Houston.

Now cross Capitol to the right to the dark tinted-glass towers with sloping glass roofs.

This is the famous Pennzoil Place which prompted a leading architectural critic to acclaim that "Houston is the American future." These trapezoid-shaped towers are the creation of world-renowned architects Philip Johnson and John Burgee who, like many of their counterparts, have made Houston an architect's playground.

Return Through the Tunnels

For the return trip south, we take you into the world's longest single-level pedestrian tunnel, already more than six miles and still expanding.

This is unique as tunnels go in that each city block is privately designed, being built by the overhead buildings' owners; therefore, no two segments are identical. Some are old, while others are glimmering, mirrored corridors that have been used in sci-fi films such as *Futureworld*.

As you enter the arcade, just to your right is the escalator to the Tunnel System. **As you come off the escalator, walk straight ahead to the tunnel on the left marked "Well—Tech—Two Shell—One Shell"; enter and proceed** along the curving path south; follow the jog to the right and then to the left, straight around to still another curve to the right and then left to a junction with the East/West tunnel at the Ice Cream Parlor, under Two Shell Plaza; **turn left passing the B. Dalton bookstore,** and you will find a variety of shops and a gourmet foodstore in this mall; **proceed along this tunnel toward the Esperson Building** to another junction going North/South under the Esperson; here you **take a right at the corner** headed south and **continue straight ahead for one block,** passing under the Bank One Building, where you see another small complex of shops; continue straight ahead past the Bank One station on the right to the tunnel continuing south; this passes an energy system visible through a large window on your right; it dead ends with a tunnel going west; **go through the double glass doors and turn right,** then **proceed one block** past the Tenneco Employee Center, **through another set of glass doors where you must turn left;** this is a straight course headed south where you will see a security guard immediately on the right.

To the left is another assortment of shops with a newsstand at the center. **Proceed past the Republic Bank escalator on the left to the South Concourse** which jogs right, then left.

Go to the security-guard desk ahead on the right, and turn left into a large open mall under the 1100 Milam Building.

Go back to the guard station in the tunnel and continue on your course south just a short distance, passing several boutiques.

At the end of this tunnel you come to a junction with another East/West tunnel under the Entex Building; **turn right and go through the double glass doors straight ahead and take the escalator up.**

A View from the Top

This then brings you into the lobby of the spectacular Hyatt Regency Houston Hotel with its 350-foot high atrium lobby. To recapitulate some of the sights of the day visit the revolving "Spindletop" bar atop this hotel, where you can relax and watch the frantic traffic far below on the freeway "spaghetti bowl." An express, outside elevator is on the wall opposite the bank of inside elevators.

Continuing On

If you would rather forego the lift to the top then **exit the hotel** through the glass doors on the opposite end of the lobby **onto the motor lobby.** In the outside lobby **take a right, and at the sidewalk turn left and go one block to the corner of Polk. Then cross over Smith Street to your right.**

Here you see the R. E. "Bob" Smith fountain and beyond that is the Cullen Center, another of downtown's multi-million-dollar developments.

Walk straight ahead to the Corten steel sculpture, *High Plains Drifter* by Peter Reginato. If you stop and look back to your left here, you will see the Exxon Building just to the right of the Hyatt. From the position of the sculpture, look across the street to see Antioch Baptist Church and Park. This is Houston's oldest black church.

Now proceed past the Citicorp Building to the bronze exterior of MCorp Plaza.

Here you **turn right into the gardens behind the Doubletree Hotel,** which is on your left and the Allen Center on the right.

Walk toward Allen Center past the fountain and sunken garden then **turn right under the covered walkway** past a reflection pond.

Continue north on Smith, **turn left to the corner of Dallas** and look up here for a good view of the pink marble InterFirst bank building.

Walk to the left on Dallas past Allen Center and the Doubletree motor lobby **before arriving back at the Long Row** on the adjacent corner.

METRO DRIVING TOUR

In a couple of hours driving, you should be able to capture a very good overview of this dynamic city. You can stop midway at The Galleria for lunch. If you do, add another hour to the driving time for a total excursion of approximately three to four hours, depending on traffic.

Leaving Downtown

As in the walking tour, you may begin at Sam Houston Historical Park. Simply proceed north on Bagby to Lamar and turn left headed west.

You are now following the winding path of Buffalo Bayou on your right, which, just a few miles downstream, has been converted into a major world port. Development plans for the bayou call for a landscaped river walk, complete with boat landing, amphitheater, and other people amenities.

Watch on the right now for a small children's park on the bayou banks. About two-tenths of a mile from the park on the right is a large bronze sculpture called *The Spindle Piece,* by British artist, Henry Moore. It is directly across the street from the now-defunct Jefferson Davis charity hospitals. It was at Jeff Davis that author Jan de Hartog worked in emergency, incognito, to research his book, *Hospital.*

Coming into view on the right is a white complex, the American Rice Mill, an incongruous sight this close to downtown. With our abundant rainfall, and flat marshlands, the Houston area has proven ideal for growing rice crops, and this has served as one of the centers for milling and storage.

As you come out of the underpass up ahead, American General Companies and the office of Riviana Foods are on your left. Agricultural products and food processing are important industries in Houston. The Gus Wortham Memorial Fountain across from American General, which Wortham once headed, makes a beautiful spray like a dandelion.

Printing is another major industry here and on your left you will pass Gulf Publishing, one of the oldest such firms in town, and behind that is Gulf Printing Company, which has produced most of Houston's telephone directories.

Making the bend here around to the right you will see a marker for The Greensheet and the Center for the Retarded on the left. One of the city's oldest Jewish cemeteries, Beth Yeshurun, is directly across the street on the right.

River Oaks

At the next intersection with Shepherd are gates leading into River Oaks. This is Houston's most exclusive residential district, planned by Will Hogg and Hugh Potter. Here, the many mansions are shrouded by huge oaks, magnolias, pines, and other native and imported trees and flora, making this an idyllic, well insulated escape from the bustle of Houston.

As you enter the gates, Allen Parkway becomes Kirby Drive, then curves gently around to your left.

Go one short block and turn left onto the first street which is Troon. Follow this street around to the right two long blocks to a stop sign at the corner of Pine Valley. Turn right onto Pine Valley and proceed one block to Kirby Drive. Across Kirby you see a green esplanade, cross over to the right side of the esplanade. Now you are on Lazy Lane.

It will take you into the citadel of Houston's elegant living, called "Contentment." The Ima Hogg mansion, known today as Bayou Bend, is all but hidden from view just ahead on the right where the street address in the driveway is 2940 and 2950. These ground markers are immediately adjacent to the tip end of the rose garden just ahead. Miss Hogg was the sister of Will and Mike Hogg and for many years was a dominant influence in the cultural development of Houston. Bayou Bend is now part of the Museum of Fine Arts collection and houses one of the nation's finest collections of American artifacts and furnishings.

Continue to the end of Lazy Lane at the intersection of Inwood. Turn right on Inwood and proceed to the first stop sign at the corner of River Oaks Blvd.

As you pause here, look to your right to see the River Oaks Country Club and some of the mansions along this boulevard. It is Houston's most prestigious street and, of course, has some of the city's most expensive real estate.

Continue on Inwood until it forks, then bear right onto Willowick.

This takes you along a winding, heavily forested rustic trail, one of the most scenic streets in the district. There is an abrupt break in the trees up ahead and the end of Contentment as you come to San Felipe.

Turn right on San Felipe. There is an Exxon station across the street, which should help you identify this intersection—it is difficult to spot the street sign.

Just across the railroad tracks up ahead you come to the I-610 Loop. **Stay on San Felipe, passing under the Loop, and follow the curve around to the right then left, crossing Post Oak Road and Post Oak Lane.**

At this point note the twin tower condos on the right. These are called Four Leaf Towers and on the plaza in front is a 60-foot scuplture by Beverly Pepper titled *Polygenesis.*

Stay in the left lane and at the next light past the Towers turn left onto Sage, continue to the end and turn left on Westheimer.

A Break for Lunch ——————————————

On your right is The Galleria Complex, with numerous choices for dining. You might prefer to end the tour at this point if you are lodged in this area of town. Just past the Lord & Taylor store on Westheimer are several entrances to parking. If you're going for the remainder of the tour, **continue down Westheimer, passing The Galleria.**

Westheimer's Variety ——————————————

Westheimer is one of the longest streets in Houston and is named after the family of author David Westheimer. With miles of restaurants, nightclubs, stores, and galleries, this is the shopping, dining, and entertainment mecca of Houston and is one of the busiest streets in town.

Just past The Galleria on your right is the Neiman-Marcus flagship store in Houston. At the corner of Neiman's turn right onto Post Oak. Ahead one block on the right is the facade of the 65-story art-deco Transco Tower, the nation's tallest building outside of a central business district. In the next block on the right is the five-story Transco Fountain, known as the Water Wall, a popular stop for visitors in The Galleria area.

Proceed a short distance and move over into the far left lane in preparation to turn left onto Richmond. This avenue also is lined with a huge assortment of restaurants and nightclubs.

At Weslayan, the next major intersection, the fortress-type building to the left is the Houston Independent School District headquarters.

Farther east is a cluster of silver reflective glass buildings, the first two phases of the Greenway Plaza development. After you pass them you will see a dark glass-curtain building beyond to the right. That is Stouffer's El Presidente Hotel and behind that, out of sight, is the Houston Sports Arena (The Summit), home of the NBA champion Houston Rockets basketball team and scene of major headliner concerts.

Continue along Richmond, crossing Buffalo Speedway and Kirby. At Shepherd, turn right.

Shepherd curves around to the right, then back to the left, so just follow it

until you cross under the Southwest Freeway and over some railroad tracks; two blocks later take a left onto North Boulevard. Gradually, the trees become more dense until, toward the end of North, in a division called Broadacres, the mammoth old oaks come together over the street, forming a natural canopy. At the end of the boulevard take a right on Parkway. Proceed to the next block and notice that South Boulevard, to your right, has similar tree formations.

At Bissonnet make a left turn. Continue down Bissonnet five short blocks.

Museums and Rice U.

At that point you will see an aluminum building on the left with a sculpted Palm Tree in back. This is the contemporary Arts Museum and adjacent to that on your right is a new wing of the Museum of Fine Arts building, one of only two museums designed by famed architect Mies van de Rohe. The other is in Bonn, Germany. Pass this museum and turn right onto Main Street.

Straight ahead are the Mecom Fountains, a gift to the city from the late John Mecom, Sr., who opened the luxurious hotel on your left.

Go around the circle of fountains and continue on out Main past another old establishment neighborhood on the right called Shadyside with its privately owned streets.

At the next light, at the corner of Sunset Boulevard, look to the right and note the long tree-lined drive that leads up to the administration building of Rice University. The land for this school was willed to the city by William Marsh Rice, the man for whom the old Rice Hotel was named.

At the end of the Rice campus you come to the area of business supporting the mammoth Texas Medical Center on the left. (We will return to the Medical Center.)

Stay in the left lane, after the stoplight at Braes Bayou turn left on Kirby Drive.

Astrodomain

As you turn, you will see looming up ahead the world's first and originally the largest covered air-conditioned arena, the Astrodome or Harris County Domed Stadium. It is the home of the Houston Astros, the Oilers, college games, and many other spectacular year-round events. Daily tours are available.

Next to the Astrodome is Astrohall, actually larger in area than the Dome and the home of the Houston Livestock Show and Rodeo. It is here that thousands of delegates gather from around the globe annually to see the latest in equipment during the Offshore Technology Conference. Next to the hall is the third building in the complex, Astroarena.

At the I-610 Loop up ahead on your right is the Astrodome hotel complex. Note the dark windows along the full length of the top floor of the tower. That is the "Celestial Suite," once listed in the *Guinness Book of World Records* as the world's most expensive hotel accommodation ($3,000 per night).

Go under the Loop and turn left onto the feeder road.
Now you will pass directly in front of Six Flags AstroWorld family amusement park with more than 100 rides and shows. The overhead bridge leading into the park is the only privately owned bridge over an interstate highway. It is used by tram cars that take guests from the parking lot into the park. Next to AstroWorld is Six Flags WaterWorld, still another theme park full of rides, thrills, and water-oriented activities and eateries.

Watch now for the Fannin Street sign as you proceed down this feeder road along the freeway. Turn left at the light onto Fannin and get over into the right lane. Ahead at Fannin and Greenbriar on your left is the 30-foot Jesse H. Jones Fountain, named for the man who built 33 skyscrapers on the city's early skyline.

As you move along, note the cluster of buildings up ahead; they constitute still another major commercial development underway called Plaza del Oro.

At a fork in the road, bear right to stay on Fannin. Exit right onto Holcombe just at the point where Fannin dips into an underpass.
As you do, you may notice on the right the tall building with a stone sculpture fountain in front called *The Family*.

Proceed to the second street on the left and at the light turn left onto Bertner, which is the street with the overhead garage.

Texas Medical Center

Now you are in the world-famous Texas Medical Center, the largest of its kind in the United States. Off to the right is a pink-colored, modernistic structure which is M.D. Anderson Hospital & Tumor Institute, noted for cancer research. It is one of more than 40 different hospitals and institutions in this complex.

The first hospital on your left is St. Luke's, which is where the heart surgeon Dr. Denton Cooley is based, and next to that is Methodist Hospital, the principal point of operation for Dr. Michael DeBakey. Anyone who has read the book *Hearts* is familiar with these names and hospitals.

Bertner curves to the right, passing a vest-pocket park in front of the Religion Institute. **Drive along Bertner through Moursund and M.D. Anderson to a dead-end intersection with E. Cullen. Turn left to leave the Center.** As you turn, notice the McCollum Plaza on the right with the kinetic sculpture by Mark di Survero. **Exit, turning right onto Fannin, and stay in that lane for one long block to Outer Belt Drive. Turn right there and get in the left lane.**

As soon as you turn, notice the Hermann Hospital on the right and a statue of George Hermann to the left. He was the donor of both the hospital and Hermann Park, which you are about to enter. Continue along, passing Texas Children's Hospital on the right and next to that, set back off the road, Ben Taub General Hospital.

At the Ben Taub entrance there is a log cabin home, which is headquarters for the Daughters of the Republic of Texas. **At the sign "Zoo—Miller Theatre," make the bend to the left onto Golf Course Drive.** You will pass the Zoological Gardens on the left and the park golf clubhouse coming up on the right. **Follow the signs to Miller Theatre.**

Hermann Park

Pull up and park at the theater if you like, to stretch a bit and to take a closer look at this innovative auditorium. There are restrooms and a snack stand if you care to pause before the remainder of the tour.

Miller Theatre has permanent seating for 1,700 but many thousands show up regularly for free summer performances by Houston Grand Opera, Symphony, Ballet, Broadway musicals, Gilbert & Sullivan, and a wide range of other entertainment.

To continue, follow the small white sign pointing left toward the Zoo. Take this turn onto the one-way street one short block, then turn left again crossing back over onto Golf Course Drive. This puts you on your way out of the park.

As you proceed, note the Houston Garden Center to the right and the Planetarium and Museums of Medical Science and Natural Science.

At the park exit, there is an equestrian bronze of Gen. Sam Houston, the hero of Texas independence from Mexico.

Turn right there onto Fannin, which in one block becomes San Jacinto as it curves around to the left.

The fountain on your left is the Mecom-Rockwell Colonnade, titled the "Oracles of Delphi." The columns came from the original Miller Theatre facade.

To Return

Stay on San Jacinto. It will take you past the Sacred Heart Co-Cathedral at the I-45 elevated freeway; under the street span of the cornerstone buildings of the Houston Center; past the South Texas College of Law on the right and the Texaco Building on the left; and finally straight down to Commerce Street just this side of Buffalo Bayou where you turn left two blocks to the entrance of Allen's Landing Park where Houston was founded in 1836.

ONE-DAY EXCURSIONS

Dramatic changes in scenery and a slower paced life-style are within an easy one-hour reach north and southeast of Houston. The city sits astride a natural divide where the pine forests of northeast Texas meet the semi-tropical terrain of the upper Gulf Coast. These contrasts become more pronounced as you go farther in either direction.

Two suggested excursions offer a different mix of things to see and do, as well as a change in scenery. Our recommendations include dining experiences.

Taking these trips during early spring, adds the pleasure of seeing the highways in bloom with Texas wild flowers. The northern route's pine forests become a fantasy land with dogwoods and Texas bluebonnets, and the southeastern route weaves a patchwork of Indian paintbrush, winecups, and dandelions.

We hope you enjoy these excursions as much as do the locals who head for the hills or the coastline on weekends.

NORTH TO WOODVILLE
(7 to 8 hours or overnight)

The Alabama-Coushatta Indian Reservation –

On any highway north of Houston it doesn't take long before the coastal flat lands meet gentle rolling hills. Likewise, Houston pines are dwarfed by their country cousins in northeast Texas.

There should be no need to stop until arriving at the Reservation unless you have the urge to check out some of the roadside stands along these East Texas highways. People in pickup trucks, vans, and lean-to shelters sell everything from hot boudin (Acadian sausage made with pork, rice, and cayenne) to juicy Texas navel oranges. It's fun to poke around even if you don't buy.

Take US 59 North out of Houston and continue straight ahead.

On the edge of the city limits you will pass the town of Humble off to the right. This was the site of one of the greatest oil discoveries in Texas after the

163

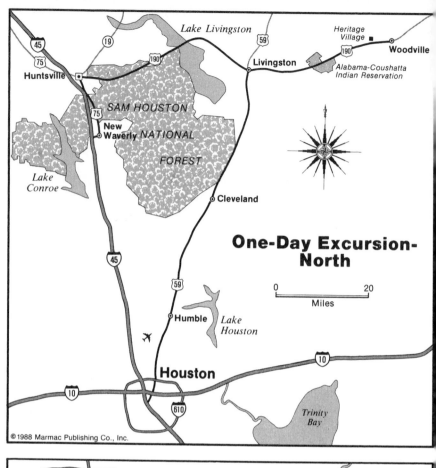

One-Day Excursion-North

0   20
Miles

© 1988 Marmac Publishing Co., Inc.

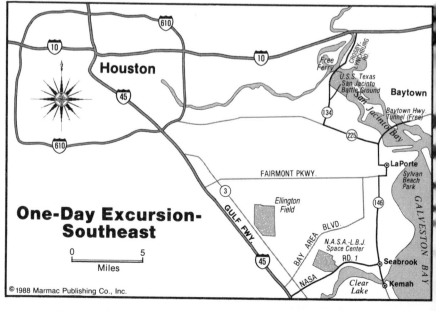

One-Day Excursion-Southeast

0   5
Miles

© 1988 Marmac Publishing Co., Inc.

history-making Lucas gusher blew in at Beaumont in 1901. Several Houston families involved in this oil boom banded together to name their company Humble Oil & Refining, later to become the giant Exxon Company U.S.A.

About 25 miles farther is the town of Cleveland, headquarters for several mammoth forestry industries such as Champion International. Here you will begin to see railcars and trucks brimming with fresh-cut logs headed for nearby mills.

After Cleveland, settle back to cruise this excellent highway to low-lying hills at Livingston, another forested town nestled between the Big Thicket National Preserve and Lake Livingston.

Be sure to take US 59 Business Route into Livingston and at the third light turn right onto US 190 East.

From here on you will see towering pines, magnolias, oaks, and palmettos growing in the Big Thicket swamps.

Watch for directional signs to the entrance of the Reservation on the right, then park in front of the museum gift shop.

The Alabama-Coushatta Indians currently number about 550, the larger of only two tribes left in Texas. They were presented their land by Gen. Sam Houston for remaining neutral in Texas' battle for independence. Today they farm and operate the "Living Indian Village." Call 1-409-563-4391.

Here you have a variety of things to see and do. Check at the ticket booth for the programs of interest. We especially urge you to take the Big Thicket tour, either on open bus or aboard the miniature train, for a close-up view of the beauty of these forests and swamps much as they existed when the Indians first arrived more than 300 years ago.

Before leaving the reservation, follow the delightful drive circling Lake Tombigbee Campgrounds. If you're driving a camper and wish to spend the night, check at the Village Office.

Heritage Village

When you exit, take a right on US 190 East and continue another 12 miles to the Heritage Village. A huge wooden overhead gateway shaped like an ox yoke is the main entrance on your left.

We suggest you have lunch at **The Pickett House,** a typical, old communal dining hall for lumberjacks. The meals are served family-style, all you can eat, for one nominal price. Guests sit together at long wooden tables, and, while waiting for lunch, it's fun to look around the walls at the impressive collection of old circus posters. Plan to arrive before noon or around 2 pm to avoid long lines, especially on weekends. Food service is from 11 am to 8 pm, seven days.

After lunch you may feel like walking a bit. At the museum and gift shop, you may purchase nominally priced tickets for the Heritage Village tour.

This restoration of an early East Texas sawmill town looks as if the townspeople suddenly abandoned it, leaving everything in place. At the center is the huge old City of Houston town clock that for many years was believed lost. It turned up here, rebuilt as the world's largest mantle clock, so enormous you can climb inside to see its inner movements.

If you decide to stay overnight **turn left from here onto US 190 East, and go one mile to the town of Woodville.** The **Woodville Inn** has comfortable rooms, swimming pool, and country breakfasts.

Returning to Houston

To return to Houston, **turn right onto US 190 West heading back toward US 59.** Turn south on US 59. To try a **different route, stay on US 190 West** a few miles until you cross Lake Livingston on the way to Huntsville. After the crossing you will be in the **Sam Houston National Forest,** another scenic drive.

Huntsville is the home of Sam Houston State University and the Texas Department of Corrections.

This town takes its place historically as the site of the homestead of Gen. Sam Houston, Texas' hero of independence. Most interesting is the architecture in the old **"Steamboat House,"** which contains his personal effects. This attraction is across the campus from Sam Houston State University.

Driving directions: After passing the prison you come to the Walker County Courthouse on the left. At the light past the Courthouse, turn left onto Sam Houston Ave. Stay on the Avenue to Sam Houston State University, which is at the third light on the left. Across the street from that is the Sam Houston Monument, which is open from 9 am to 5 pm. *NCH.*

Behind the Monticello-style museum are Sam Houston's home, his unique steamboat house, and several other structures that constitute the historical complex.

Leaving the museum, turn right on Sam Houston Ave. and continue to the overpass which is TX 19 South, connecting with Houston and New Waverly via I-45 South.

SOUTHEAST TO GALVESTON BAY

(8 to 9 hours)

If you could leave downtown Houston at about 9 am, preferably on a weekend when traffic is not so congested, and take all of the tours offered on this excursion, you could be back downtown by approximately 5:30 or 6.

NASA/Space Center

Take Jefferson, which is a crosstown one-way street southeast from downtown that puts you directly **onto I-45 South (Gulf Freeway).** After Bay Area

Blvd. **get into the right lane for the next exit will be marked "NASA— Alvin—1 mile." Exit and stay in the middle lane on the feeder road until you go under the overpass, then cloverleaf to the right** onto NASA Rd. 1 headed east. Continue for about three miles.

On your right across from the Space Center is a tall building—brick, with white trim and with mortared arches painted white. This penthouse used to be all glass and was the network pool for all television stations for shooting the exterior of NASA during the Mercury, Gemini, and Apollo space flights.

Watch for signs directing you to the entrance of the spectacular new Space Center Houston, which serves as visitor and interpretive center for the Johnson Space Center. (See SIGHTS for details.)

Allow at least 3-4 hours for visiting the center and its various activities and attractions.

Time for Lunch

Try one of Space Center Houston's eateries or leave the Space Center **turn left onto NASA Rd. 1 and head east toward Galveston Bay.**

This road curves frequently, passing Clear Lake on the right and the Lunar Planetary Institute across the street on the left. The Institute was formerly the summer home of the late Houston millionaire, Jim West. West had a ranch at the site where the Space Center is located. He sold it to Humble Oil, which later gave 1,000 acres to Rice University; Rice in turn donated the land to the US government, which then purchased more acreage to bring its land commitment up to the 1,642 acres required to build what was originally called the Manned Spacecraft Center.

As you get closer to the bay you will begin to see marinas and other water-oriented businesses. **Continue until you cross some railroad tracks, then turn right at the traffic light onto Texas 146 South.** As soon as you make the turn you'll see a tall bridge that crosses Clear Creek.

Stay in the left lane, cross over the bridge, and you will be in Kemah, an Indian word meaning "Facing the Wind." **Just across the bridge is a stoplight, turn left there and go to the end, then take another left. Go to the end** and on the right you will see a cluster of restaurants.

Beyond choices dominated by fresh seafood or fish, Kemah eateries offer variations of grandstand views of pleasure boats entering and leaving Clear Creek and Galveston Bay all year 'round.

The bay is rich in lore from the days of pirate Jean Lafitte, who headquartered at Galveston Island nearby. There are numerous known plus a few legendary treasures throughout this area. Some caches remain buried on land. Others lie at the bottom of the sea on galleons wrecked during hurricanes. The last treasure discovered in the Kemah area was a cache of gold and silver Spanish coins found in 1965. (See GALVESTON for more on pirate days.)

Old Houston Town Clock in Heritage Village *Dale Young*

Sylvan Beach Park and Sterling Home ———

Leaving here, return to Texas 146 and go back north over the bridge; continue for about five miles. Turn right at sign indicating "146 Business—¼ mile to the right"; follow to dead-end junction with Broadway; turn left; then turn right at Sylvan Beach sign onto Fairmont Parkway leading to Sylvan Beach Park. Drive through the Park, around the circle to the left, out the other end, and turn right onto Bayshore Drive. Past the church on the left, turn left onto Oak Grove for one block, right onto Park Ave. This road makes two "s" curves and crosses two small canals before you come to the Sterling mansion on the right with the historical marker in front of a hurricane fence.

This famous home was built in 1927 by Houston architect Alfred Finn for former governor Ross S. Sterling. The portico faces the bay, and in its day it was the largest home in Texas. Its 34 rooms included a dining room seating 300 for dinner. The mansion had silver and gold sconces and Tiffany chandeliers. It is an exact, one-fifth scale replica of the White House.

In the '20s and '30s this stretch between Sylvan Beach and Morgan's Point was known as the Texas "Gold coast," and at Sylvan Beach many of the great names in big bands played to high society.

San Jacinto via a Tunnel and Oil Derricks —

From the Sterling home turn around and go back south on Park Ave., across San Jacinto St. to Fairmont and turn right. Continue on Fairmont to TX 146 and turn right again. After you pass the sign that reads "Barbour's Cut," go two miles before coming to a fork in the road, just past the railroad underpass. Bear to the left to TX 225.

Shortly you will begin to spot plastics and chemical plants.

In about five miles turn right onto Texas 134 north toward the San Jacinto Battleground. Proceed north on Texas 134, which is part of the State of Texas Independence Trail. Just past a polymer plant on the right, you will see the towering San Jacinto Monument. Shortly this highway veers off to the right onto Battleground Road, leading straight to the base of the monument.

San Jacinto Battleground, Monument, and USS *Texas* ———

For a tour around the battleground, turn right at the sign with directions to Battleship Rd., just after the park gates. Drive into the **game preserve,** cross over a spillway, and go to the end at the water's edge, where there is a cul-de-sac to turn around. You will see people out in the water fishing, as this San Jacinto River is very popular with sportsmen. Turn back and go to the **Monument.** You can ride to the top of the 570' tower for a great view of the marshes stretching for miles around. On a clear day you can see downtown Houston. *CH.* The **Regional Museum of History** is at its base, *NCH.* (See SIGHTS for details on the battleground, monument, museum, and battleship).

Leaving the monument, **go to Battleship Rd. and turn right.** Follow the signs to **USS *Texas.*** Tickets are available at the foot of the gangplank.

Return to Houston

Leaving here, you will see a historical cemetery and picnic grounds along the banks of the Houston Ship Channel. At the gate **turn left onto TX 134** and shortly you will be nearly surrounded by the back bay waters and the San Jacinto River.

To cross the channel, board a ferry, one of the few remaining small, free, vintage ferries in the United States.

On the other side you will be on the Crosby-Lynchburg Road, which also is elevated above water on both sides. **When you come to I-10 East (East Freeway), cross over and turn left onto the freeway to head west back into Houston.**

Watch the overhead signs for the lane into downtown. You may take the Capitol St. exit off the freeway which puts you in the heart of downtown Houston, and over to Main Street. As you exit you will spot the massive George R. Brown Convention Center.

THE INTERNATIONAL VISITOR

In recent times Houston has been dubbed a humming world marketplace where the world beats a steady path to place its stake in the city's business and industrial circles.

Recognizing this emergence as an international gateway, Houston's civic and business leaders have taken steps to assure the international traveler a convenient, rewarding, and enjoyable stay. The U.S. Customs facilities at Houston Intercontinental Airport accommodate 1,000 foreign passenger arrivals an hour. In addition, there are directional signs in several languages and foreign currency exchange facilities.

The **Greater Houston Convention & Visitors Bureau** maintains a multilingual staff and distributes brochures in several languages at its offices at 801 Congress and at the airport.

TEXAS in the U.S.A.

Travelers Aid Society provides social services 24 hours, seven days. It offers emergency aid and translations and can put the traveler in touch with consulates, 2630 Westridge; 668-0911.

Business travel constitutes the bulk of international arrivals. Presently there are hundreds of foreign companies from more than 50 nations with offices in Houston.

But all foreign travel here is not just commercially oriented. Many visitors come to Houston for their health. The Texas Medical Center wields a sizeable impact on the city's international visitor industry. Thousands of foreign patients visit Houston annually for medical reasons. The vast network of colleges and universities contribute as well, with perhaps 10,000-plus students registered from abroad. And apart from international business people, patients, and students, more than 200,000 foreign seamen call on Houston every year via the Port of Houston.

As the city's international image grows, Houston is realizing significant increases in foreign tourism.

Of all the organizations involved in programming international visits to Houston, the forerunner is the **Institute of International Education**, 515 Post Oak Blvd.; 621-6300. The IIE works closely with the medical centers, the Greater Houston Partnership, the Port of Houston, and others in planning such visits. Under a program sponsored by the U.S. Information Agency, the IIE follows up on requests from consulates, bi-national chambers, major business firms, and others requesting assistance in planning visits for guests and specialists in such areas as medicine and education. Working parallel to the IIE is the **Houston International Protocol Alliance**, 801 Congress, Suite 270; 227-3395.

The alliance is the city's protocol office and serves as liaison with the consular corps, as well as with Houston's 12 Sister Cities and visiting dignitaries. The alliance also advises city officials, as well as the corporate and public sector, on matters of protocol and cultural sensitivities.

Consulates and Trade Offices

Houston has the fifth largest consular corps in the U.S. and the largest in the South. There are 56 consulates and 27 trade offices here. The following is the latest Houston International Protocol Alliance list of consulates, consulates-general, and honorary consulates arranged alphabetically by country. Most function as, comprise, or can direct callers to trade offices for their respective countries.

Albania, 7400 Fannin; 790-1341.
Argentina, 1990 Post Oak Blvd.; 871-8935.
Australia, 1990 Post Oak Blvd.; 629-9131.
Austria, 7887 Katy Fwy.; 688-1126.

Belgium, 2929 Allen Parkway; 529-0775.
Belize, 7101 Breen; 999-4484.
Bolivia, 8811 Westheimer; 780-8001.
Botswana, 4615 Post Oak Place; 622-1900.

Brazil, 1700 W. Loop S.; 961-3063.

Cameroon, 2711 Weslayan; 961-5263.

Chile, 1360 Post Oak Blvd.; 621-5853.

China, People's Republic of, 3417 Montrose; 524-0780.

Colombia, 2990 Richmond; 527-8919.

Costa Rica, 3000 Wilcrest; 266-0484.

Cyprus, P.O.Box 9049, Houston 77011; 928-2264.

Denmark, 5 Post Oak Park; 622-7514.

Dominican Republic, 3300 Gessner; 266-0165.

Ecuador, 4200 Westheimer; 622-1787.

Egypt, Arab Republic of, 1990 Post Oak Blvd.; 961-4915.

El Salvador, 6420 Hillcroft; 270-6239.

Finland, 2190 North Loop W.; 680-2727.

France, 2777 Allen Parkway; 528-2181.

Germany, 1330 Post Oak Blvd.; 627-7770.

Greece, 1360 Post Oak Blvd.; 840-7522.

Guatemala, 10200 Richmond; 953-9531.

Haiti, 2422-A Nantucket; 781-7407.

Honduras, 4151 Southwest Freeway; 622-4572.

Hungary, P.O.Box 27253, Houston 77227; 961-1929.

Iceland, 2348 Settlers Way; 377-6393.

Indonesia, 10900 Richmond Ave.; 785-1691.

Ireland, 2711 Weslayan; 943-2200.

Israel, One Greenway Plaza East; 627-3780.

Italy, 1300 Post Oak Blvd.; 850-7520.

Japan, 1000 Louisiana; 652-2977.

Jordan, P.O. Box 3727, Houston 77253; 224-2911.

Korea, 1990 Post Oak Blvd.; 961-0186.

Liberia, 3300 S. Gessner; 952-5959.

Malta, 654 N. Belt East; 999-1812.

Mexico, 3015 Richmond Ave.; 524-2300.

Morocco, 5555 Del Monte; 963-9110.

Netherlands, 2200 Post Oak Blvd.; 622-8000.

Nicaragua, 6300 Hillcroft; 272-9628.

Norway, 2777 Allen Parkway; 521-2900.

Panama, 24 Greenway Plaza; 622-4451.

Paraguay, 14770 Cindywood Lane; 558-9878.

Peru, 5847 San Felipe; 781-5000.

Portugal, 1100 Louisiana; 759-1188.

Saudi Arabia, 5718 Westheimer; 785-5577.

Spain, 1800 Bering Dr.; 783-6200.

Sweden, P.O.Box 899, Bellaire, TX 77402; 295-5747.

Switzerland, 1000 Louisiana; 650-0000.

Syrian Arab Republic, 5615 Richmond Ave.; 781-8860.

Tunisia, 7500 San Felipe; 782-9021.

Turkey, 1990 Post Oak Blvd.; 622-5849.

United Kingdom, 1000 Louisiana; 659-6270.

Venezuela, 2700 Post Oak Blvd.; 961-5141.

Auto Rentals

There are dozens of auto rental firms in Houston that follow standard procedure for rentals to international travelers. They require a valid driver's license, and, if you have no major credit card, passport, proof of a return ticket to your country of origin, and a cash deposit. It is advisable to ask for insurance when you take a car.

Bank Hours

Houston's banking hours are generally from 9 am to 5:30 pm. Some branches of some banks remain open on weekends as well. For Currency Exchange and International Banking, see below.

Currency Exchange and International Banking

It is possible to exchange foreign currency either at Houston Intercontinental Airport or in a bank, but to obtain the best rate, try an exchange specialist such as Thomas Cook. Some major hotels may post signs indicating the currencies they accept with current information on the daily rate of exchange, but such willingness is subject to wide and unpredictable fluctuation. See the section on LODGING for this information, but do not count too heavily on it.

At Intercontinental Airport there are foreign exchange facilities at the International Airlines Building dealing in currencies of nations linked by air with Houston, plus selected others.

Several private firms that handle foreign currency and/or buy and sell travelers checks, drafts, or gold coins include: **International Money Exchange,** 1130 Travis, 654-1900; **Thomas Cook Currency Services,** 11077 Westheimer, 782-8091; and **American Express,** 1200 McKinney, 658-1114.

Some Houston banks have international banking departments that include services such as buying and selling foreign currencies, foreign travelers checks, transfers, Eurodollar service, foreign drafts on overseas banks, foreign collections, import/export financing, acceptance financing, and issue of commercial letters of credit.

There are 39 foreign-owned banks operating in Houston. For more information and a list of these banks contact the **Greater Houston Partnership International Business Dept.** at 651-1313. In addition there are four Edge Act banks authorized to handle exclusively international commercial transactions.

Customs Allowances

Foreign nationals are allowed to bring certain items into the United States duty-free for personal use only:

One liter of alcoholic beverages per adult non-resident; 200 cigarettes, 50 cigars, or 2 kg smoking tobacco or proportionate amounts of each; articles up to $100 in value for use as bona fide gifts. Items or products made from endangered species are strictly prohibited and subject to confiscation.

It is highly recommended that international visitors learn all of the details on customs allowances before departing for the United States A handy guide is titled "Know Before You Go." You may secure a free copy by writing the **U.S. Customs District Office,** 1717 East Loop #401, Houston, TX 77029, 713-671-1000, or from your nearest U.S. Embassy or consulate.

Driving

Driving in the United States is in the right lane. You will need a valid international driver's license, which should be secured before you leave home.

Gasoline stations along the highways are usually open daily, on weekends, and in the evenings. Some, often self-service operations, remain open 24 hours. At nearly all U.S. stations, patrons enjoy the money-saving option of pumping their own gasoline.

The urban 55 m.p.h. maximum speed limit is enforced on Houston freeways and expressways. The speed limits decrease as you get into the city. Watch for posted signs to be sure you are driving at the correct speed.

In Houston you may turn right on a red light after stopping and looking in both directions; you may turn left on a red light only when turning onto a one-way street from another one-way.

Electricity

110 volts 60 cycles A.C. You will need a plug adapter and a voltage converter for foreign electrical appliances.

Hospitals—Emergency

Certain hospitals have 24-hour, fully comprehensive emergency centers.

Ben Taub (D3), 1502 Taub Loop, 791-7300; **Hermann Hospital** (D3), 6411 Fannin, 704-4000; and **Lyndon B. Johnson Hospital,** 5656 Kelley, 636-5000.

For general information on these and other hospitals call the **Greater Houston Hospital Council,** 526-9031.

In case of emergency call 911 or the **Houston Fire Dept.** paramedics ambulance service, 222-3434.

International Publications and Newspapers

Some bookstores, newsstands, universities, hotels, libraries, and consulates have international publications either to purchase or that may be read on location.

The **Central Public Library** (J9), 500 McKinney, has foreign language newspapers on the "First Floor" and magazines and journals are in different departments by subject throughout the library.

Deutsche Welt, P.O. Box 35831, Houston, 77235; 721-7277. A monthly newspaper in German.

Korean Journal, 1241 Blalock; 467-4266. Korean weekly newspaper.

Guy's News Stand (F3), 3700 Main; 528-5731. Spanish publications.

Several Chinese newspapers are available at stores and restaurants.

Medical Clinics

With the large number of foreign nationals coming to Houston for check-ups, several clinics cater to international patients. Among them are **Diagnostic**

Clinic (D3), 6448 Fannin, 797-9191; **Kelsey-Seybold** (J10), Two Houston Center, 909 Fannin, Suite 310, 654-4401; and **Kelsey-Seybold** (D3), 6624 Fannin, 791-8700.

Medical Insurance

Medical insurance should be secured prior to arrival. There is no national health service. Health care is costly and payment is often required immediately.

Money

The U.S. dollar ($) is divided into 100 cents (¢). The coins are the penny worth 1¢ (copper-colored), nickel 5¢, dime 10¢, quarter 25¢, half-dollar 50¢ (all silver-colored), and occasionally a silver dollar coin. The bills or notes are predominantly printed in green and black ink on special white paper in denominations of one dollar, five dollars, ten dollars, twenty dollars, fifty dollars, one hundred dollars, five hundred dollars and one thousand dollars.

Pharmacies

With the large number of international patients visiting Houston, it is good to know of a 24-hour pharmacy for emergency needs, and medical supply rentals such as crutches and wheelchairs.

All Night Eckerd Pharmacies.
Eckerd Drug (E1), 8062 S. Gessner; 774-6326.

Postage

Mail service is generally good, and letters can cross the country in one to three days. Zip codes must be used for guaranteed delivery. Express mail (guaranteed overnight delivery) is available. Two-day Priority Mail transports up to two pounds in two days for $3.00 with surprising dependability. Check with the nearest post office on information on rates. **Central Post Office** (H10), 401 Franklin, 227-1474 and **Sam Houston Sub-Station** (I10), 701 San Jacinto, 226-3452. Both of these are downtown. Note: Days and hours of collection vary by location.

Public Holidays

The following holidays are considered legal holidays in most businesses including government offices. Some holidays are celebrated on the closest Monday to the holiday in order to give working people a long weekend. This is indicated in the listing.

January 1, New Year's Day.
January 18, Martin Luther King Day.
February 22, George Washington's Birthday, celebrated as Presidents Day on closest Monday.
May 30, Memorial Day, celebrated on closest Monday.
July 4, Independence Day.
September, Labor Day, first Monday after first Tuesday.
November 11, Veteran's Day.
November, last Thursday, Thanksgiving Day.
December 25, Christmas.

Shopping

Several major stores have taken that extra step in catering to international travelers by employing interpreters, accepting foreign currencies, and providing rapid credit. (See the SHOPPING section for more information.)

Taxes

In Texas there is an 8.25% state sales tax on purchases except non-restaurant food and prescription medicines. There is an additional 15% tax on hotel and motel rooms in Houston.

Telephone and Telegrams

Pay phones require a 25¢ deposit. When calling long distance, first dial 1, then the area code number, then the telephone number. Telephone numbers preceded by an (800) number are toll-free. You dial 1, (800), and number.

To send a mailgram (guaranteed next-day delivery by mail and less expensive than a telegram), telegram, international message, or charge-card money order, call **Western Union,** 654-8087.

Tipping

Some businesses such as restaurants and bars automatically add a gratuity to a check, so be mindful of this and look at your bill before you pay the normal 15% tip for services rendered. Tipping may exceed the standard 15% when and if you observe that service has been exceptional. Bellhops and porters generally receive $1.00 per bag and, while it is not required here, taxi drivers appreciate a nominal tip.

Tours

Several sightseeing firms offer special tours of the city with narration in foreign languages.

Custom Convention Service, a subsidiary of Kerrville Bus Co.; 228-9449. Private tours in French.

Gray Line Tours of Houston, 223-8800. Most languages.

Translators

AE Inc. Translations, 14780 Memorial Dr.; 870-0677.

Inlingua Translation Services, 2500 West Loop South; 622-1516.

SpanTran Educational Services, 7211 Regency Square Blvd., Suite 205; 266-8805. Unusual firm evaluates foreign educational credentials for purposes of further study, immigration, employment, and professional licensure in the United States. Also certified translations of educational and non-educational documents. Deals with all languages.

The Language Co.; 952-6704. Translations and interpreters for most languages.

Transportation

Fiesta Cab, 225-2666. Bilingual drivers.

Metro Transit Information in Spanish; 635-4000.

TV Channel and Radio Stations Broadcasting in Foreign Language

Radio and television stations vary news, entertainment, and talk shows in Spanish, Mandarin Chinese, Cantonese, Vietnamese, and other languages. See local listings for current programming.

KXLN-TV Channel 45 and KTMD-TV Channel 48 broadcast almost 100% in Spanish.

METRIC CONVERSIONS

Length

1 millimeter	=	.039 inch (in.)	1 inch	=	2.54 cm.
1 centimeter	=	.39 in.	1 foot	=	0.30 m.
1 meter	=	3.28 feet (ft.)	1 yard	=	.91 m.
1 kilometer	=	.62 mile (mi.)	1 mile	=	1.61 km.

To convert miles to kilometers, multiply the number of miles by 8 and divide by 5.

Weight

			1 oz.	=	28.35 g.
1 gram	=	.04 ounce (oz.)	1 lb.	=	.45 kg.
1 kilogram	=	2.2 pounds (lbs.)	1 ton	=	.91 metric ton

Liquid

		2.11 pints (pt.)	1 pt.	=	.47 liter
1 liter	=	1.06 quarts (qt.)	1 qt.	=	.95 liter
		.26 gallon (gal.)	1 gal.	=	3.79 liters

Temperature

To convert Fahrenheit temperatures to Centigrade (Celsius): Take the Fahrenheit temperature, minus 32 and divide by 1.8 equals the Centigrade temperature.

CONVERSION CHARTS FOR CLOTHING

Dresses, coats, suits and blouses (Women)

British	10	12	14	16	18	20
American	8	10	12	14	16	18
Continental	40	42	44	46	48	50

Suits and overcoats (Men)

American/British	34	36	38	40	42	44
Continental	44	46	48	50	52	54

Shirts (Men)

American/British	14	14½	15	15½	16	16½	17	17½
Continental	36	37	38	39	40	41	42	43

Shoes (Men) for ½ sizes add ½ to preceding number

British	6	7	8	9	10	11
American	7	8	9	10	11	12
Continental	39½	40½	41½	42½	43½	44½

Shoes (Women) for ½ sizes add ½ to preceding number

British	3	4	5	6	7	8	9
American	4½	5½	6½	7½	8½	9½	10½
Continental	35	36	37	38	39	40	41

THE SPECIAL TRAVELER

SENIOR CITIZENS

Senior citizens are a vital segment of the tourist industry according to the nation's travel-market experts, who are developing programs and bus tours aimed at this sizeable and growing group of travelers.

Houston has a host of exciting things to see and do and certain amenities and special considerations will make your stay more comfortable and rewarding. For these Special People there are many services in social, recreational, and educational outlets, as well as assistance programs of every description.

As in other parts of the country, senior citizens find various establishments here offering discounts on tickets, ranging from airlines to attractions.

Few phenomena have proven flightier than airline fares.

Some **airlines** quote a significant discount off regular fares for coach class, but we suggest you be more investigative before buying to make sure you get the best possible offer.

AMTRAK may offer discounts off full fares for seniors. Check with Amtrak for details, 1-800-872-7245.

Greyhound has a terminal here. Inquire about alternatives to regular rates. 1-800-231-2222.

Metropolitan Transit Authority public bus system allows senior citizens to ride anywhere in the city at a discounted fare providing they have a Senior Citizens identification card issued by Metro. Call 635-4000 for details.

Many **movie theaters** give a discount upon such proof of senior citizenship as driver's license or Medicare card.

Most cultural performing arts groups offer discounts. Check with them for individual policies. **Houston Ballet,** 523-6300; **Houston Grand Opera,** 546-0200; **Houston Symphony,** 227-2787; **Society for the Performing Arts,** 227-5134; **Theatre Under the Stars,** 622-8887. Frequently other groups have discounts and for specific information check with a ticket company such as **Ticket Center,** 965-0161, or **Houston Ticket Co.,** 877-1555.

Newcomers with special needs will find an abundance of agencies offering varied assistance programs, ranging from nutrition to recreation.

If an emergency arises while traveling through Houston, contact **Traveler's Aid Society,** 668-0911.

Another fine agency is **Sheltering Arms,** providing telephone assurance, foster home programs, homemaker series, and casework counseling, 956-1888.

Texas Department of Human Resources Comunity Care for the Aged offers home and community-based services to help the aged remain in their own homes, as an alternative to nursing homes and hospitals. Another important aspect of their program is protective services for the physically and mentally disadvantaged, 692-3236. Ask for ABD.

For those unable to get around there is a **"Meals-on-Wheels"** service by Interfaith Ministries of Greater Houston, 520-4641.

If you need job assistance, call **Goodwill Industries,** 692-6221.

For reading materials call **"Books by Mail,"** 869-0318, of the **Houston Public Library.**

The **American Red Cross** provides transportation to and from clinics and hospitals for those with no other means.

Of course, **United Way** is the clearing house for numerous agencies and information on various types of assistance, 957-4357.

HANDICAPPED PERSONS

With today's advances in medical technology, innovative space-age aids, the multiplicity of self-help programs, the will to see the world, and new laws on their side, the handicapped are finding a very special welcome mat in most major cities in the country.

In Houston, not only the traveler, but also the newcomer will find an open-door attitude and a desire among the citizenry to accommodate the disabled in every way possible.

Handicapped persons arriving at **Intercontinental Airport** will experience little difficulty getting around. This facility has international signage clearly marking spaces for wheelchair accessibility.

The **Metropolitan Transit Authority** operates a new fleet of buses, some equipped with "lifts," and the handicapped need only call the Metro dispatcher at 225-6716 for pick-up service.

Houston has many attractions that, from the outset, were designed with the handicapped in mind.

The **Space Center Houston, Astrodome,** and **Six Flags AstroWorld** all receive excellent marks for their effort in planning and allowing for the disabled to fully enjoy their visit.

Most new hotels, restaurants, and shopping malls provide wheelchair accessibility and are increasingly barrier-free. For more complete information see the chapters on LODGING, DINING, and SHOPPING.

The City of Houston continues restructuring curbs at downtown intersections and other projects to assure that the Civic Center, parks, streets, and public buildings are wheelchair accessible and reasonably barrier-free.

Those who enjoy cultural performances will discover excellent conditions in venues such as **Jones Hall, The Summit, Wortham Theater Center,** and others.

One could spend a day or more at **Hermann Park** alone with its museums, zoo, planetarium, garden center, and other attractions and encounter few difficulties getting around.

Handicapped newcomers to Houston will find bountiful social, recreational, and educational programs available. The following are just a few suggested agencies offering a broad range of assistance.

Houston Center for Independent Living, 974-4621. Among its many key services is a TTY communications system enabling the deaf to call in on their teletype machine for a voice exchange. Job referrals, information on accessibility to buildings, and care counseling are just a few of their programs.

Lighthouse of Houston, 527-9561. This agency offers the blind vocational evaluation, instruction in the use of the cane, and how to travel independently.

Texas Rehabilitation Commission, 977-2613. With offices all over town, this group works with the physically and mentally disabled who want to enter the world of work in Houston. It serves all eligible clients except the blind.

Texas Department of Human Resources Community Care for the Aged and Disabled, 692-1635. Ask for ABD. This department provides home- and community-based services, helping the disabled to remain in their own homes as an alternative to institutional care. Alternative living plans include clusters of apartments modified for the handicapped.

Center for the Retarded, 525-8400. Apart from providing high-rise living for qualified clients, this agency assists with job counseling and a placement center. It offers a workshop for vocational rehabilitation and a day-care and training center at its Pasadena location.

All is not geared to education and community assistance, however. The **Wheel Blazers** meet once a month to learn dancing or simply to exercise.

A good central source for information and referrals is **United Way** (C3), 957-4357.

The **Coalition for Barrier Free Living** has researched a variety of stores, hotels, restaurants, apartments, theaters, and other facilities and makes recommendations, but bear in mind that this is a rapidly changing city and you should always double check on suggested locations for possible changes.

An expanding list of hotels and motor hotels offers comprehensive facilities for the handicapped. Check the LODGING chapter, contact your choice, and ask what facilities they offer guests with whatever disability concerns you.

CHILDREN

Houston holds special promise of fascinating times for the young. The city's many playgrounds, pools, watercoasters, putt-putt golf courses, rinks, pony rides, and nearby beaches all hold real appeal for children of all ages. Among primarily adult attractions that also appeal to youngsters, the following stand out:

Space Center Houston, despite evolving from a universe of high technology and NASA jargon, gears much of its effort to exciting, fascinating, and captivating children by making space science fun.

Museum of Natural Science keeps adding exhibits that youngsters love—exhibits such as the dinosaur hall and a miniature sub for oceanographic studies.

At **Hermann Park,** children delight in walking through the Aqua Tunnel entrance to the **Children's Zoo.** Also they can watch birds fly freely through a Tropical Bird House or take a miniature train ride through the park and around a lake where only children are allowed to fish. Everyone enjoys the aquarium at the Zoo entrance, and you might even plan a picnic in Hermann Park, where there is a pavilion next to the children's playground.

A day or two could be spent exploring the various theme parks at **Six Flags AstroWorld.**

Every day can be a changing world of fantasy for the kids, and what child doesn't enjoy a boat ride? Perhaps the Sam Houston excursion boat at the **Port of Houston,** or a free ferry ride across **Galveston Bay.** (See chapter on GALVESTON.)

Throughout most of the year there are plays, musical events, dance, and exhibits oriented to youth. A few such outlets include the **Alley Theatre, Houston Symphony,** the **Houston Ballet** and **Museum of Fine Arts.** Check the calendar of events for a listing of monthly happenings, available at the Greater Houston Convention & Visitors Bureau, 801 Congress.

Finally, amidst all of this space-age fantasy, rides, games, and events, you can retreat to the wilderness along nature trails and maybe catch a glimpse of small wild animals at the **Houston Arboretum and Nature Center** or **Armand Bayou Nature Preserve.**

STUDENTS

With Houston's median age only 30, it follows that there are numerous youth-oriented outlets for students from teens to 20s. There are 35 colleges and universities in the area, and the University of Houston, alone, posts a wide variety of programs year 'round.

Many discounts offered to senior citizens are available to bona fide students as well, so bear this in mind and inquire wherever you go. Invariably, valid student identification is required and must be presented in order to get a student discount.

Lodging

Houston has limited youth hostel accommodation. Contact **American Youth Hostels** at 523-1009 or 520-5332.

Days Inn (B3), 100 West Cavalcade; 869-7121. **Days Inn** (D4), 2200 S. Wayside; 928-2800. These two Days Inns of America have reasonable rates, comfortable rooms.

Days Inn (F6), 2020 NASA Rd. 1; 332-3551. Near Space Center and close to Clear Lake Park.

Grant Motor Inn (E2), 8200 South Main; 668-8000. Close to the Astrodome and AstroWorld theme park.

The Roadrunner Motor Inn Astrodome South (E2), 8500 South Main; 666-4971. Reasonably priced rooms, close to the Astrodomain/ Astroworld complex, and bowling center. Twenty-four-hour restaurant nearby.

YMCA (K9), 1600 Louisiana; 659-8501. A limited number of rooms reasonably priced. Benefits include access to the physical fitness facilities downtown.

Metro Colleges and Universities

Each campus has a student center and a director of activities, and most publish calendars and newspapers and sometimes advertise on radio and in newspapers to promote student programs of general interest.

Student travelers in Houston are often welcome to participate in a wide variety of such events. The following is a select list of area campuses with similar schedules of entertainment and recreation. Contact the student activities or program director's office for a calendar of events.

Houston Baptist University (E1), 7502 Fondren Rd.; 774-7661. This is a small liberal arts institution on Houston's southwest side, which welcomes out-of-town students to some planned activities. Good architectural museum here (see VISUAL ARTS).

Rice University (D2-3), 6100 South Main; 527-8101. Opened in 1912 as Rice Institute, this university has a history of quality education with emphasis on science, engineering, and the humanities. Its Mediterranean-style architecture and tree-shaded campus make this an interesting stop whether or not one participates in student events. Several museums of art (see VISUAL ARTS). The Rice Owls are in the Southwest Conference with home football games at Rice Stadium.

San Jacinto College Central Campus (E6), 8060 Spencer Highway, 476-1501; **North Campus** (B6), 5800 Uvalde, 458-4050; and **South Campus** (F5), 13735 Beamer, 484-1900. This is a freshman and sophomore community college with full academic, vocational, and technical programs.

Texas Southern University (D3), 3100 Cleburne; 527-7011. This is Texas' largest predominantly black and minority-oriented campus with a wide range of cultural, recreational, and entertainment activities.

University of Houston—Univ. Park (D4), 4800 Calhoun Blvd.; 743-1000.
University of Houston—Clear Lake (F6), 2700 Bay Area Blvd.; 283-7600.
University of Houston—Downtown (G10), One Main Street; 221-8000. This is the state's second largest institution, with still another campus at Victoria, and a total enrollment of over 47,000. Begun as a junior college in 1927, the University of Houston campuses offer a very large program of student activities of every description, including Southwest Conference sports.

University of St. Thomas (D3), 3800 Montrose Blvd.; 522-7911. This is Texas' largest Catholic institution and is convenient to downtown. Among its many student programs are mini-concerts at noon, major drama events, and guest artist concerts.

Popular Student Hangouts

The variety of discounts and range of entertainment in Houston's student hangouts is incredible. One club may happily tell you it offers free drinks all night on Sundays, while one movie house quotes two films for one cheap price, and all sorts of eateries and drinkeries use discounts on food, drink, dance lessons, and other gimmicks to draw youthful clientele. The majority have entertainment ranging from punk to classical and from country to reggae. Several book star entertainment. Also see DINING and NIGHTLIFE chapters.

Birraporetti's (C2), 1997 W. Gray; 529-9191. Several other locations. Italian food and Irish bar—great pizzas and meatball sandwiches. Can be loud—very popular hang-out.

Butera's (F3), 4621 Montrose Blvd.; 523-0722. (See DINING.)

Cody's Jazz Bar & Grill (D3), 3400 Montrose Blvd.; 522-9747. Big jazz bands, restaurant, bar. Very popular Happy Hour. Fantastic view of city from penthouse level—open terrace plus indoors. Packed house weekends—dressy crowd. An older group with some college age, especially early during Happy Hour.

Fitzgerald's (C3), 2706 White Oak; 862-7580. Mixed crowd of college age and older for dancing. Changing bands almost nightly (rhythm-blues, rock, etc.) Reduced drink prices for Happy Hour 4-8 pm.

Marfreless (C2), 2006 Peden Avenue (no sign, enter on McDuffie); 528-0083. Mixed crowd of college age and older. Intimate surroundings with classical music and conversation bar. No food.

Numbers (F3), 300 Westheimer; 526-6551. Saturday night younger crowd.

River Oaks Theatre (C2), 2009 W. Gray; 524-2175. Avant-garde films.

Rockefeller's (C3), 3620 Washington Blvd.; 861-9365. A star-studded concert hall that packs in all ages. Dancing in the aisles and music ranging from Puerto Rican "salsa" to Ella Fitzgerald. Cover charge.

NEW RESIDENTS

AN INTRODUCTION TO HOUSTON LIVING

Much already has been written for the newcomer, and it is our aim to offer additional information and as many referrals as possible so that you may at least have a feeling of familiarity with the terrain and climate, plus an acquaintance with some of the laws, and an idea where to drop oar in this sea of limitless possibilities.

Geographical Profile

While everyone has at least heard of Houston, many don't know what to expect in the lay-of-the-land.

Geographically, the city is situated at about 29 degrees latitude and 95 degrees longitude or on a line approximately equal with Cairo, Daytona Beach, and New Delhi. Houston sprawls across flat coastal prairie and marshes with many various size streams called bayous and creeks. Much of the northern half of the city is wooded, and the metro area encompasses several lakes including Lake Houston, Lake Conroe, and Clear Lake. The southern half is largely built over salt-grass prairies and marshlands with wooded areas along waterways in the southeastern extremes.

The altitude in Houston ranges from near sea-level to 55 feet. This means that certain areas are subject to flooding and lie in what is known as the "100-Year Flood Plain."

Houston's year-round temperature averages 68.6°F. The spring and fall seasons are delightful but brief, while summers are prolonged with mild to hot weather prevailing from March to November. During much of this time the humidity factor presents a problem for many new residents and even some of the oldtimers. The solution is air conditioning, and Houstonians burn lots of money on it to stay cool.

Thanks to abundant rainfall, Houston is green nearly year 'round and neighboring farmlands yield bountiful crops of rice, soybeans, grains, cotton, and some vegetables. Fruit and flowering trees that do well here include pecan, fig, pear, peach, crepe myrtle, mimosa, Japanese yew, magnolia, Chinese tallow, rain trees, and tapioca. Certain hardy species of palm also thrive in this semi-tropical climate. Houston's prevailing soil is a thick black clay called "gumbo," although in sections close to the coast it becomes more sandy. Because of contractions and expansions in the soil, there are scattered ground faults that can cause foundation problems. Prospective buyers need to be aware of such problems, or the potential for such problems, when considering a home site.

People Profile

Southern and Southwestern accents still prevail here, but they are joined more and more by the distinct accents of Midwesterners and Easterners who seem to predominate Houston's newcomers. The burgeoning international community, too, adds to this medley of accents, at times creating a real polyglot in malls, markets, and other people places.

Despite—or perhaps because of—the urban growth, Houstonians continue to cling to the traditional Southwestern love for the open spaces. Since the city regularly exercises its legal right to annex unincorporated communities, Houston continues to offer plenty of room for homeowners to maintain yards and gardens. Indeed, you will find few sections without well-manicured lawns and some degree of landscaping.

The more affluent districts are most exemplary of this management of surroundings. In areas such as River Oaks, property restrictions aim specifically at preserving nature and the aesthetic appeal of the neighborhood. The beautiful estates of River Oaks, Memorial, and much of the West End lend credence to this passion Houstonians have for the outdoors.

The temperate climate leads many people here to be extremely outdoor conscious. When they are not in their gardens and on their patios, they are likely involved in various other forms of recreational activity. This goes particularly for the young who account for a large portion of the populace.

In Houston you find unprecedented growth and variety among ethnic communities. A long-standing exception, however, lies in several sections that are made up predominantly of Latin Americans.

The racial mix here is 67.57% white, 17.3% black, 3.56% Asian and Pacific Islander, and 10.95% other races. The largest ethnic group is the Hispanic, regardless of race, which constitutes 20.81% of the population. The majority of foreign Houstonians originated in the Middle East, Latin America, the Caribbean, and Southeast Asia.

Houston Insight

This town is crazy about sports, particularly basketball and football, but almost any sporting event will draw a crowd. You'll find few cities where the rodeo following is as avid as it is here. During the annual Houston Livestock Show & Rodeo Houstonians nearly go overboard going Texan. And that has nothing to do with what's "in" or with trends in fashion, for just under that skin-deep layer of sophistication simmers a boisterous frontier spirit. Houstonians, especially many newcomers, willingly stampede to become born-again Wild Westerners.

A flair for casual living is sometimes disconcerting to new residents until, they too, finally relinquish their more serious ways, relaxing to let go and enjoy the Houston style. Not peculiar to Houston, but certainly a major social style, is the round-up of patio and pool parties, usually accompanied by outdoor barbecues. Of course, boating, fishing, picnicking, and other forms of outdoor recreation are popular weekend pastimes during warmer months and days. In the winter most folks turn inward to the theater and other cultural activities. Many of Houston's well-to-do still put on "tea dances" in country clubs and in some of the mansions, and these share in popularity with garden parties.

In all of Texas, folks think nothing of driving long distances, and our sense of mileage and how long it takes to get from point "A" to point "B" can be very misleading, particularly if you are an Easterner where cities are more compact and states are considerably smaller. Immediately, newcomers may be jarred by Houston's addiction to the automobile. The locals click off about 22.3 billion miles a year commuting, and this is usually with only one or two people in a car. You rarely see anyone walking, and it has been said that Houstonians are born with wheels instead of legs; the farther from the center of town you go, the more folks you see riding bumper-to-bumper up and down neighborhood arteries. The law of the West seems to prevail in spite of Texas Highway signs which remind us to "Drive Friendly." The Southwesterner's mythical rugged individualism prompts far too many to make up their own set of rules, and some drivers take to freeway traffic as if they were running a herd of cattle.

Perhaps the most amazing insight for newcomers is that Houston has somehow survived without zoning laws. This is one of the last outposts of "laissez faire," and with a lingering pioneer spirit, just about anything goes except putting up a bar too close to a church or school. Historically, Houston has shied away from, indeed fought, high-handed government interference, both in civic and private business affairs.

Social changes may erode some of this individualism. But new folks like you may be just the thing to keep it alive. Since a big part of Houston style means accepting and appreciating you for being you, welcome!

HOUSTON FACTS

Automobiles

Auto Insurance

Texas law requires drivers to carry "Minimum Liability" insurance, and you must have a **Texas Automobile Insurance Identification Card** in your possession at all times while driving. These cards are issued at the time of purchase of insurance. Such coverage is called 15-30-15 or $15,000 each person bodily injury, $30,000 each accident, and $15,000 on property damage liability. Check with the insurance agent of your choice for more details.

Auto Registration and Vehicle Inspection

Before you can obtain registration tags for your automobile you must first acquire a valid **Inspection Sticker.** The Texas Department of Public Safety requires all vehicles to pass inspection once a year through a licensed station. On approval you will be issued a VI-30-A form which you must take, together with car papers from your home state, to the **Harris County Tax Assessor and Collector.** Call 224-1919 to determine the office most convenient to you.

You must also have a valid Texas driver's license, a current odometer reading, proof of liability insurance, a sales or tax-use affidavit, and, if importing the vehicle from outside the United States, proper customs documentation before you can get Texas license plates.

When registering your car you are issued front and rear tags. Your new title will be sent in 60 to 90 days. The license fee depends on the weight of your automobile. In addition, there may also be a new resident fee, and transfer and filing fees. (Cash or money order only—no checks accepted.)

Auto, Reporting of Accidents

In an accident involving another vehicle, if you can move your car, pull over to an emergency lane and exchange insurance identification and other prescribed information.

You have 24 hours to report an accident to the Houston Police Department or to the law enforcement agency in whose jurisdiction the mishap occurs.

If there is bodily injury, remain in place and contact the emergency office of the Police Department, 911 or 222-3131; or dial the operator for emergency assistance.

If it appears that the other party is intoxicated on alcohol or on drugs or can show no valid driver's license, you must report the incident immediately.

Should you require emergency ambulance service, call the **Houston Fire Department** paramedics division at **911** or **222-3434**; or dial the operator for assistance.

Driver's Licenses

Out-of-state drivers have 30 days after establishing residency in which to obtain a Texas driver's license. The basic license to operate a motor vehicle is valid for four years (it expires on your birthday) and costs $16 (personal check accepted). There are Texas Department of Public Safety licensing offices for testing throughout the city. For license information call 681-6187; for the location and hours of the nearest DPS driver's license office call 957-6196.

Banking ───────────────────────────

Houston is a leading banking center in the Southwest, and the Houston-Galveston SCSA ranks high among the nation's metropolitan areas in total deposits. The Federal Deposit Insurance Corporation reports that as of June 1993, Harris County's 96 commercial banks with 505 offices had total deposits exceeding $28.1 billion. Every conceivable financial service is rendered, catering to all domestic and foreign needs. For answers to specific banking questions go to the bank most convenient to you or call the **Texas Bank Association** in Austin; 512-472-8388.

Chambers of Commerce ──────────────

Chambers of Commerce are ideal sources of general information for newcomers and prospective home buyers. They are vital to the development of business, and most companies subscribe to their many services to the community.

The following is a list of chambers in principal areas of metropolitan Houston:

Alief-Southwest Houston C of C, 498-6071.
Bellaire C of C, 666-1521.
Clear Lake Area C of C, 488-7676.
Deer Park C of C, 479-1559.
Friendswood C of C, 482-3329.
Galena Park C of C, 672-6443.
Greater Houston Partnership (Houston C of C), 651-1313.
Houston Citizen's C of C, 522-9745.

Houston Northwest C of C, 440-4160.
Houston West C of C, 785-4922.
Katy C of C, 391-2422.
North Channel Area C of C, 452-2800.
Pasadena C of C, 487-7871.
Pearland C of C, 485-3634.
South Montgomery County—Woodlands C of C, 367-5777.
Tomball Area C of C, 351-7222.

Churches, Synagogues, and Temples ─────────

Practically every religious denomination in the world is represented in Houston with more than 1,000 churches, synagogues, temples, mosques, and ecumenical chapels.

The **Houston Metropolitan Ministries Association** has a listing of its members including most Christian and Jewish groups; 520-4603. It operates as a coalition to work on social projects helping jail inmates, Senior Citizens, youths, and refugees.

Among the major denominational and ecumenical organizations here are:

Assemblies of God South Texas District Council; 455-1221.

Beth Yeshurun (conservative); 666-1881.

Church of Jesus Christ of Latter Day Saints—Texas Houston Mission; 440-6770.

Eastern Orthodox Church;721-3824.

Episcopal Diocese of Texas; 520-6444.

Islamic Society of Greater Houston; 524-6615.

Lutheran Council—Houston Area; 864-6987.

Methodist Board of Missions of Texas; 521-9383.

Presbytery of the New Covenant; 524-6632.

Roman Catholic Diocese of Galveston-Houston; 659-5461.

Rothko Chapel (ecumenical); 524-9839.

Sri Meenakshi Temple Society of Houston (Hindu); 489-0358.

St. Basil's Byzantine Rite Center (Ukrainian); 697-7109.

Temple Emanu El (Reformed); 529-5771.

Texas Baptist Convention; 674-9091.

Theosophical Society—Houston Branch—Non-Denominational; 861-8526.

Union Baptist Association—SBC; 957-2000.

United Orthodox Synagogues; 723-3850.

Clubs and Associations ─────────────

Once you've settled down in Houston and want to get involved in any community activity, whether social, educational, recreational, or civic, you may not know where to begin the search. It helps to know your neighbors and your community leaders who can steer you in the right direction with area civic organizations.

The **Greater Houston Partnership Publications Department** maintains a roster of women's clubs and downtown service organizations; 651-1313.

Sports enthusiasts may want to link up with little leagues, ski clubs, or maybe join a private golf or tennis club. For details on such contacts see the chapter on SPORTS.

There are various art groups in the city such as the **Art League of Houston,** 523-9530.

The **YMCA, YWCA,** and their branches are always great places to become involved in dance groups, exercise, and other special programs, as is the **Jewish Community Center.**

The **Houston Zoo** has a society of friends of animals; you may patronize museum organizations or other cultural groups such as the **Houston Friends of Music,** the symphony, opera, or ballet, or begin a dig with one of the garden clubs such as **River Oaks Garden Club Forum of Civics** and the **Houston Garden Center.**

Senior Citizens may wish to become involved with the **Golden Years Council,** and single parents may inquire of the orientation programs presented by **Parents Without Partners of Greater Houston;** 663-7971.

Education

Schools, Primary and Secondary

There are 23 school districts partly or entirely within Harris County, with the **Houston Independent School District** accounting for some 200,000 students, the fifth largest district in the United States with more than 240 schools.

Education is free in Texas for children from kindergarten through the 12th grade. Most systems have four levels of education, including elementary (grades K, 1-6), middle school (grades 6-7), junior high (grades 8-9), and high school (grades 9/10-12). The HISD has the most extensive magnet school program of any school district in the area. There are 88 such programs available at every level, plus Vanguard programs for the gifted, and remedial classes for the handicapped. Several HISD schools operate solely under the magnet program system such as the **High School for the Performing and Visual Arts,** the **High School for Health Professions,** and the **High School for Law Enforcement and Criminal Justice.**

School programs are funded by the state of Texas and, in Houston, by school taxes assessed on property.

Newcomer students must have a birth certificate or equivalent, doctor's certification of immunization, and a final report card from the last school attended.

For more detailed information on **HISD** call 892-6390.

Another 25,000 students are enrolled in non-public schools, one-fourth of which are parochial. Among the major denominational schools are those run by the **Galveston-Houston Catholic Diocese,** 659-5461; the **Episcopal Diocese of Texas,** 520-6444; **Lutheran High School,** 645-4178; **Union Baptist,** 984-2327.

Schools for the deaf and handicapped are **Houston School for Deaf Children,** 523-3633; **St. Dominic's Deaf Center,** 741-8721; **Speech and Hearing Institute,** 792-4500; **Center for the Retarded,** 525-8400.

For information on child care contact the **Child Care Council of Greater Houston,** 266-6045.

For information on the name and number of the school district that serves your preferred area of relocation, call the closest community chamber of commerce. Then be sure to investigate the school program thoroughly, as it can be a major factor in determining where you buy or rent.

Colleges and Universities

Houston is a major center for higher education with 26 colleges and universities in Harris County.

The senior institutions are the **University of Houston** (University Park, Downtown, Clear Lake and Victoria), 749-1011; **Rice University, 527-8101; Texas Southern University, 527-7011; University of St. Thomas (Catholic),** 522-7911; **Houston Baptist University, 774-7661; South Texas College of Law,** 659-8040.

Junior colleges are: **Houston Community College System,** 265-5343; **Lee College in Baytown,** 427-5611; **San Jacinto College** (three campuses), 476-1501; and **North Harris-Montgomery County College District,** 591-3500.

Houston is famous for a number of major medical schools, most of which are within the vast Texas Medical Center complex. While practically every institution in the Center maintains some form of education and training program, the leading colleges and universities are **Baylor College of Medicine, Prairie View A & M School of Nursing, Texas Heart Institute, Texas Institute for Rehabilitation and Research, Texas Research Institute of Mental Sciences, Texas Woman's University, University of Houston College of Pharmacy, University of Texas Health Science Center,** and the **University of Texas System Cancer Center.**

Still other medical schools are on the periphery of the Center.

In addition there are several theological schools here such as **Gulf Coast Bible College, St. Mary's Seminary, Southern Bible College,** and **Texas Bible College.**

Extra-Curricular Educational Programs

At some time in life many would like a refresher course or an opportunity to learn something entirely new, say, art, a foreign language, photography, word processing, or real estate. Various colleges and universities provide such opportunities, as do community centers.

These are available during the fall, spring, and summer for nominal fees. For information call the school of your choice.

Government —————————————————————

City Government

The City of Houston is governed by a mayor and 14 council members who, together with a city controller, are elected every two years. Nine of the members represent their own districts, while five are council members at large.

The public is invited to appear before Council with problems, complaints, or other matters, every Wednesday in **Council Chambers at City Hall** (J9), 901 Bagby, starting at 9 am. Each person is allowed from one to three minutes to state a case. You may reserve time by calling 247-1840 (City Secretary's Office).

Houston government is officially independent of political party alignment, and city employees have a choice of belonging to a municipal union or not. The police and firemen have stronger union links. They may not, however, strike.

Labor unions in general are comparatively small here, primarily because Texas still is a "Right to Work State."

County Government

Harris County is governed by a county judge and four commissioners elected by the citizenry every four years. They are all members of the County Commissioners Court.

Congressional Districts

Metropolitan Houston according to the 1990 census has six Congressional districts.

Those districts are: **District 7** whose precincts include parts of the southwest side of the city; **District 8** generally covering the northeast quadrant including Spring, North Shore, Aldine, Baytown, Deer Park, and a northern part of the city of Pasadena; **District 18** covering everything from about Sims Bayou to Tidwell Road and from the Houston Ship Channel to Buffalo Bayou and on over to Kirby Drive; **District 22** which covers the southeastern portion, including part of Clear Lake and all of Ft. Bend and Brazoria counties; and **District 25** with precincts in the southwest, Medical Center, and Astrodome area, Sunnyside, part of Pasadena and Deer Park, all of La Porte, the Southeast corridor, and the NASA-Clear Lake area; and **District 29.**

U.S. Senators from Texas

Senator Kay Bailey Hutchison, Republican, 1919 Smith; 653-3456 (Houston), and (202) 224-5922 (Washington D.C.).

Senator Phil Gramm, Republican, 712 Main; 229-2766 (Houston), and (202) 224-2934 (Washington D.C.).

Both of the Houston offices are downtown.

Health Care

Houston is known the world over for its excellence in health care, medical research, and specialization in certain surgical techniques. In Harris County alone there are more than 60 hospitals with 19,000 beds. In addition there are numerous convalescent homes and children's care institutions.

Several Houston pilot programs have spread throughout the nation. One is the Houston Fire Department paramedics teams with specially built and equipped ambulances. Another is Hermann Hospital's "Life Flight" program, which provides emergency medical transport via helicopters and small jet airplanes.

Among hospitals with 24-hour emergency care are:

Bellaire General, 669-4040.
Ben Taub General, 793-2000.
Hermann Hospital, 797-4060.
Lyndon B. Johnson General, 636-5000.
Spring Branch Memorial, 467-6555.
Twelve Oaks Hospital, 623-2500.

Among hospitals and clinics with full services are also many with established specialties, such as cancer treatment, plastic surgery, treatment of psychiatric disorders, drug and alcohol abuse, children's diseases, and rehabilitation.

The following is a select list of hospitals by locale:

Northwest—Memorial Hospital NW, 867-2000.
Southeast—Memorial Hospital SE, 929-6100; 1 Humana Clear Lake Hospital, 332-2511.
Southwest—Bellaire General, 669-4000; Memorial Hospital SW, 776-5000; Rosewood General, 780-7900; Twelve Oaks Hospital, 623-2500; and Westbury Hospital, 729-1111.
South and Central—Park Plaza Hospital, 527-5000; St. Joseph's Hospital, 757-1000; Methodist Hospital, 790-3311; Medical Center del Oro Hospital, 790-8100; St. Luke's, 791-2011; Hermann, 797-4100; and Texas Children's Hospital, 791-2831.
Spring-Tomball—Parkway Hospital, 697-2831.
Richmond-Rosenberg—Polly Ryon Memorial Hospital, 342-2811.

Information, emergency, and referral organizations throughout Houston cover various areas of specialization:

Crisis Hotline (counseling and referrals), 350-0700. Bay area, 333-5111.
Greater Houston Hospital Council, 526-9031.
Harris County Hospital District, 793-4243.
Harris County Medical Society (doctor referrals), 790-1885.
Houston Dental Society, 961-4337.
Houston Health Department (private ambulance information), 794-9645.
Poison Control Center of Southeast Texas, 654-1701.

Home Decorating

Several major department stores have interior design studios in their branches as do some of the fine furniture outlets.

They include **Foley's, Dillard's** and **Sears Roebuck.**

You may prefer to hire the services of an interior design expert and, if you take your designer along, you may stop by the **Decorator's Walk** decorative center at 5120 Woodway where there are more than 30 different showrooms for both commercial and residential design. This is a wholesale to-the-trade-only outlet; 629-6340.

Jury Duty

Juries are called on weekdays for civil and criminal cases.

The selection is made from the driver's license list.

Persons 65 or older are, if they wish, exempt from serving jury duty. Also a parent with a child under 10, who has no way of leaving the child at home with proper supervision, is exempted. Other possible exemptions include those attending school (at any level), and the infirm. Persons may call in and request an "excuse slip" and such requests are handled individually. Information: 755-5000.

Legal Services

For reference, the **Harris County Bar Association** is available to mediate minor legal disputes; 236-8000.

The **Houston Lawyer Referral Service** can assist with the selection of an attorney, and there is a nominal consultant's fee; 237-9429.

Libraries

The administrative offices for the city library system are downtown at the **Central Public Library** (J9), 500 McKinney; 247-2222. There are 34 branch libraries. Services include books by mail and bookmobiles. The Central Library has ongoing programs of educational and cultural interest to the community; call for a schedule of events.

In addition **Harris County** maintains 23 libraries with administrative offices at 8080 El Rio; 749-9000. The system includes a bookmobile.

Local Laws

Texas, like every state, has laws special unto itself.

Liquor Laws

Certain establishments have beer, wine, and champagne only permits while others are licensed to sell mixed drinks. Most bars operate with full services, including the sale of mixed drinks, and remain open until the absolute curfew which is 2 am daily. No business may begin selling alcoholic beverages on Sundays until after 12 noon. Those places without late-hour permit must stop serving at 1 am on weekends and by midnight weekdays. Bars with beer, wine, and champagne only permits usually sell "set ups," and customers may bring hard liquor in their own bottle, but it must be concealed in a "brown bag" and poured personally.

Certain areas in and around the city are "dry" by choice and no alcoholic beverages are sold whatsoever.

Package stores are open from 10 am to 9 pm daily, except on Sundays and certain holidays such as Christmas. When Christmas and New Year's days fall on Sunday, then liquor stores must remain closed for the following Monday.

The minimum legal age to order, buy, possess, or consume any alcoholic beverage in Texas is 21, including the military.

Property Laws

The following laws should be checked with an attorney for Houston/Texas variations:

Community Property—Texas enforces this law because of its strong Spanish-Colonial influence; **Dower; Curtesy; Eminent Domain; Easements; Homestead Rights; Deed Restrictions,** which various civic groups establish and record for protection against commercial encroachments in residential areas. The latter is something to check out thoroughly before purchasing a home or property for a home.

Property Taxes—Homeowners have the responsibility to keep the tax departments of the city and county informed of any changes in address or status in ownership, and must also see to it that a proper tax bill is forthcoming. Failure to receive such a bill is no excuse for not paying taxes, and failure to pay on time results in the owner being assessed a fine plus interest on each month remaining unpaid.

Owners have the right to request appointment to render the value of their property as assessed and may call for a hearing within a time prescribed by the city; 892-7700.

Property Tax Exemptions—An owner using his home for no purpose other than as a residence may apply for a "Homestead" tax exemption with the city and the county on an annual renewal basis. Call the **Harris County Appraisal District** for details, 957-7800; or the **County Tax Assessor/Collector,** 224-1919. Other exemptions are also available. A property owner over the age of 65 and/or totally disabled may qualify for special tax exemptions.

Rentals—Contact the **Houston Apartment Association,** 933-2224, for information. You should know, however, that if you sign an application to rent that binds you to an agreement, then change your mind, the landlord may not have to return your deposit. Know before you sign.

Medical (see Health Care)

Newspapers and Publications

Houston has one major daily newspaper plus numerous weekly and monthly publications serving various neighborhoods, the city, and the metro region plus special interest groups.

The major local newspaper is the **Houston Chronicle** (I10), 801 Texas Ave.; 220-7171, with weekday, Saturday, and Sunday editions.

The leading weekly is the tabloid **Houston Business Journal**; 688-8811. This was the first of its genre.

The **Greensheet** is Houston's most widely circulated free "want ads" paper; 655-3100.

There are two black-oriented newspapers: The **Forward Times**, 526-4727, and the **Informer,** 527-8261.

Two leading Spanish language publications are **El Sol,** 224-0616, and **La Voz,** 644-7449.

Serving Houston's Asian community are the **Chinese Daily News,** 771-4363, and the **Korean Journal,** 467-4266.

The Greater Houston Partnership compiles a **Houston Area Media Guide** to local and neighborhood publications; 651-1313.

Pets

The law requires that pets be properly licensed and vaccinated against rabies. Leash laws are in effect in Houston, and if violated the owner is subject to fine.

For information, contact the **Harris County Rabies Control Center,** 999-3191, and the **City of Houston** for more specifics on owning pets, 547-9400.

The **Houston Humane Society** is located at 14700 Almeda; 433-6421.

The **Society for Prevention of Cruelty to Animals** is at 519 Studemont; 869-8227.

Public Services

Houston's utilities are supplied by **Houston Lighting and Power Company,** 228-7400; **Southwestern Bell Telephone Company,** 1-800-499-7928; **Entex** (gas), 659-2111; **City of Houston Water Division,** 754-0500; **City of Houston Sewer Repair,** 754-0509; and **City of Houston Solid Waste Management Department** (garbage and trash pick-up), 865-4100.

There are private companies serving some outlying areas.

Deposits are required of newcomers with no former record of service, and there is a start-up fee as well. These vary according to each individual case. An advance notice is required to start services.

Free garbage pick-up is twice weekly in Houston and for unusual loads the city takes requests for special handling; 699-1114.

Regular garbage must be bagged securely in plastic.

Most garbage collections are curbside, or, in some neighborhoods, in alleys. New residents should call to find out which are the pick-up days for their area. Residents outside the city of Houston usually get water and sewer services by contract with independent districts.

Residential Cleaning

In Houston there are a number of major firms catering to personal cleaning needs. Bonded and licensed by law, they go beyond cleaning and can assist with party help in bartending and sprucing up the garden, as well as providing cooks, butlers, and even chauffeurs and companions for the elderly.

Maid In Houston (serving the Greater Houston area); 266-3400.

Associated Building Services, 227-1261.

Taxes

City/State

Many newcomers are happy to learn that Texas has no state, county, or city income tax. Our sales taxes are 8.25% from which most food and prescription drugs are exempt. One percent of that sales tax goes to the Metropolitan Transit Authority. Of the remaining monies, 6.25% goes to the state and 1% to the city. Information, 868-9112.

The city tax rate on land and real estate is 63 cents per $100 value. The city also collects taxes for the Houston Independent School district and that rate is 47 cents per $100. For further information call the **City Tax Department** at 892-7700.

County

At this writing, the county property tax rate on land and real estate is 60.032 cents per $100, with the owner paying 100% of assessed valuation. For further information call the **Tax Assessor and Collector's office**; 224-1919.

Legally declared homesteads qualify for exemptions of about 20% of assessed valuation.

TV and Radio
(see MATTERS OF FACT chapter)

Volunteering

If you have a special gift and a sense of service, opportunities to serve abound in Houston.

You may consider the following suggested areas in which to volunteer your services:

Big Brothers and Sisters of Houston; 468-8010.
Harris County Heritage Society Preservation Alliance; 655-1912.
Greater Houston Chapter of the American Red Cross; 526-8300.
United Way of the Texas Gulf Coast; 685-2300.

With Houston's large medical center complex, hospitals are always in need of various volunteer services. If you have a special gift in foreign languages, numerous patients from around the world come to Houston for treatment; and you might consider translation/interpretation services.

Consider being an usher in one of the city's theaters or training to become a docent or guide in a museum, visitor attraction, or nature center.

If you are sincerely interested in volunteering, it won't be long before you find your niche by inquiring around.

Voting

Citizens may apply for a Voter's Registration Certificate. Voting rights become effective 30 days after receipt of the application by the tax office. Once a valid certificate is received, it remains permanent, but a change of domicile must be reported; a new certificate is then issued. A new certificate is automatically issued every two years if the voter does not become disqualified. Voters are disqualified when they move and leave no forwarding address. Application is made through the office of the **Harris County Tax Assessor-Collector** (H10), 1001 Preston; 224-1919. Voting is done by precinct.

The **League of Women Voters** can be most helpful with voter's guide and other information prior to elections; 784-2923.

HOUSTON REAL ESTATE

An Overview

There are more than 500 subdivisions with building activity in Houston, the majority being in the outlying areas and in particular the west, southwest, and northwest regions extending out some 20-plus miles into other counties in the metro region.

The median home price in 1992 ran $80,349. According to the latest statistics, the average income in the Houston-Galveston area per household after taxes is nearly $44,600.

Throughout the city and in surrounding metropolitan areas the buyer will find a wide variety of homes, in style and in size, and the prices range accordingly. Most newer homes are a combination of wood and brick, and the majority are on concrete slabs and have central air conditioning and heating. Sizes generally range from 1200 square feet up.

Information and Referrals

There is a host of both civic and private sources with information, leads, consultation services, and referrals, some free and some by fee.

But first we would like to mention that many Houston hotels and motor hotels may offer special "relocation rates" for newcomers who wisely take their time to shop around and investigate before making the plunge into buying a home. Contact individual hotels or motels for details.

Other good sources of information on Houston are:

The **Better Business Bureau** (Consumer Protection Division); 868-9500.

Chamber of Commerce Division of the Greater Houston Partnership (Houston facts and newcomer data); 651-2100.

CSC Credit Services; 878-1900.

Federal Housing Administration/U.S. Dept. of Housing & Urban Development; 653-3274.

Greater Houston Builders Association (information on builders); 776-1445.

Greater Houston Convention & Visitors Bureau (lodging and other general information on Houston); 227-3100.

Harris County Flood Control (information on flood plain); 684-4000.

Houston Apartment Association (information on types of apartments available); 933-2224.

Houston Association of Realtors (information on realtors); 629-1900.

Houston Air Quality Control; 640-4200.

Houston Public Library (various referrals); 247-2222.

State Department of Human Services (information on licensed care facilities); 526-3531.

Texas Attorney General (Consumer Protection Division); 223-5886.

Travelers Aid Society (all types of emergency services); 668-0911.

United Way (information and referral services); 957-4357.

Veterans Affairs Department (benefits and assistance); 664-4664.

Buying and Renting

Apart from the desirability in a home and its cost, the new home buyer should make a close study of several variables before entering into a contract to purchase. Important considerations include the proximity of the place of employment; the disposition of the school district, and the availability of college prep programs, higher education, and libraries; the tax structure; the type of insurance required; the existence of deed restrictions; land level and soil conditions; and the availability of shops, churches, schools, and public transportation.

When searching for a home you may see the HOW seal. This is a good indication since, for a builder to qualify for the Home Owners Warranty approval, he must meet certain high-level performance standards in materials and workmanship.

In Houston the renter will find everything from garage apartments to luxury townhomes. Some older neighborhoods have duplexes and four-plexes with efficiency apartments in back. In addition, in areas such as Montrose and the Heights where many old houses have been torn down to make way for apartment complexes and townhomes, there are numerous attractive patio dwellings with clubs and recreational facilities popular with young professionals. This type of complex is also widely available in much of the West End where many singles reside.

The overall average rent in Houston ranges around $450 per month for a 2-bedroom/1 bath, good-quality apartment.

Regional and Neighborhood Profiles

The following is an analysis for familiarization with certain sections of metropolitan Houston. However, this section in no way pretends to fully define the vast environs of Houston with its hundreds of new subdivisions plus older neighborhoods. For a comprehensive understanding of what the city has to offer, read all available newcomer material, the newspapers, and magazines oriented toward Houston living, and, of course, confer with your realtor or an independent locator service firm.

In order to understand the layout of Houston, imagine, if you will, one loop circling the city at a radius of approximately six miles from the Central Business District. This is Interstate 610, referred to as "The Loop." For the purpose of locating and referencing, specific points are either "inside the loop" or "outside the loop."

Southwest Region—Inside the Loop

This vast region encompasses an area from near downtown all the way out west some 20-30 miles into Ft. Bend County, and includes many separate villages and incorporated communities. The southwest sector has long been among the most active areas of the city for the development of planned communities and subdivisions, particularly at its southwestern extremity bordering Ft. Bend County.

The Montrose area is closest in to downtown. There are many older homes dating back some 60 years with an enormous mix of single-family dwellings, townhouses, condos, and two-story brick duplexes, four-plexes, and garage apartments for rent. This area has been under vigorous restoration for the past 20-30 years with many young couples and singles moving in to refurbish and expand existing structures. It offers unique urban home sites in neighborhoods interspersed with a potpourri of commercial interests. It is a highly mobile area with many tree-lined streets, and its inhabitants cover a wide range of the social strata.

West of the Montrose lies **River Oaks,** Houston's bastion of wealthy citizens, whose mansions rival anything in Beverly Hills. A board of directors maintains stringent deed restrictions governing everything from the height of a hedge to putting up signs. The area is dense with foliage, and the winding streets are lined with huge old oaks and magnolias. It generally parallels the path of Buffalo Bayou. At the outset, River Oaks was carefully planned for the preservation of the natural environment and to protect it against commercial encroachment or other threats to residential planning.

Residents of the neighborhood enjoy elite social and fine recreational outlets as found in the River Oaks Country Club. Relative security is enforced by an auxiliary police force.

Just north of River Oaks and on the eastern edge of the city's largest park, **Memorial,** are several smaller quiet neighborhoods dating from the post World War II era. Such are **Crestwood** and **Glencove,** with family dwellings nestled away in the beautiful park surroundings with many trees along the bayou.

These sections have their own small shopping outlets nearby plus the facility of fast commuting into downtown.

Southward across the Southwest Freeway are still other fine old neighborhoods such as **Southampton** and the area known as **Rice University Village** or, more often and more simply, the Village. Southampton is especially majestic with massive oaks spreading across quiet streets with esplanades and large estates with formal gardens and pools.

The homes in the Village area are somewhat smaller but still offer a mix of lovely two-story dwellings with a wide variety of architectural styles. They range from modest one-story frame family homes to two-story brick executive-type structures.

The area is especially popular with students and faculty at nearby Rice University and professionals and staff at the Texas Medical Center. The Village has one of Houston's most provocative commercial centers with many unique boutiques, cafes, stores, and galleries.

The city of Houston has grown to envelop a number of smaller, incorporated communities, and two of them fall within the boundaries of this region, both inside and outside the Loop.

Typically, **West University Place** is a quiet older residential district, well planned and minus much traffic beyond a couple of key arteries. Most of the homes are one- and two-story handsome frame and brick structures with well-manicured lawns, as are the homes in the adjoining **South Side Place.**

The **City of Bellaire** straddles the Loop, and it, too, is an old residential community with many modest frame homes and some brick. As in other areas, Bellaire too is becoming popular with young move-ins who prefer to take a house in need of repairs and remodel according to their own designs. Many others have bought, demolished, and completely rebuilt just because they like the location. Some have bought multiple adjacent lots to site one house.

South of these communities is a section of one of the most lovely swaths of home sites found in the city, extending as far west as Braeburn Valley.

Brays Bayou winds east and west across the southern half of Houston, and along its entire course stand numerous beautiful home sites, some dating from World War II.

In this region are **Braes Heights** and **Link Wood** with small but gracious homes on lovely grounds. The majority are of brick, and the styles range from California Ranch to Spanish stucco. The banks of the bayou are popular with joggers and bicyclists in the neighborhood, and residents are convenient to such commercial complexes as Meyerland and Meyer Park.

To the east of these sections across Main Street is the famous Astrodomain complex, whose northern edge nearly reaches the Texas Medical Center.

Just north of both the Medical Center and Hermann Park is an area known as **The Binz.** Preservationists have been buying the older homes and small apartment complexes of the Binz for restoration and conversion.

Just across Main Street from The Binz is another of the oldest and wealthiest sections of town called **Shadyside.** It was planned about the same time as River Oaks, and some of Houston's most famous families dwell here within the confines of a high brick wall that serves as a buffer against traffic along Main.

Shadyside borders Rice University and property owners maintain their own private streets with alleys of old oaks.

Southwest Region—Outside the Loop

Toward the south **Willowbend** and **Westbury** both lean heavily to strictly single-level homes of brick and frame combined. A few townhomes are beginning to crop up in the area, but it still is geared to single family living with scattered shopping centers.

Farther south and southwest of Westbury are several incorporated towns crossing over the Harris County line and extending into Ft. Bend County.

Among them are older communities such as **Missouri City** and **Stafford** with many single family modest frame homes. Farther out, however, some 20-plus miles from the center of town, are beautifully planned communities in the area of **Sugar Land.**

Sugar Creek, for example, is one of the most prestigious area communities outside the Loop. Here the homes are built around the Riverbend Country Club golf course and many face canals running through the district. The average home is two-floors with loft and some have as many as eleven principal rooms. The styles range from Tudor to Colonial and most are of brick or stonework, with handsome galleries and patios.

Next to this is **Venetian Estates,** another most desirable area with waterfront homes. Some date back 20 years, but there has been considerable newer building activity, too.

This path of immense new subdivisions continues north, following the route of Highway 6, and includes an array of home sites and developments such as **Towne West** just outside the Houston City Limits, **Sugar Mill** which is in Sugar Land, **Wilcrest Park,** and **Alief,** most of which enjoy settings with plenty of open space, perhaps even a vegetable farm nearby. Homes in such areas are mostly brick and frame combinations, two-story. Throughout the area are new shopping centers, new schools, and new apartments and townhouses, usually built along commercial strips.

Sharpstown, one of the first planned areas in Houston, covers many thousands of acres, many of them taken up with such commercial developments as malls, hotels and motels, and restaurants. While there are plenty of single-family homes ranging from modest frame/brick to executive, most of this area is made up of apartment complexes, patio homes, and condos, some geared to adult living or "singles only" complexes around swimming pools. The area boasts one of Houston's busiest, most comprehensive shopping malls: Sharpstown Center.

Near and just west of Sharpstown Center, stores and signs proclaim the influential influx of Asians into the community. Even some street signs are bilingual English-Chinese.

One of the longest streets in Houston is Westheimer Road which becomes Highway 1093 and extends all the way from the Montrose, through the Galleria/Post Oak area, and way out west some 20 or more miles before poking into the rural farm and ranch areas.

Parallel to its course on both sides are pockets of middle-class to upper middle-class residential areas from just outside the Loop west through **Tanglewilde, Woodlake Forest, Rivercrest, Briargrove Park, Southlake,** and **Ashford West** as Dairy-Ashford Road.

These and many other neighborhoods share innumerable commercial centers, with a vast array of shops including The Galleria, restaurants, night-clubs, hotels, and small businesses.

Rivercrest offers valuable wooded home sites for the likes of highly paid executives, while **Woodlake's** townhome developments lean more to younger career types.

Except enclaves restricted to single-family dwellings, the bulk of the West-heimer corridor is devoted to large apartment complexes and townhouses.

The northern tier between the Westheimer Strip and the Katy Freeway is the beginning of forest lands that constitute much of Houston's northwest and northeastern quadrants.

Here you will see villages with a bayou or creek running through them and hundreds of houses hidden in dense thickets that are home to many small animals as well.

The principal artery cutting a winding path across this section is **Memorial Drive,** which begins on the edge of downtown and continues west all the way to State Highway 6, sometimes known as the Outer Belt, looping around the southwest and northwest region where it then becomes FM-1960.

Starting closer in to town at the western edge of Memorial Park are beautifully wooded sections known as **Post Oak, Briar Grove,** and **Tanglewood,** which are just south of Memorial along an extension called Woodway.

Many of the expansive homes on winding streets along Buffalo Bayou in the **Post Oak** have an almost rural setting with fine ranch-style houses on spacious grounds covered with pines. Most are brick and many date back to the 60s and 70s. Going west into **Briarcroft** and **Briargrove,** the homes are closer together and on smaller lots but still are beautiful brick, one- and two-story dwellings. Abutting all of this are many new high-rise condos, huge townhouse developments, and apartment complexes, particularly along **Fountainview.** Some quiet streets lead onto cul-de-sacs.

North and west of Briargrove is a handful of private villages that have grown up around the Memorial/Buffalo Bayou corridor, including **Hunter's Creek, Piney Point, Bunker Hill, Hedwig** and **Willowick,** which is next to the Houston Country Club. The area offers many tennis, racquetball, golf, and swimming facilities, while, of course, many of the beautiful estates have private pools.

These villages boast tall pines and even wildlife. Some of the homes rival those in River Oaks with a wide assortment of architectural styles.

They are largely highly restricted areas, and many lots cover half-an-acre, which adds to the rustic flavor of the communities.

Between **Hunter's Creek** and the Loop are the older homes that grew up along Memorial, many of them hidden away in dense foliage and thickets along cul-de-sac streets. Subdivisions in this area tend to be strictly private with guarded gates and high brick walls.

West of the villages the trees get smaller and there is less natural foliage, but the homesites are still beautiful, neighbors to a large selection of townhomes such as in the Woodlake area.

Northwest Region—Inside the Loop

Inside the Loop this area is wooded and lined with bayous. It features some of the oldest and most historical neighborhoods in Houston, more recently joined by apartment complexes.

One particularly noteworthy section, called **The Heights,** has numerous old frame Victorian-type homes and cottages, drawing floods of restoration-minded young couples and other folks.

Nearby, the **Sabine** district also has many old frame, two-story houses with a turn-of-the-century look and is undergoing restoration by new owners.

The **Woodland Heights,** along White Oak Bayou, is made up largely of single-family brick and frame homes dating back to the 1930s. Family home sites mix with rentals in duplexes, apartments, and condos.

Northwest Region—Outside the Loop

This immense region also has proven one of the fastest growing in all of Houston, both commercially and residentially. It extends 20 to 30 miles out, all the way west to Cypress, north to Tomball, and to Conroe in Montgomery County. The major freeway artery cutting through the region is Highway 290 to Austin, and on either side are many sub-divisions both old and new. Much of the region is dense with tall pines and big thickets, more so closer to metro Houston's northern extremes.

Closer in toward the Loop are fine old residential districts dating back to post World War II such as **Garden Oaks** and **Oak Forest** with many one- and two-story frame and brick homes along tree-lined streets. Some of the houses in these areas are executive level, and residents find convenience in major shopping malls and other commercial centers nearby.

The districts are divided by large business center strips along such thoroughfares as North Shepherd, Ella Blvd., and T. C. Jester Blvd.

Farther west is **Spring Branch,** which contains a couple of incorporated villages just north of I-10 West. Affordable homes and apartments abound.

At the western extreme of this region are vast new sub-divisions from the Addicks area 20 miles out to Katy. These farm and ranch land communities are springing up all over the prairies with corn fields and gullies in between. Close by are Lakeside Airfield and the mammoth Bear Creek Park at the Addicks Reservoir. The majority are brick or a combination of frame and brick. In addition to the many fine new homes, there are new townhouse and apartment complexes with units for rent and for sale.

North around FM-529 some of the largest subdivision developments have grown under the banners of **Copperfield** and **Colonies.** The area is pocketed with office parks and strip developments along FM-1960.

Area recreation facilities include the prestigious Champions Golf Club. There are great executive homes in the **Champions** area, some facing right onto parkways and with lovely wooded gardens.

Keeping up with this growth are shopping malls and high- fashion stores. Here, too, are plenty of townhomes for sale and for rent.

The majority of the executive homes off FM-1960, or Bammel Road as it's known at this point, are of a wide variety of styles and materials, mostly two-story and invariably with well-cared-for lawns and gardens, many with pools in the back.

In the area of **Cypress** are fine colonies such as **Steeplechase.**

Also in divisions such as the newer **Hastings Green** homes are affordable and the majority are single-family units, but multiple-family dwellings are being built here as everywhere else.

North into the **Tomball** area are homes ranging from modest tract houses to large-acreage estates. Tomball boasts clean air, plenty of wooded areas, a golf club, shopping, and a small-town atmosphere.

Continuing north and just west of I-45 North are the resort living areas around **Conroe,** namely **April Sound,** a private community; **Walden,** with its excellent golf facilities and yacht club; and others capitalizing on the water-front lots and wooded acreage all around Lake Conroe, one of Houston's most popular recreation spots.

While there are many resort homes, there also are plenty of rustic-type condos.

Finally, 27 miles northwest of downtown Houston is the famous celebrity golf course and conference center called **The Woodlands,** around which is growing a totally planned community on some 23,000 acres of forest land. Here you will find a wide range of homes and affordable lots. Residents commute to Houston via van pools, cars, and park-and-ride buses.

Northeast Region—Inside the Loop

This is a comparatively small area and principally made up of old neighborhoods with many frame houses widely mixed with commercial enterprises ranging from warehouse districts to shopping parks. The area closest to I-45 North around **Moody Park** can be pleasant with residential areas dating from pre-World War II. Most of the homes are one-story, single-family frames with some apartment complexes mixed in. This region heavily intersperses residential, industrial, and major rail transportation sites.

Northeast Region—Outside the Loop

This region extends north and east into both Montgomery and Liberty counties, and much of the territory is covered with tall pines since it abuts the southern fringe of the East Texas piney woods. In addition, many canals, bayous, plus Lake Houston and the San Jacinto River, water the area. It encompasses Houston

Intercontinental Airport at the western edge and includes such incorporated towns as Humble and Spring.

The area just south of the airport includes older sub-divisions such as **Aldine** with its own independent school district, **Western Homes,** and **Woodsdale.** Between these large subdivision areas and the airport is the H and H Guest Ranch and Country Club set in forest bordering Intercontinental. **World Houston** is still another major development near the airport.

North of the airport are **Westfield** and **Spring.** Significant strip development along this corridor follows I-45 North all the way to Conroe, which straddles our regional divide.

Old Town Spring reflects the early days of this rural community. The area is full of Victorian-style houses. Nearby are newer developments such as **Inverness Forest. Spring** has an independent school district and is served by North Harris County College. Shopping centers and other commercial developments are nearby along the I-45 corridor.

To the east and just outside Intercontinental is the old town of **Humble,** site of one of Texas' greatest oil discoveries, whence eventually Exxon flowed.

While this area blooms with new shopping malls, apartments, and condos, it maintains its small-town flavor. It, too, has an independent school district serving planned communities farther north. **Kingwood** is one of those fast-growing residential communities with close to a dozen different villages along forested trails. Homes range from modest to upper level.

Another such community is **Atascosita,** a community synonymous with golf, tennis, and other great recreational features on Lake Houston. There are fine resort homes in sections such as Atascosita Shores.

Southeast Region—Inside the Loop

Much of this region is devoted to industry and is populated by families of workers in the surrounding refineries, chemical plants, and other installations that compose the mighty industrial districts of Houston and Pasadena.

In fact, nearly all of the sector between I-10 east and I-45 south is such big business. Few of the once-lovely old East End neighborhoods remain intact.

Areas such as **Pecan Park, Mason Park, Forest Park,** and **Idlewood** are especially scenic, with Brays Bayou winding through and lots of quiet, tree-lined residential streets.

There still are one- and two-story 1940s brick homes in good condition, and at the center is the lovely wooded area around Gus Wortham Golf Course.

South of the Gulf Freeway is **Riverside Terrace** with both Texas Southern

University and the University of Houston at its door. It borders still another recreational facility at MacGregor Park.

North and South **MacGregor Way** and their environs boast some of the most lavish old mansions in Houston. This scenic wooded setting follows the path of Brays Bayou, and some of Houston's wealthiest black families reside here. They, together with a growing number of whites, are restoring these great homes on their spacious grounds.

Farther south these sections become **Forest Place** and **MacGregor Terrace** toward the Loop.

Southeast Region—Outside the Loop

Most of this land is coastal prairie and marshland. Numerous waterways include scenic bayous with moss-covered trees; the Houston Ship Channel lined with heavy industry; the San Jacinto River, which is popular with fishermen and skiers; and Clear Lake, with man-made canals in neighboring subdivisions. Homeowners park their boats at the front door.

Just outside the Loop, **Park Place** and **Glenbrook Valley** typify modest residential areas developed during and right after World War II. They remain peaceful neighborhoods with tree-lined streets and primarily with frame and some brick two- and three-bedroom homes. **Park Place** borders Pine Gully and Glenbrook Golf Course.

To the south is ever-expanding Hobby Airport with small industrial strips, newly developed hotels, restaurants, and shopping centers along Mykawa and Almeda-Genoa roads.

From the Gulf Freeway East is the **City of South Houston,** another World War II-era product, a bedroom community with modest frame homes and small shopping and business centers. It is close to Houston's newest airport, Ellington Field.

Pasadena is another pre-existing city Houston has virtually surrounded. It retains its own school district, city government, law enforcement, shopping venues, and a general hospital.

It is in the heart of the industrial quadrant, where a number of similar small cities are home to refinery workers and their families—**Deer Park, Galena Park,** and **Jacinto City.**

Just to the east of San Jacinto Battleground, across the channel is **Baytown.** Formerly called Goose Creek, this city derives its economic backbone from such big industries as Exxon and Chevron. The community offers some very pleasant residential areas, with urban amenities in a small-town aura. It is the home of Lee College.

South of Baytown and following Galveston Bay into Galveston County, small villages intersperse with incorporated towns: **La Porte, League City, Dickinson, Webster. Texas City** is at the tip of the mainland some 45 miles from Houston.

The area known as **Clear Lake** grew with the establishment of the Lyndon B. Johnson Space Center, when hundreds of related industries moved in with NASA. This catalyzed the region as a preferred residential area catering to employees of the center and of other area businesses. Principal streets through the district are El Dorado, Bay Area Blvd., and NASA Road 1. The latter slices through the center of such towns as **Webster, Nassau Bay, El Lago,** and other resort-type communities that offer a wide range of middle- to upper-income brick homes, many in forested bayou settings, many on lakefront property.

The entire area has stimulated bordering towns such as **League City.** Marinas and apartment and townhouse complexes have sprung up along with business and the single family dwellings. The University of Houston Clear Lake campus provides higher education to the communities in this area, as does the College of the Mainland.

La Porte is a very old community with many small frame houses dating back more than 60 years. Its coastline, however, is still a popular resort area with some large homes and mansions along winding, wooded streets on Galveston Bay.

Just south is a string of villages with weekend homes and cottages, along with plenty of shopping to support the recreational business.

Many Houstonians buy property in **Bayview, Bacliff,** and **San Leon,** and commute to work in Houston.

Galveston Island is our last outpost in this vast region, 50 miles from downtown Houston. Long deemed a resort and port, Galveston boasts many new developments in condos, townhouses, and restorations of old historical homes—all becoming immensely popular among Houstonians commuting to work in the big city and living by the sea. Much growth has been along Seawall Blvd. and toward the western tip of the island.

We have taken you in whirlwind fashion over many miles of metropolitan Houston, barely skimming over all the options available to new residents. But as stated at the outset, our intent is to offer you an overview of the topography and a glimpse of neighborhood profiles.

Such information should at least help you nail down a starting point in your search for new quarters, whether you are buying or renting.

Whatever your needs, whatever your income bracket, and whatever your preference, Houston can deliver practically anything but mountains and snow.

HOME AND GARDEN SHOPPING NEEDS

It pays to shop around but for starters—the author's or editor's choices:

Air Conditioning Repairs—Air Quality Assurance, 14102 Susan Court, Sugar Land; 240-1204.

Automobile Repairs—Import Repair Center, 9048 Long Point; 467-2171.

Building Materials (old and new)—Olshan Lumber Co., 2600 Canal; 225-5551.

Carpet & Rug Cleaning—Superior Rug Cleaners, 4208 Washington; 524-7529.

Doors (new and damaged/repairs/build)—The Detering Co., 3028 Center; 869-3761.

Electrical Repair—McBride Electric Inc., 1229 W. 34th; 864-7800.

Furniture Rentals—Finger Furniture Rentals, 8155 Kempwood (other showroom locations); 468-5411.

Gas Leaks (repairs)—Entex—emergency only, 659-3552.

Glass (auto repairs)—Lone Star Glass Co., 3804 Bissonnet; 661-0091.

Glass (home)—Binswanger Glass Co., 3333 Holly Hall South Loop (other locations); 747-5430.

Hardware—Wagner, 5233 Bellaire; 667-5868. Also other locations.

Hardware (decorative)—Bruce Adkins Architectural Antiques, 3515 Fannin; 522-6547.

Lamp Repairs—Alcon Lightcraft, 1424 W. Alabama; 526-0680.

Leather Cleaning—John's Leather Cleaners & Dyers, 1402 Welch; 528-1209.

Lights (service trouble)—Houston Lighting & Power Co.; 228-7400.

Luggage Repairs—Bag 'n Baggage, 3900 Polk; 223-2181.

Paintings Restoration—Fine Arts Center, 1639 Bissonnet; 529-9411.

Party Decorations (home and patio)—Southern Importers, 4825 San Jacinto; 524-8236.

Party Rentals/Supplies—Abbey Party Rents, 8634 Westpark; 266-3910.

Pest Control—B.T. Beier Pest Control, 723-0172 or 440-0156.

Picture Frames (sales and repairs)—Allart Framing & Gallery, 2635 Revere; 526-3631.

Plumbing—Grizzly Bear Plumbing & Heating, 496-3295 or 356-4835.

Printing (offset, small jobs)—Heights Litho, 365 W. 19th; 880-0002.

Recreational Vehicle Supplies—RV Suppliers, 6220 N. Shepherd; 691-3789.

Rentals (tools, machines, cleaning equipment, etc.)—A to Z Rentals, 1301 W. Alabama (other locations); 523-4459.

Shoe Repairs—Houston Shoe Hospital, 5215 Kirby (other locations); 528-6268.

Stained Glass (custom made and repairs)—Texas Art Glass, 1211 Illinois in South Houston; 944-2805.

Telephone (service trouble)—Southwestern Bell; 1-800-246-8464.

Veterinarian—Southwest Freeway Animal Hospital, 10710 W. Bellfort; 495-0130.

LET'S HAVE A PARTY

Tired of giving parties in your home, at the club, or at your place of business? Wracked your brain for original ideas but still want to do something really daring and different? There are innumerable possibilities for themes and locations, for small and large gatherings. You can settle for cake and ice cream or go for it all with something like "Coon and Collards Under Glass" in your own privately catered function.

Perhaps the following list will prick your imagination and steer you in the right direction for your next extravaganza.

A Day in the Park

This one is for children (no one below 3rd grade), and a great way to educate as well as entertain your youth groups.

The **Houston Arboretum and Nature Center** at 4501 Woodway (C2), will set up a program combining a lecture on nature and tours through the botanical gardens conducted by trained guides. You could wind up with a picnic in Memorial Park next door, and you can arrange this for groups up to a maximum of 60.

During the school year give two to three months notice. There may be a nominal charge per child for the educational programs. For information: 681-8433. Call for reservations.

A la New Orleans

Brennan's of Houston, whose fame originated in New Orleans, can help you pull off a real corker with your own "Breakfast at Brennan's," perhaps in their wine cellar. Or it could be lunch or dinner or a jazz brunch if you please. Call 522-9711 for arrangements.

All Skate!!

Grab a partner and all skate at **Bear Creek Park** out on Highway 6 just north of Bear Creek. You can have the whole rink with catering and beverages (soft drinks only) and have a rollicking good time roller skating for your next get together. Check hours, days available. Call 496-2177.

An Historic Brunch

You can have a nostalgic knock-out of a party privately catered in **Sam Houston Historical Park** downtown. In a replica of the first commercial building in Houston, The Long Row, is an old-fashioned tea room for luncheon or dinner. Members of the Harris County Heritage Society may be available to serve, dressed in vintage attire, and arrangements can be made for a private tour of the historical buildings in the park. Ask about early Houston-style recipes. Call 759-1287.

Come to My Chateau

If you can't afford your own French chateau, would you settle for the old Fondren Mansion in Houston? **La Colombe d'Or Restaurant and Hotel,** one of the world's smallest luxury hotels in the heart of The Montrose, will let you take over the whole place for a Chateau Ball or set you up in The Penthouse or one of the other deluxe suites for elegant cocktails and dinner party by candle-light. Call 524-7999.

Fine Arts Fest

You too can be a patron of the arts by making a donation to the **Museum of Fine Arts** and holding your next corporate or organization party here, with museum instructors taking your guests on tour for a special showing. Pick your theme—avant garde, Oriental, Old World—the Museum will assist with cater-ing and decorations to fit the bill. Call the Director of Special Events; 639-7300.

Frontier Days Are Here Again

Go really Texan and stage your own rodeo for up to 3,000 or have a bang-up barbecue in an enclosed pavilion for as many as 2,000. Whatever you've got in mind, **Double LL Western Productions** will assist, including entertainment, decorations, concessions, hay rides, games, and children's rides at the tree-cov-ered 123-acre **Houston Farm & Ranch Club** on Highway 6 or at the Western Park on FM 1960. Call for details; 524-4727.

Go Posh in the Park

Why be so plebian as to picnic on a blanket in the park? **Miller Outdoor Theatre** has numerous spectacular evening productions in Hermann Park, from opera to ballet to symphony to Broadway musicals. Take your pick and plan ahead, if you dare, with a formal, catered picnic on the grassy knoll while enjoy-ing any of the above shows under the stars. It's been done with white-gloves service, candelabras, champagne, and everybody done up real elegant—you could try a Southern-Southwestern-style gala with magnolia corsages and a mess of fried chicken, okra-and-tomatoes and jalapeno cornbread.

I'll Have My Vin Blanc in the Vault Please—

Have you ever dreamed of being locked in a bank vault with all the money you could ever want? Well, how about being set in a vault with all the Italian food and wine you want? It could happen at **Ballatori's** famous Italian restaurant on Houston's East Side. The Ballatoris moved their entire family and all of their old recipes from their famous stake in Rome to this former East Side bank. There you may close in on 30 of your best friends in the former vault—now a private dining room—for a specially prepared menu of Northern Italian cuisine. Call: 224-9556.

Meet Me in the Zoo

Don't monkey around with old-hat birthday ideas for the kids—bring your own cake and as many youngsters as you want to the **Children's Zoo** at **Houston Zoological Gardens** in Hermann Park for some real treats and a chance to play among the animals in the contact pens. Then take the miniature train ride through the park and wind up at the Children's Playground Pavilion for a picnic. A very reasonable and unique way to make your child's next birthday extra special.

Moon Over Galveston Bay

If the moon and the stars are out, you can dance the night away at romantic **Sylvan Beach Park** in La Porte, scene of many a fancy ball in the good old days when this was the "Gold Coast" of Texas with big-name bands of the 40s. This is a large indoor Sylvan Beach Pavilion with an open deck overlooking the bay; ideal for parties of all types including theme, dinners, cocktails, and dances. Pavilion can accommodate a maximum of 650-700 party guests. Call the **City of La Porte Parks & Recreation Dept.**; 470-7275.

Nice `N' Spicy

The fragrant spice gardens of old Ceylon have nothing over **Hilltop Herb Farms** on FM-787, about 18 miles east of Cleveland, Texas, and about 60 miles north of Houston. There your group may dine on foods specially prepared, with fresh herbs grown right here. Hours, days, and meals served vary greatly, so reservations are necessary. Tour the gardens before or after your meal, and be sure to check out the unique gift store. The gift shop and the greenhouse are both open daily 9 am-4 pm regardless of whether the restaurant is serving. Call 1-713-592-5859.

Opt for Opera

You don't have to be an opera buff to enjoy the **Great Caruso** in the beautiful Carillon West Center just off Westheimer Road. Your friends will never forget such a sumptuous dinner party complete with your own corps of opera singers on stage, Continental lunch or dinner, and a beautiful opera bar for latecomers SRO. This is how to go first class in one of the nation's most strikingly beautiful and unique restaurant show bars filled with European antiques. So dim the house lights, cast a spotlight, and shine as the host of the season for your next group function. The Caruso manager can assist with the arrangements; 780-4900.

Stairway to the Stars

Atop the **Sheraton Astrodome Hotel** sits the Celestial Suite, once designated the world's most expensive hotel quarters by the *Guinness Book of World Records*. It may not fit your budget to take the entire floor, but you might have part of it—maybe the Mini-Dome, a split-level party room for your next dinner dance and cocktails, complete with electronic scoreboard to welcome guests and closed-circuit television. Amenities and polices subject to change without notice. Call 748-3221.

Come on Down to Galveston

An abundance of unusual party places on the island can make your next group occasion truly an event to remember.

Consider taking over **Seawolf Park** on Pelican Island with food, beverage, and entertainment for up to 200 in a party room on the second floor of a three-level pavilion overlooking Galveston Bay, right next to a World War II submarine and destroyer.

Board a vintage railroad car going nowhere at the **Center for Commerce and Transportation,** available for cocktails and hors d'oeuvres.

Or take a slow boat to nowhere with up to 100 on the *Elissa,* a four-masted schooner that made ports of call around the world in the 1800s. Stand-up buffet and cocktails can be arranged on this, the third oldest tall-sail ship in the world.

A slow way to go on a leisurely cruise around Galveston Island is aboard the Victorian paddlewheeler, *The Colonel,* which caters to parties for up to 800.

Early German immigrants to Galveston built a traditional community recreation house called the **Garten Verein,** still in use and focal point of Galveston's municipal Kempner Park. This octagonal antebellum building is a perfect setting for a garden party for lunch, dinner, or cocktails and entertainment, serving up to 250. Available through City of Galveston Parks & Recreation Dept., and you book your own entertainment. Call 1-(409) 763-1261.

Or how about an elegant party, with a view of both the Gulf and the Bay? Invite as many as 60 guests to a seaside soiree in the **Presidential Suite** atop the Hotel Galvez, scene of many a fancy affair around the turn-of-the-century.

For information and assistance, start with the Galveston Island Convention & Visitors Bureau at 1-409-763-4311.

GALVESTON

GALVESTON PAST

Not only is Galveston one of Texas' oldest cities, it is among the most colorful with a long history of exploration, buccaneer days, wars, fortunes made and fortunes lost, natural disasters, and the struggle to remain in the competitive mainstream of major ports.

While the City of Galveston was created in 1838, its trail through history really started off in 1528, when Spanish explorer Cabeza de Vaca arrived.

Fewer than 40 years after the first voyage of Columbus to the New World, de Vaca became the first white man to set foot on Texas soil. Galveston at the time was a favorite dwelling for a fierce tribe of cannibalistic Indians known as Karankawas, who lived primarily in nomadic fashion along the coast, existing on fish and small game.

French and Spanish Claims

Later, Cavalier Sieur de la Salle came to the Texas coast and he gave the island its first name, San Luis, in honor of his French sovereign. The name is still in use today for a bay opening at the west end of Galveston. It is also borne by a deluxe resort hotel.

By 1777, Texas and Mexico came under Spanish claim and it was Count Bernardo de Galvez, viceroy of Mexico under Spanish dominion, who ordered the first survey of Galveston Bay. The island's name changed to Galvez in his honor, and it eventually metamorphosed into "Galveston."

The island was then largely ignored until a Frenchman named Louis-Michel Aury was made resident commissioner by rebel Jose Manuel de Herrera, who proclaimed the land for the non-existent Mexican Republic. Aury, who was involved in contraband and slave smuggling, left the island temporarily on an unsuccessful mission to help free Mexico from Spain. On his return, he found that a rival band of bounty hunters had taken over.

217

A Pirate Rules —————————————————————

Jean Lafitte, one of history's most famous pirates and a man whose name has become synonymous with Galveston, perhaps even more than Galvez himself, made this his island domain. He was named governor by the Mexican Patriot Government and called his little kingdom "Campeche." An imposing but suave man, feared by seafarers and statesmen alike, Lafitte attracted a sizeable settlement of buccaneers who went along with Mexico's idea of sweeping the Gulf clear of Spanish ships.

Earlier, an English officer had approached Lafitte to take up arms against the United States at the Battle of New Orleans. But instead Lafitte befriended Gen. Andrew Jackson and, overnight, became a hero of the War of 1812. He was left with impunity, then, to rule Galveston with an iron fist. He ran raids on sea traffic and, according to legend, built up a mighty cache of gold and silver that many today believe is still buried somewhere around Galveston.

Lafitte vowed to Jackson that he would commit no act of piracy against U.S. vessels, but several secret raids by some of his men eventually led the United States to demand that he abandon Campeche forever. With this downfall he ordered his settlement burned to the ground, then quietly put out to sea with his chosen freebooters. Finally, in broken health, he reportedly died in Venezuela.

Galveston Comes into its Own —————————————

The Galveston of more recent times had its beginning on the heels of Texas winning independence from Mexico. In 1836, the same year that the Allen brothers founded Houston, a French-Canadian named Michel Menard bought a league of land from the new republic for $50,000. Two years later he formed a partnership to organize the Galveston City Company and immediately opened a port facility with private wharfing.

During the early days of the Texas Republic, Galveston conducted a fair amount of trade, shipping hides, cotton, wool, and cattle, and bringing in foodstuffs and other goods needed by the Southwestern colonists. Following Texas' annexation by the United States and the subsequent war with Mexico, Galveston continued as a leading port, and the largest and richest city in the state.

By 1850 it was known as the "commercial and cultural emporium of the Southwest." Cotton was king and many a fortune was made with cotton presses, storage, and shipping.

Texas by then was a full-fledged slave state and, despite strong opposition from Governor Sam Houston, who was deposed because of his refusal to sign allegiance to the Confederacy, Texans voted to secede from the Union. From the outbreak of the Civil War, Galveston was blockaded by the Federals, and the most important engagement in Texas took place when the U.S. Navy captured

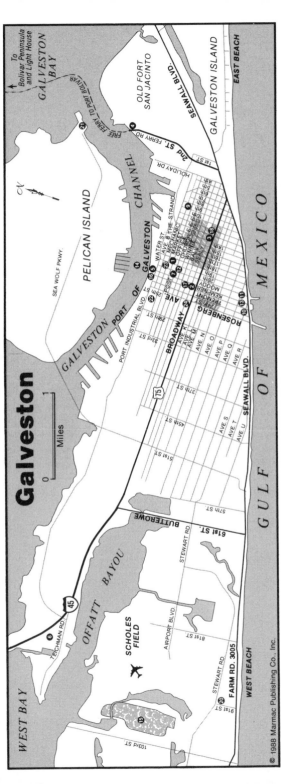

Galveston

Miles
0

© 1988 Marmac Publishing Co., Inc.

Western Galveston Island

Miles
0

Galveston. It later was regained by Confederate troops out of Houston, who used vessels fortified with cotton bales to ward off enemy fire.

Later during the Spanish-American War, when it was feared that Galveston might again come under siege, earthen-camouflaged gun mounts were set up along the seawall. They were never fired except in practice, but the mounds remain as points of interest, and they are part of the landscape design of today's San Luis resort hotel.

Galveston freely concentrated on her port development and other industrial efforts until 1900, when one of the most destructive natural disasters in American history struck.

Galveston's Nemesis

The calamity came suddenly in September.

Despite warnings of an approaching storm, Galvestonians, who were accustomed to such tropical invasions, went on about their business with little heed to the rising tides and increasing winds.

A few cautious souls headed for higher ground in Houston, but the majority retired as usual, only to be awakened early in the morning, trapped by two gigantic forces converging on Galveston; one, a West Indian hurricane out of the Gulf, and the other, a northeasterly gale descending from the Bay, driving a wall of water 15 feet high across the island.

When the waters finally met, the island was completely inundated with a swirling sea. Before the storms subsided, Galveston was almost completely wiped off the map. More than 6,000 people perished in just a matter of hours.

An outpouring of aid from around the world relieved the suffering and immense damage to a degree, but it was years before Galveston recovered completely. At least the storms prompted the city to build a 12-mile-long, 17-foot-high seawall along the Gulf, and workers literally raised the island grade level by up to 12 feet, using many tons of landfill—quite an engineering feat for those mostly horse-and-buggy days!

Recovery

While Galveston was rebuilding, Houston surged ahead with its port development and wrenched the title of number-one shipping center in Texas. But then Galveston was resourceful and rebuilt itself into importance in world trade as well as other realms. Her list of firsts in Texas history and the great contibutions by her citizenry could not be erased by a few strokes of ill fortune.

GALVESTON TODAY

This island is a natural sandy barrier about 32 miles long, following the curve of the mainland, and is accessible by a causeway across the bay off I-45 from Houston, by a bridge over San Luis pass at the western tip, and by ferry at the eastern end from Bolivar Peninsula or Highway 87.

The Galveston-Texas City SMSA population was 217,399 in the 1990 census, of which Galveston itself accounted for 59,070, with an area of some 400 square miles at an altitude ranging from sea level to 50 feet.

Like Houston, Galveston enjoys or endures a sub-tropical climate, but temperatures here tend to range ten degrees warmer in winter and ten degrees cooler in summer.

The coastal, sandy loam soil is fertile ground for tropical vegetation and produces a sizeable annual income from rice, soybeans, and grain sorghums plus good grazing grounds for cattle.

In business, Galveston ranks high among world cotton centers with immense storage facilities and mammoth presses.

Resort City and Educational Center ——————

Long a resort city attracting millions of tourists annually, Galveston also was once on the international gambling circuit with beautiful casinos, nightclubs offering star-studded entertainment, and slot machines on every corner.

Many thought that the closing of gambling by state troopers would be the final death knell for Galveston, but since that time she made still another comeback as an important center for medical research and education.

In fact, Galveston opened the first medical school in Texas, an ornate red-brick structure locals call "Old Red." That school is still in use today, and around it is built a vast medical center complex with the University of Texas Medical Branch and the world-famous Shrine Burn Center.

Galveston also harbors other educational institutions, including Galveston College, the National Maritime Research Center, and the Texas A&M Maritime University. Galveston is also home of Texas' first library, the Rosenberg.

While its deep-water port is best known for cotton shipping, Galveston also moves considerable tonnage in oil, petrochemicals, grain, sand, gravel, and other commodities.

It is ideally situated for studies in oceanography and, of course, the fishing industry. Visitors may catch a glimpse of some of Galveston's famous "mosquito shrimp fleet" tied up along the piers on the bay side of the island.

But surely the industry most closely identified with Galveston is tourism, for it continues to grow as a mainstay in the city's overall economy. Tourism and its related industries have mushroomed throughout Galveston, expanding its repertoire to appeal to all tastes and ages in all seasons.

Fine lodging facilities include some of the most unusual and historic in Texas. Diners can catch the super seafood here. Shoppers can go nuts in shops, boutiques, and stores offering a range of goods from seashells to Steuben.

From its grand and glorious days as an early cultural center of the Southwest, Galveston carries that tradition forward with the 1894 Galveston Opera House restored to offer stellar entertainment; outdoor symphonies; fine art and antiques exhibits; and galleries for arts and crafts.

It is a natural for sports enthusiasts who enjoy horseback riding, tennis, golfing, soccer, squash, racquetball, rugby and, of course, watersports galore. Visitors may enjoy a family bike ride or skating along the famous seawall, surf or swim in the tepid Gulf waters, or fish from long, low jetties. Party boats are available for bay or deep-sea fishing jaunts, and there are several excellent charters.

Galveston's rich history comes to life on guided tours of old mansions or on miniature train and trolley rides through the historical districts.

However you choose to see Galveston—by private auto, by boat, in the air, on guided tours, or afoot—there are many facets and many frames.

We invite you to peruse the following checklist of things to see and do on Texas' most exciting resort island.

While some establishments in Galveston maintain Houston phone numbers, to call most other Galveston numbers from Houston, you must first dial (1), then the area code (409), and the number.

LODGING

There are numerous hotels and motels of all sizes and priced to fit most any budget. Our recommendations are merely a selection. We do suggest that you make reservations well in advance if you are planning to visit here during the summer months. Consult your travel agent or airline or call direct for information on the seasonal rates, the numerous weekend packages, special promotions, and for reservations; rates vary considerably. The price categories we have affixed here reflect average summer rates and can be considerably less during the winter—except during Mardi Gras.

E—Expensive, $70 and up for a double.
M—Moderate, $50-70 for a double.
I—Inexpensive, less than $50 for a double.

The Flagship Hotel, 2501 Seawall Blvd.; 488-2555 (Houston) or 1-409-762-9000 (Galveston). M *to* E. A remodeled hotel on a million-dollar pier. The only one of its kind in the nation, it is built on an 1,100-foot pier over the Gulf, with seven stories and 220 rooms, offering a spectacular view of the surf.

Features include fresh Gulf seafood dining, fishing from the T-head pier, surfing, and nearby golf. Popular for wedding receptions and its Chef's Sunday Champagne Brunch. Many specials and honeymoon packages.

Gaido's Seaside Inn, 3828 Seawall Blvd.; (409) 762-9625. *I to* M. Long a popular family-operated motel. Boasts 110 comfortable rooms. Pool. Coffee shop plus *Gaido's* fine seafood restaurant next door.

Holiday Inn on the Beach, 5002 Seawall Blvd.; (409) 740-3581. *M to E.* An eight-story hotel overlooking the Gulf offers 180 rooms, landscaped pool area, restaurant, cocktail lounge. Also gift shop and free parking. *BF, FL.*

La Quinta Motor Inn, 1402 Seawall Blvd.; (409) 763-1224. *I to* M. Overlooks the Gulf of Mexico. Has 115 rooms and suites. Restaurant adjacent. Pool on premises. One-half mile from Stewart Beach. Also close to Moody Convention Center.

Hotel Galvez, 2024 Seawall Blvd.; 765-7721. *I to E.* The grand and historical old Galvez has been totally renovated, restoring the look of its youth. A terrace lounge provides a marvelous view of the Gulf. Outdoor pool. Sports and recreational outlets nearby. Adjacent to the Moody Convention Center. Limos to and from Hobby Airport.

The San Luis Resort & Conference Center, 53rd and Seawall Blvd.; 774-1500. *E.* This hotel offers 244 rooms, all with balconies overlooking the Gulf. Also a tropical garden with heated pool, swim-up bar, and waterfall. Dining rooms, lounge, in-room movies, ballroom, meeting rooms, gift shop, whirlpool spa, non-smoker rooms available. Free parking.

Tremont House, 2300 Ship's Mechanic Row; (409) 763-0300. *E.* Deluxe rooms and suites in the heart of the historical area. The *Merchant Prince* provides continuous service for breakfast, lunch, and dinner.

DINING

Apart from the above-named hotels we have selected what we consider to be some of Galveston's most famous and best restaurants, offering a cross-section from sandwiches to gourmet dining.

Rates are based on appetizer, entree, and dessert, no beverage.

> *E*—Expensive, $20 plus per person.
> *M*—Moderate, $10-$20 per person.
> *I*—Inexpensive, less than $10 per person.

Clary's Restaurant, 8509 Teichman Rd. behind Galveston Daily News building; 1-409-740-0771. *M.* A favorite with the locals and many Houstonians who drive down for fine fresh seafood. Small dining room, attentive service. Good gumbo, and oysters and crab (in season). Also steaks. Dress casual. Lunch Mon-Fri; dinner Mon-Sat. Closed Sun. Reservations recommended.

Gaido's Seafood Restaurant, 3800 Seawall Blvd.; 762-9625. E. A tradition in good seafood and fresh Gulf fish. A large family restaurant overlooking the Gulf's rolling surf. Always popular with locals and visitors alike. Specialties include stuffed broiled flounder and, of course, fresh oysters and crab (in season). Casual. Open for lunch and dinner daily, except Monday.

Hill's Pier 19, Port Industrial Blvd. at 20th St.; 763-7087. I. A unique eatery with a view of the docking area for Galveston's shrimp fleets. Seafood platters, fried oyster poorboys, boiled shrimp, crab, gumbo, fried fish, and more. Very casual. Great place for the family. Lunch and dinner daily.

Old Strand Emporium, 2112 Strand; 763-9445. I. This is a must stop when strolling the Strand. Sidewalk tables under the big veranda or tables inside. Terrific deli sandwiches and other unusual treats. A treasure trove of import items from around the world plus many gifts and souvenirs. Hear the old piano roll and sip a glass of wine while you browse through yesteryear. Very casual. Open daily.

The Wentletrap, 2301 Strand; 765-5545, Houston number, 225-6033. M. This is Galveston's most beautiful gourmet dining room, housed in the League Building, which was completed in 1871 on the site of the old Moro Castle. The cast-iron facade makes it a treasure among Galveston's famous Strand structures. Wonderful Sunday brunch spot and an elegant atmosphere for dinner. Lunch Mon-Thu; dinner Mon-Sat. Sunday brunch 12-3. Evening dress code.

SIGHTS TO SEE
AND MUCH TO DO

We have selected a cross-section of the major sights including parks, historical sites, aquatic shows, cultural outlets, and various tour possibilities from Galveston's myriad attractions and tours.

We offer our own version of an overview of the island in the SELF-GUIDED TOUR below if you prefer to see Galveston in the familiar comfort of your own automobile.

1859 Ashton Villa, 2328 Broadway; 762-3933. CH. Located on Galveston's "mansion row," this historic Italianate home predates the Civil War and has withstood the ravages of both man and nature. An excellent film prefaces the tour with good insight into the city's history, including the wrath of the 1900 storm and the incredible rebuilding efforts that followed. Open Mon-Fri 10 am-4 pm, Sat and Sun 10 am-5 pm.

Bishop's Palace, 1402 Broadway; 762-2475. CH. This has been the only house in the country listed both in the Library of Congress and on the American Institute of Architecture roster of the most architecturally significant 100 homes in the United States.

Built in 1886, the Bishop's Palace was erected by Col. Walter Gresham at a mere cost, in today's terms, of only $250,000. Designed by the well-known Nicholas Clayton, the palace features many mantels from around the world, one of which is lined with pure silver. It was later purchased by the Catholic Church to serve as a bishop's residence and today houses a Newman Center in the converted basement. Tours Mon-Sat 10 am-5 pm, Sun 12-5 pm (summer); tours daily 12-4 pm in Winter (closed Tue).

Bolivar Peninsula—Ferry Boats and Lighthouse, at the end of Ferry Rd. (2nd St.) from Seawall Blvd. *NCH*. A fleet of free, state-run ferries continuously plies the three-mile crossing over the channel to the Bolivar Peninsula onto Highway 87, providing a fun experience for the entire family.

You may leave your car and stroll the deck for an occasional glimpse of playful dolphins, a good view of Pelican Island, and a survey of the merchant ship activity in the Port of Galveston.

At Point Bolivar there is an abandoned lighthouse that is one of the few of its era still intact. Built in 1872, it miraculously survived the great 1900 hurricane that swept over the peninsula with massive tides and gales.

The *Elissa*, Pier 21 just off the Strand. *CH*. The *Elissa* was built in Scotland in 1877 and is one of the world's few remaining tall ship square-riggers. A four-masted schooner, she served under five different flags and has called on many of the exotic ports of the world. She visited Galveston twice during the 1800s, when ships of her class, their masts towering over the Strand, were common sights. After nine years of restoration and expenditures amounting to close to $4 million, she once again rests proud and tall. Tours daily, 10 am-5 pm.

Galveston Island State Park, at 13 Mile Road and FM 3005 on West End of island; 737-1222. *CH*. Situated among the natural dunes, bay marshes, and along clean sandy beaches, this 2,000-acre park is popular with campers and nature lovers.

This vast park reaches from the bay to the Gulf beaches. At its center is the multi-million-dollar **Mary Moody Northen Amphitheatre**.

Grand 1894 Opera House, 2020 Post Office St. Restored by the Galveston County Cultural Arts Council, this European-style opera house, built in 1894, spotlighted many of the world's great artists over the years. Lillian Russell, Anna Pavlova, Sara Bernhardt, and Otis Skinner all performed here. Private tours available; just drop by. Call for a schedule of events including ballet, opera, symphony, musicals, and pop concerts. (Houston) 480-1894 or (Galveston) 765-1894.

Rosenberg Library, 2310 Sealy; 763-8854. *NCH*. Galveston gave Texas its first free library. The Rosenberg was a gift to the state from philanthropist Henry Rosenberg who emigrated from Switzerland to Galveston in 1843. Among his other gifts was the imposing Texas Heroes Monument that still dominates the traffic island at Broadway and Rosenberg. This library is noted for its collection of rare books and artifacts, including original letters of Jean Lafitte, Sam Houston, and Stephen F. Austin, among others. It also features a fine art collection and special exhibits. Open Mon-Sat.

Seawolf Park. Take Seawolf Parkway from 51st and Broadway to Pelican Island, the other island off Galveston; 744-5738. *PKG CH.*

Pelican, during the early years, was Texas' version of Ellis Island in New York. Thousands of immigrant families were detained here in the 1800s for quarantine before being admitted to the United States and moving on to settle in their new homeland.

World War II-vintage vessels and other military equipment now have a permanent resting place in the park. You may peer through the periscope of the USS *Cavalla*, a submarine distinguished in battle against the Japanese Navy, or learn how the USS *Stewart* destroyer came to serve under both the U.S. and the Japanese flags. *CH.*

Then take to the T-head for fishing in the fertile waters of the bay or simply relax, picnicking at a three-level modern pavilion from which point you can sight the *Selma* or what remains of a World War I concrete vessel that sank here long ago.

All of this on a windswept, palm-lined, sandy bar of Pelican offers a great way to spend a day on the island off the island.

The Railroad Museum, at the foot of the Strand on Rosenberg; (409) 765-5700. *CH.*

This art-deco museum focuses on the golden era of railroads. The entrance to the Center for Transportation and Commerce is a restoration of the city's 1875 train depot. The backside of the museum has a working model railroad of the Port of Galveston, and a large collection of vintage cars including a dining car. The interior of the museum tour begins with several rooms equipped with multimedia shows depicting Galveston history, dating back to Indian lore. Moving along into the People's Gallery you come upon innovative audio systems enabling life-size sculptures of historical figures to carry on conversations. Also gift shop and snack stand. Open daily.

Historical Districts

East End, bounded by market, Broadway, 19th, and 11th.

Silk Stocking, south of Broadway, between 23rd and 26th.

Strand, historic district along Strand and Ship's Mechanic sts. between 20th and 25th (Rosenberg).

There is hardly a site on the island without some tale, romantic myth, legend, or historical note. Many of the homes date back more than 140 years and range in style from Moorish to Queen Anne.

Some open to the public seasonally for tours including such architectural treasures as the **Bishop's Palace, Ashton Villa, Samuel May Williams home,** and the **Powhatan House,** which is now the Galveston Garden Club.

In addition to hundreds of homes, there are magnificent commercial structures with ornate iron facades, also dating back to the early 1800s. Through the efforts of the Galveston Historical Foundation these buildings plus many other sites have been restored to conform to their original designs.

Early immigrants to Galveston built churches along the grand European style and particularly the **East End** contains beautiful examples reflecting various styles popular at different stages of island development. Historic churches include **St. Mary's Cathedral,** which was the first Catholic cathedral in Texas (1848), 21st and Church; **First Presbyterian Church** (circa 1840), 19th and Ave F; **Trinity Episcopal Church** (1857), 22nd and Winnie; and **St. Joseph's Church,** built by German immigrants in 1859 and now open for tours through the offices of the Galveston Historical Foundation, 765-7834, located at 22nd and Ave K.

The most outstanding church on the Galveston skyline is the **Sacred Heart Church and School** at Broadway and 14th, across from the Bishop's Palace. It is painted stark white with onion-shaped cupolas in the Moresque style.

Along the **Strand** exciting shops, boutiques and other retail outlets intersperse with artists' studios, apartments, and even small industry. This gaslight-punctuated street of living history sparkles with activity in cafes, galleries, specialty stores, bars, and even an old-fashioned candy factory, where you may indulge in an ice-cream soda and witness candy creations in progress.

Tours

Galveston offers not only many sights to see, but also many ways to see them: by harbor cruise, by Galveston Air Center helicopter flight, by trolley and miniature train, by bus, by guided walking tour, by your own vehicle, or even by van or bus out of Houston.

Pick whichever way best suits your time, taste, and temperament, but know that really getting into the heart and soul of Galveston means striking out in your most comfortably sturdy walking shoes.

Aimless wandering has both its adherents and its merits, but organization or at least initial guidance can spare you needless frustration and grief.

The **Galveston Historical Foundation,** located at 2014 Strand, offers assorted brochures on all aspects of the island.

The **Visitor Information Center** at 21st and Seawall also has brochures, maps, and Galveston information.

The information specialists at both centers are most helpful and happy to assist with a variety of requests.

From Houston there are several Galveston tour possibilities, and we recommend that you call on **Houston Gray Line** for information on their schedule; 223-8800 (reservations must be made the day before by 5 pm). Gray Line picks up at most major hotels. *CH.*

A day cruise or evening dinner and dance cruise can be savored aboard the Victorian-styled *Colonel paddlewheeler.* Docked at Pier 22 next to the *Elissa,* the Colonel floats day cruises seven days a week, leaving at 12 noon and at 3 pm.

Dinner and dance cruises are scheduled weather permitting. Board one hour prior to departure time of all cruises. Reservations required. Call (Houston) 280-3980 or (Galveston) 763-4666. CH.

On the island there are several ground tours such as the **Treasure Isle Tour Train**; 765-9564. Departures from the Moody Center, Seawall Blvd. at 21st St. CH.

Another popular way to see Galveston is aboard the **Galveston Island Trolley,** a trolley ride that will drop you off at any point along the way and let you reboard at any point, at no extra charge. Primary boardings are at either the Strand Visitor Information Center or at 21st and Seawall. The trolley runs continually daily. You don't need to call; just step aboard and pay the conductor. Information 763-4311. CH.

The friendly folks at the **Strand Visitor Information Center** can fill you in on the audio walking tours in the East End Historical District. CH.

SHOPPING

Seawall Boulevard is lined with shops—some on piers—for souvenirs, seashells, and all the traditional coastal resort items.

The **Strand** has a most interesting assortment of boutiques, art galleries, a very fine old jewelry and gift store, arts and crafts shops, clothing, cards, gourmet foods, and antiques.

The downtown area close to the Strand has clothing stores, plenty of beachwear, and full-line department stores plus pharmacies, florists, and gift shops.

Just after crossing the causeway onto the island you'll spot Galvez Mall with its variety of stores.

SPECIAL EVENTS

Galveston is a city of festivals and with its temperate climate these events may be enjoyed year 'round. For the most current information we suggest you check with the visitor information centers for a calendar of events. Besides festivals there are many annual events of interest at the Moody Center, ranging from antique shows to road show concerts.

We have selected just a few of the major annual items to give you an idea of the range of festivals by seasons.

Mardi Gras. February. Week-long festivities. Big nighttime parade, street dances, entertainment.

IslandFest. In March. This is a two-day environmental spectacular of music, dance, arts, children's activities, and food at the gigantic Moody Gardens Rainforest Pyramid. Information: 744-4673.

Blessing of the Shrimp Fleet. First Sunday after Easter. Shrimping is one of the city's major industries and at the beginning of the season, thousands flock to see the beautifully decorated boats on parade, to enjoy dancing in the street, gumbo cook-offs, and a music festival in the Strand district. At the conclusion the boats are blessed for a productive and safe season. *CH.*

Galveston Historic Homes Tour. Early May. A marvelous opportunity for an inside view of famous historical homes not generally open to the public.

AIA Sandcastle Competition. Early June. About 50 teams of architects and designers compete for the Golden Bucket Award for castles or sculptures built of Galveston beach sand. *CH.*

Fourth of July. Ashton Villa stages an annual old- fashioned Fourth picnic and an Ice Cream Crank Off on the lawn. *NCH.*

Dickens Festival on the Strand. First weekend in December. Merrye Olde England and the days of Charles Dickens come alive with performing artists, food booths, chestnut roastings, poetry readings, and fun for all ages—all on one of Galveston's most historical streets. *CH.*

SELF-GUIDED TOUR

If you are coming from Houston stay on I-45 South (Gulf Freeway), which, after crossing the causeway, becomes Broadway. Even if you are already on the island, start at the foot of Broadway near the causeway. This will give you a comprehensive overview of Galveston.

From this tour, then, you tailor the time at each point according to your interest. Depending on the waiting time for the ferry, and the volume of traffic on Broadway and along the Seawall, this tour should take five or six hours, including a stop for lunch or dinner.

Along Broadway

As soon as you get off the causeway the first thing to catch your eye, if they are in bloom, will be the oleanders along the esplanade. This is the Galveston city flower and they provide a profusion of color during the summer.

A short distance ahead, as you come to the Port Industrial Blvd. exit, you'll see to your right the Galveston *Daily News* on a slight knoll. The News is the oldest daily newspaper in Texas. Farther in and on your left stretches a long row of windowless warehouses with bougainvillea growing up the sides. These are among the world's largest cotton-press and storage houses, which have long been a vital element in the city's economy.

Moving along Broadway to its intersection with Rosenberg, you will see a tall bronze statue on a handsome pedestal with four panels depicting the highlights of the Texas Revolution. Galveston philanthropist Henry Rosenberg gave it to the state to commemorate the heroes of the Battle of San Jacinto which, just a few miles inland, won Texas' independence from Mexico in 1836. In the next block past the statue you will begin to see beautiful old mansions on your left. Galveston is filled with 19th-century architectural wonders as evidenced by these homes. At 24th Street, one block past the statue, is Ashton Villa, a Mediterranean-style Italianate home with wrought-iron balcony, dating from 1859. Today it is a museum depicting the lifestyle of Galvestonians at the turn of the century.

Bishop's Palace is next at 14th Street across from Sacred Heart Cathedral, which is a key landmark on Galveston's historical skyline. The palace was built in 1886 by U.S. Congressman Walter Gresham, and, in architectural significance, ranks among the top 100 homes in the United States.

The church is Moresque architecture and has beautiful stained-glass windows.

Continue to the end of Broadway and turn left onto Seawall Blvd. Proceed two more stoplights to Ferry Road (2nd Street), which leads to the free, state-run ferry boats to Highway 87 on the Bolivar Peninsula.

Take the Ferry to Bolivar

Turn left at Ferry Road and go to the end to reboard the ferry. The actual crossing of the three-mile-wide channel to the peninsula takes about 20 minutes. A good view of Pelican Island is one advantage, A chance to see dolphins cavort alongside the moving vessel is another.

At Bolivar there is an abandoned 1872 lighthouse, one of few left intact. You may turn around at the lighthouse for the return trip, but if you need film or other sundries first, continue just past the lighthouse to Fisherman's cove on the right.

Back on the island, take Ferry Road 14 blocks and turn right onto the Strand.

The Strand

On the left is a cluster of buildings that constitute the Galveston Medical Center, including the University of Texas Medical Branch and the Shrine Burn Center.

Look to the left to see "Old Red," a tile-roofed, red-brick building that was the first medical school in Texas.

You are now approaching the section of the Strand that is most historical and which has been under massive and continuous restoration by the Galveston Historical Foundation since before the 1976 U.S. Bicentennial celebration.

When you get to 19th Street we suggest you find a parking spot and stretch your legs a bit, for this is an ideal place to start a stroll along the Strand. Stop by the clearly marked Visitor Information Center at 2016 Strand. Besides providing helpful and informative brochures, the knowledgeable staff can assist with all types of recreational referrals. We will proceed only a short distance from here to give you an idea of what to expect in the Strand area.

The Old Strand Emporium exemplifies early Galveston commercial interiors and houses a yesteryear shop with a deli. Walk past the Emporium to the corner, cross the street and turn right. At the next doorway on the left is a relic space capsule marking the entrance to one of the most fascinating stores anywhere: Col. Bubbies Surplus Senter, a warehouse filled with antique military gear from around the world.

Now continue to the dead end of this street to Fisherman's Wharf at Pier 22 for a look at a typical seafood market. Just to the right of Pier 22 is the entrance for tours aboard the *Elissa.* The restored square-rigged merchant ship that called at Galveston during the 1800s permanently berths here as a maritime museum.

Back over to the Strand and just across 23rd Street is a marvelous restaurant, the Wentletrap. It is named for a rare Texas seashell and, indeed, lunching or dining here is a rare treat. In the large central room at the entrance is a massive mirrored bar that won first prize at the St. Louis Hemisfair. Over the bar is a three-story atrium, walls, and arches of Houston brick.

All of the Gulf fish and seafood here is fresh and we highly recommend the local crabs and oysters when in season.

Now head back to your car and proceed on down the Strand to the end at Rosenberg.

The large art-deco building you see there is the Shearn Moody Plaza, formerly the Gulf, Colorado, and Santa Fe Terminal. It now houses a railroad museum called the Center for Transportation and Commerce. Innovative audio systems and vintage railroad cars make this a fascinating tour stop.

East End

To continue on, turn left on Rosenberg and go five blocks to Winnie Street. Turn left and just ahead you will see a couple of old churches with beautiful stained-glass windows. Winnie is one of several interesting streets in this historical East End. You will see many homes with "gingerbread" facades, wrought-iron fences, galleries, turrets, towers, and gables.

Continue on Winnie to 19th Street and turn right. Then go two blocks to Sealy and turn left. This is one of the most beautiful streets in all of Galveston. Just as you turn, notice the Gothic house on the left with its intricate woodcarving. On the right, at 17th Street, another unique edifice mixes Moorish style with Gothic design.

When you get to 14th (Christopher Columbus), take a left and go to Market Street. There turn left again and, on the right at 15th, note the white-frame home with columns and ornate front. This home has a state historical marker, as do so many of its neighbors.

At 19th Street, the modern building (Galveston's tallest) on the right is the headquarters of American National Insurance Company, one of the largest insurance firms in Texas. If you go inside, ask whether they still publicly display the insurance policies they issued on the infamous 1930s criminals, Bonnie & Clyde.

Turn left onto 19th, go one block to Post Office Street, then turn left again.

Note the red-brick and tile home at the corner of 16th, unusual for this area since most houses are of wood frame construction. Built in 1887 in the Richardsonian Romanesque style, it offered refuge for some 200 Galvestonians during the 1900 hurricane.

To Seawall Boulevard

Follow this street now all the way to University, turn right there and get into the middle lane. Pass the light at Broadway and turn right onto Seawall Boulevard.

Stewart Beach Park will now be on the left. This is a very popular summer beach and it offers a number of conveniences including bathhouse, snack stands, giftshop, life-guard stations, umbrellas and chaises for rent, and children's playground with rides and games. It is also alcohol-free, which means it is illegal to have any alcoholic beverage there.

Seawall is lined with cafes, hotels, motels, restaurants, souvenir shops, and commercial piers that, in Galveston's heyday, swarmed with gambling activity.

The Seawall, 12 miles long and 17 feet high, was built following the devastating 1900 storm to protect property along the beachfront.

If you missed the Visitor Information Center on the Strand, you have another information resource at another Galveston Island Convention & Visitors Bureau center at 21st St. (Moody) and Seawall.

Across the street from the Galveston Information Center you will see the restored and remodeled Hotel Galvez on your right.

The Flagship, just ahead, is a newer landmark property, unique in all the nation as the only hotel built completely over a body of water.

If you arrive at this point late in the afternoon or early evening, consider a stop at Gaido's for a late lunch or dinner. This is the city's oldest family-operated restaurant (see DINING above).

When you are ready to move along **continue down Seawall Boulevard.** Note a couple of artillery bunkers in the area of 45th St. These are left over from the Fort Crockett installation built for coastal defense in 1897.

To get to Galveston Island State Park this is the route you would take on to Hwy 3005, but **to return to downtown simply head back in the direction you came.**

If you are returning to Houston go back about two miles until you get to 61st Street and turn left. Pass a small Serbian cemetery on your right, continue to Broadway. Turn left onto Broadway, which will take you back to the causeway, which becomes I-45 North into Houston.

BITS AND PIECES

Intrigued with tall Texas tales, a German film company came here some years ago to research a documentary titled "Only in Houston." They found that many of the facts were harder to believe than the fictions.

The truth in telling true Texas tales is that even the most righteous tend to, shall we say, elasticize. There are several what you might term types of truth in Texas: True truth. Sorta true truth. And baldface untruth too good to shoot down with the other two.

Many Texas legends have been passed down for generations, expanding en route from past to present with romantic embellishments or other fanciful exaggerations.

So, partly for edification, but mostly for fun, here are a few that have become as much a part of this part of Texas as bayous and oil.

Each item is marked with an asterisk or two. One * means solid to semisolid truth; two ** means that, like freshly drilled oil, there may be a little gas in it.

*The Battle of San Jacinto was one of the briefest in world history. No one knows for sure, but it took the Texans either 18 or 19 minutes to rout the Mexican forces and midwife the independence of Texas as a republic.

**The song, "Yellow Rose of Texas," was written in honor of the Texas heroine, an octoroon named Emily, who, shall we say, distracted Mexican general Santa Anna sufficiently to enable Gen. Sam Houston to launch his victorious surprise attack at San Jacinto.

**The Episcopal Diocese of Texas may be the only church anywhere that has a pair of Texas Longhorns on its official seal. It reportedly commemorates the day of groundbreaking for Houston's Christ Church Cathedral when a Longhorn heifer broke away from a Texas Avenue cattle drive and scampered right through the formal gathering. Church leaders took it as a good omen.

*Houston has more than one million trees on public rights-of-way and is one of few major cities still celebrating Arbor Day by dispensing free trees to citizens.

*One of the most expensive pieces of land in Houston history was a half block purchased by the Woolworth Company. The price paid: $3,050,000, or about $2,000 a front inch. This is significant when you consider that the initial league of land for the city cost only around $9,000.

*President John F. Kennedy spent the last night of his life, Thursday, November 21, 1963, in Houston at the now-defunct Rice Hotel. The next day, he was assassinated in Dallas.

**Hermann Square in front of City Hall was a gift to Houston from philanthropist George Hermann, with the stipulation that it would always remain a refuge park for transients and the like. He had trouble getting his hands back to work in the cotton fields after a weekend binge downtown that usually wound up with a night in jail. So he bought a parcel of land with firm instructions that his help should head for the square to avoid encounters with the law. If they got drunk they could sleep it off in the park and make it back in time for muster on Monday morning.

*The Flagship of the Texas Navy is the battleship USS *Texas*, permanently moored as a museum near the San Jacinto Battleground.

*Buffalo Bayou was once a source of drinking water for Houstonians. Later it was dubbed "The worst polluted such body of water in the nation." More recently Houston has cleaned it up and some marine life has returned to the still murky waters.

*In 1882, Houston became one of the first two cities to build an electric power plant. The other, shockingly enough, was New York.

*Houston was the first city to induce the Federal government to come up with a matching-funds grant. Children with tin cans and adults alike hit the campaign trail at home to raise funds necessary to match Federal monies, which paid for the final development of the bayou into a world port.

*Gail Borden, the inventor of the process for condensing milk, was hired by the Allen Brothers to produce the original plan for Houston streets. Texas Avenue was the only street he made 100 feet across . . . that was to accommodate 14 head of Longhorn cattle, horntip-to-horntip, during cattle drives.

*The Kellum-Noble house in Sam Houston Historical Park, besides being the oldest home on its original site, has been put to sundry uses. It was at one time a private elementary school and the city's first zoo.

*The Rice-Nichols-Cherry house in Sam Houston Park was being demolished when one Emma Richardson Cherry came along and took a fancy to the front door. Unable to convince the crew to sell the door by itself, she bought the whole house for $25. Who says those weren't the good old days?

*The founders of Houston advertised their new town as being a most salubrious place to live . . . they failed to mention that so many were dying from yellow fever and cholera the city was almost abandoned.

*The first word spoken from the surface of the moon when the first astronauts landed in July 1969 was "Houston."

*Houston is called "Bayou City" with good reason. There are 26 major streams, plus a list of smaller bayous long enough to fill four typewritten pages, crisscrossing the metropolitan area.

**Stories relate how President Sam Houston entertained his cabinet and foreign ministers grandly in the city's first hotel, The Mansion. Imagine the president at that time spending six dollars on a pair of fowl, a dollar a pound for butter, and three dollars for a dozen eggs, not to mention the price he must have paid for champagne.

*The downtown block where the old Rice Hotel stands is full of history. It was once site of the capitol of the Republic.

*Houstonians are intensely loyal to their own. In World War II, when the cruiser *Houston* sank in the Java Sea, one thousand crew members were lost. Shortly after, during a rousing demonstration of patriotism, 1,189 young men were sworn in en masse at Main and Lamar to serve aboard the new cruiser *Houston*. A granite historical marker was placed at the site.

*The oldest commercial structure on its original site is a pub at 813 Congress. It once adjoined an Indian trading post owned by a John Kennedy, who ran a stage coach inn upstairs where, reportedly, Sam Houston once slept.

*Late U.S. president Lyndon B. Johnson taught school here in the old San Jacinto Senior High School, now located at 1300 Holman and San Jacinto. His home here was at 435 Hawthorne.

*Clark Gable lived here while he was studying elocution and his home was at the southeast corner of Whitney and Hyde Park.

*The late billionaire Howard Hughes was brought up in Houston. His home is now part of the University of St. Thomas complex at 3921 Yoakum. He is buried in Houston's Glenwood Cemetery.

**When a famous Houston oil baron passed on some years ago his widow decided to have their mansion torn down. The demolition squad uncovered a secret underground cache with some $10,000 in silver coins that no one, including his wife, knew was there. He used to throw such coins to the poor on his way to work, driving a different Cadillac for each day of the week.

**It is said that the two spots in the nation with the strongest ultra-violet rays are at Salton Sea, California, and Houston/Galveston. Bring your strongest sunscreen.

**The Houston Zoo has the most prolific family of hippos in the nation, with so many offspring they can't even find foster homes for them. Their rounded skylight home at the zoo is called the Hippo-Dome.

*U.S. public television began here in 1953, when the University of Houston's KUHT-TV Channel 8 went on the air as the nation's first public television station.

*Galveston-based American National Insurance Company once issued policies covering the lives of the infamous 1930s criminal couple Bonnie & Clyde, who died together in police gunfire. The policies, which have been on display at the firm's headquarters, named Bonnie Parker's and Clyde Barrow's respective mothers as beneficiary.

*Glen McCarthy, a famous Houston wildcatter from early oil-boom days, built his own Texas-size playhouse which he named the Shamrock Hotel. It sat stark on a bald prairie out on South Main, and to be sure it acquired an indelible identification, he staged a week-long party for openers. To liven up the show he brought in a trainload of Hollywood celebrities. He staged water-ski shows in the Texas-size swimming pool. The hotel has since been razed.

**Flash! It used to take steamboats seven hours to go 50 miles between Galveston and Houston via Buffalo Bayou . . . now you can make a little better time (less than an hour) if you drive via the Gulf Freeway—unless you go during rush hour, in which case you might well be better off back on the bayou!

**Cultural note: Iced tea is widely considered the "National" Drink of Texas, and Blue Bell brand Homemade Vanilla flavor ice cream is just as widely considered the "National" Ice Cream of Houston.

*The Houston Rockets, in June 1994, became the first Houston team to win a major sports championship. In the seventh game of the National Basketball Association World Championship playoffs, the Rockets beat the New York Knicks. That game was played on the Rockets' home court at the Summit in Houston. In June 1995, the Rockets won the title again, beating the Orlando Magic in four consecutive games.

INDEX

Guidebook Order Form

_____Marmac Guide to Houston and Galveston   @ $10.95 _____

_____Marmac Guide to Atlanta   @ $10.95 _____

_____Marmac Guide to Philadelphia   @ $10.95 _____

_____Marmac Guide to Los Angeles   @ $10.95 _____

_____Marmac Guide to New Orleans   @ $10.95 _____

_____Pelican Guide to New Orleans   @ $7.95 _____

_____Pelican Guide to Plantation Homes
of Louisiana   @ $7.95 _____

_____Pelican Guide to Sacramento   @ $9.95 _____

_____Pelican Guide to the Shenandoah   @ $7.95 _____

_____Pelican Guide to Maryland   @ $11.95 _____

_____Maverick Guide to Hawaii   @ $15.95 _____

_____Maverick Guide to Australia   @ $15.95 _____

_____Maverick Guide to New Zealand   @ $15.95 _____

Subtotal _____

*Shipping and handling _____

**Sales tax _____

Total enclosed _____

*Add $2.25 for shipping and handling, plus 50 cents for each additional book ordered. **Jefferson Parish residents add 8.75% sales tax, all other Louisiana residents add 4% sales tax.

Prices subject to change without notice.

TO: **PELICAN PUBLISHING COMPANY**
P.O. Box 3110
Gretna, Louisiana 70054-3110

Please send me the books indicated above.

Name _____

Address _____

City _____ State _____ Zip _____